'GRASP the Solution' and

"Chris challenges people to break from 'old ways [...]
things differently."
Brenton Nicholls, Director, Impact Unlimited

"Chris's book reminds me of one of Albert Einstein's quotes – 'If you can't explain it
simply, you don't understand it'. By dissecting a complex subject and making it easy to
understand, he proves his expertise of the systematic thought process. Now I can
structure my thoughts appropriately using GRASP and harness them in their naturally
radiant form using Mind Maps… I have just discovered the genius in me!"
Abdullahi Bello Umar, CEO, VentureSUM Global Resources Ltd

"I love the focus of this new book. There's a lot of talk in business about the increasing
need for creativity but far less informed action. In the West there's a retreat from this focus
on creativity into the apparently more predictable / comfortable ground of "productivity /
efficiency". For me this latter focus only makes sense if you've set a viable course in the
first instance otherwise any competitive advantage your strategy offers can be rather
[...] hits it right on the head."
[...] Calcutt, Managing Director of GTwM

"I am amazed how simple, easy and profound this book is. It's a remarkable tool for getting
the clarity we all need to begin living our dreams."
[...], Founder, OnePointOne Training

"In many cases the full potential of individuals and organisations remains unrealised.
'Grasp The Solution' provides the perfect introduction to the development of personal
cognitive skills. Read this book and gain new perspectives on thinking clarity and
creativity. Visualise your ideas, watch them grow and let them lead you to success!"
Simon Pearson, Managing Director, Puzzlebox Potential - Unlocking learning
[...]

"[...] impressed by Chris's ability to clearly set goals and inspire individuals seeking their
[...] ual paths and creative solutions. In 'GRASP The Solution', he captures the
[...] of his polished techniques for inducing confidence in people and guiding them to
[...] brilliant decisions. Time spent reading is worthwhile!"
[...]aroslav Senshin, PME

"The GRASP method is as simple to understand as it is revolutionary in improving
results. Chris has provided a new tool that I and my collaborators are using daily in our
professional and personal lives. I believe each one of us should have learnt it at school."
Matteo Salvo, Mind Performance, Author of 'The Secret of a Prodigious Memory'

"Chris awakened the giant within and I am planning my next move with a totally fresh perspective. Chris is not only a great human being but also a great inventor, speaker and leader."
Dina Faidi, Training Consultant, Creativity Beyond

"This book leads us to more efficient, faster, accurate and enjoyable decision making processes. In my opinion 'GRASP The Solution' can become for adults what the book 'Alice in Wonderland' is for children. A wonderful and enjoyable lifetime guide."
Michaella Hella, Managing Director, Destination Group

"I found Chris's GRASP system a great way to make our thinking more structured and simpler. It has led me to metacognition i.e. thinking about thinking".
Dharmendra Rai, Professional Trainer and Coach

"Gave me so many ideas to develop...I have been using GRASP in school at Management levels and am incorporating the technique into SLT training in September."
Sue Baker, Learning and Attainment Manager & Teacher, Kirkby Sports College

"Cogently written, attractively presented and refreshingly free of hype and pseudoscientific psychobabble....packed with practical advice and interesting (sometimes startling) insights."
Graham Buik, Consultant

"My brain has been given a boost... Very inspirational. This is as good as it gets".
Gopal Raja, CEO, Ideation Inc.

"Chris shows with clarity and persuasiveness that creative thinking is not magic, but a process that can be learned, developed, and most importantly applied to the challenges, whether business or personal, that confront us all. An excellent resource. Grasp it."
Tim Hurson, Author of 'Think Better: An Innovator's Guide to Productive Thinking'

"Now is the time when this book is most needed - we live in a fiercely competitive world, where global choice is greater than ever before. Agility in spotting trends, organising and managing multiple ideas and strategies, and smart implementation are key to success."
ReSource Magazine

"Chris and his work have changed my life, and already millions of lives for the better worldwide. His work is in the process of doing the same for YOU."
Tony Buzan, Multi-million copy best-selling Author and Inventor of Mind Mapping

GRASP
The Solution

How to find the best answers to everyday challenges

By Chris Griffiths
with Melina Costi

Proactive Press

BIOGRAPHY

Chris Griffiths is the CEO of ThinkBuzan, the organisation behind Mind Mapping, the thinking tool used by millions worldwide. ThinkBuzan have been leaders in creativity and innovation for over 40 years with the mission to grow 'minds' and help individuals 'think' and 'be' better.

Chris is an expert in combining modern brain based thinking strategies, processes and techniques with creativity and technology. He founded his first business at 16 and sold his first company at the age of 25. Companies with which he has been involved have ranked in the 'Deloitte Fast 50' and 'The Sunday Times / London Stock Exchange Fasttrack 100'. He has also won awards for innovation and creativity.

Chris Griffiths is a sought after seminar and conference speaker, inspiring audiences worldwide with his distinctive take on what stops people being creative and how to unlearn the bad habits that stifle the formation of great ideas. He has facilitated brainstorming sessions for business, academic and humanitarian events, including the Petra Conference of Nobel Laureates in 2008, which was attended by some of the world's greatest minds with the aim of finding solutions to end child poverty.

Chris Griffiths recently co-authored '*Mind Maps for Business*' with Tony Buzan, which featured on the Amazon UK bestseller list. His writing draws on his own extensive observation and experience to introduce insightfully practical concepts that empower people towards success. Chris's books have been sold in over 15 countries and translated into five languages.

His material has also been integrated into a nationally accredited qualification endorsed by a major UK Awarding Board to help students maximise their thinking skills.

He is responsible for iMindMap® – the software tool that topped the Amazon charts in Japan to become the number one ranked software product across all categories. iMindMap® has been used by over a million people worldwide in over 170 countries and 15 languages.

Chris, who is married and has two wonderful children, is a firm believer in a 'healthy body equals a healthy mind', hence his on-going study of the martial arts, which he has practised for 23 years.

In his new book, Chris explains why most people struggle to be innovative and demonstrates how anyone can let go of the unhelpful thinking habits that hold them back from applying their limitless creative potential. '*GRASP The Solution*' presents a powerful and focused four-step approach for finding the 'best' answers to any challenge.

Published by

Proactive Press

Proactive Press
Falcon Drive
Cardiff Bay
Cardiff
CF10 4RU
UK

+44 (0) 2071 177 173

www.ProactivePress.com

© 2011 Chris Griffiths

ISBN 978-1-905493-76-0

Printed in the UK by the Berforts Group.

CONTENTS

ACKNOWLEDGEMENTS

It is difficult to know where to start when pulling together the acknowledgements for this book. Creativity and innovation is not yet (and never will be) an exact science, but the time, energy and effort expended by so many sharp minds help to make it more accessible than ever before.

I must say a big thank you to my co-author, Melina, for her expert input, and for her hard work in helping to make this book a reality. Her magic with words never fails to amaze me and her generous assistance in researching the material included has been invaluable.

I owe a huge debt of gratitude to the entire team at ThinkBuzan for all of the enthusiasm and effort they put into assisting people to think and work more creatively worldwide. They are more friends than colleagues and I feel very lucky to work with such a wonderful group of people.

I have been honoured to train, and more so, to learn from the many ThinkBuzan Licensed Instructors from every continent. Their dedication to teaching others how to think better and 'bigger' has been an inspiration to many, especially me, and I'm deeply grateful for their shared insights and experiences. They are ambassadors who spread the word about creative thinking around the world and, without them, the system described in this book would not exist.

It is rare to meet an individual who can make a profound difference to the way one lives one's life. Tony Buzan, my mentor, colleague and friend, is such a man. His Mind Mapping technique is now used by hundreds of millions of people because it simply works! It is fair to say that his exceptional genius and wisdom has been the inspiration for my own creative journey.

I would like to say a special thank you to Brian Lee, my Chairman and friend. Whilst I would like to sail in every direction, seeking out the new and exciting, Brian ensures that I at least find land once in a while!

I pass on my sincerest thanks to the pioneering work being done by so many amazing individuals mentioned in the bibliography, especially to Edward de Bono, Sir Ken Robinson, Steven Johnson, Daniel Pink, Stephen Shapiro, Tim Hurson, John Adair and Tony Proctor. This book would not have been possible without their extraordinary knowledge, research and expertise. I would recommend that anyone who is truly interested in understanding creativity read the material provided by all of the above named individuals to get a fuller and deeper appreciation of the subject.

The greatest thanks of all goes to my family for their love and support, especially my wife Gaile for her clarity and patience, and finally (and most importantly!), the most creative individuals of all - my children Alex and Abbie. Alex for his ability to achieve the seemingly impossible and Abbie for her amazing imagination.

PREFACE

We've all heard the saying *"knowledge is power"* **- but what happens when everyone has access to pretty much the same knowledge and information?**

Information is becoming old news. It's no longer a differentiator, it's a commodity. With access to copious communication channels, websites and media, we can all find out what we need to know, when we need to know it. And with the aid of modern technology, there's nothing remarkable in being able to analyse, process and manipulate information. In many ways, we're all skilled knowledge experts already.[1] So where's the edge?

It's time to start facing the facts - the landscape of our society is changing profoundly. We're in the throes of an extraordinary **creative** revolution and we need a whole new set of mental and operational tools to deal with it.

People say "if you keep doing what you've always done, you'll keep getting what you've always got."

I disagree with this. In the new economy, if you keep doing what you've always done, you'll get left WAY behind.

Creativity is more than just the buzzword of the moment. Individuals and organisations are finally acknowledging just how vital it is for contending with an increasingly complex and mercilessly competitive environment. Everything is shifting around us – our markets, our tasks, our technology, even our relationships. The famous adage "change is the only constant" has never been more apt as Russian futurologists report that the frequency of social and technological change will continue to intensify rapidly in the coming decades.[2] The upshot of all this change is that we're being forced out of our comfort zone and into a higher gear to boost our chances of making it in the long-term.

1 Wolf, Guillame D. (2010), 'Why We're Entering a New Creative Age', *Creativity Boost*, 12th Oct 2010, http://www.thecreativityboost.com/why-were-entering-a-new-creative-age/
2 *Law of Time*, http://zakonvremeni.ru/law-of-time.html

Creative thinking is becoming a prime tool in these wildly uncertain times, bringing us new choices and setting us up to differentiate products and services, to envision and develop new insights and processes, and to achieve growth.[3] In surveying more than 1,500 CEOs and senior managers from around the world, IBM discovered that 'creativity' is believed to be the most crucial factor for future success. More and more senior executives are focusing on it as a key mechanism for reinventing customer relationships, producing greater operational dexterity and establishing a thriving business all-round.[4] Consequently, there's a genuine need for a purposeful and strategic approach which people can use to encourage and enhance creativity actively.

My goal in writing this book was to fill that need.

In these pages, I introduce a conclusive 'real-world' system that makes it possible for anyone to achieve the creative brilliance that's needed for personal and professional success today. Not only does it break the bad habits that 'kill' creativity, it creates the most fertile conditions for the thought process to work at its highest levels - so we can all solve problems and make decisions using our full brain power and creative potential. This is the **GRASP The Solution (GTS)** system.

In Chapters 2 to 20, you'll learn how to understand your modes of thinking **(GRASP)** and how to put them to play in a way that helps you generate more and better ideas, select the right solutions and make them happen boldly and successfully **(Solution Finder)**.

But, first things first. Before we embark on our journey of creative development, we're going to look more in depth at WHY we need to focus on our thinking and creativity in Chapter 1. We're also going to explore how our creative abilities diminish with age and how taking an active interest in our mental development can put us back in control of our creativity… and our lives.

Read on to experience the POWER of creative thinking!

Chris Griffiths

---

3 Hurson, Tim (2008), *Think Better: An Innovator's Guide to Productive Thinking,* McGraw-Hill Professional
4 IBM (2010), 'IBM 2010 Global CEO Study: Creativity Selected as the most Crucial Factor for Future Success', *IBM Press Release,* 18th May 2010, http://www-03.ibm.com/press/us/en/pressrelease/31670. wss

"*The real source of wealth and capital in this new era is not material things…it is the human mind, the human spirit, the human imagination, and our faith in the future.*"

Steve Forbes, President and CEO of Forbes Inc

INTRODUCTION

During the last decade, we underwent one of the most significant shifts ever experienced in human history – the information explosion. As a result, we witnessed the rise of what Peter Drucker termed the **'knowledge worker'**[1] - the programmers, IT workers, accountants, MBAs and lawyers who could process and manipulate this all-important resource. These individuals have been credited for achieving some of our most spectacular successes in business and industry – and rightly so. But today, this is all changing.

While the linear, logical and analytical talents of knowledge workers are still very much necessary, it's hazardous to presume that these skills will continue to shape the nature of success in a new 'creative' age. As the value of ingenuity and innovation skyrockets, the competencies of analysis and logical processing of information can no longer rule.

Why is that?

New technologies are proving that they can execute this type of sequential, analytical and computational work better, faster and more accurately than even those with the highest IQs.[2] Ask any lawyer, stockbroker, analyst or programmer and they will bemoan how many of their functions are increasingly being turned over to machines!

Knowledge is a fantastic means for aiding advancement but it's not a solution in itself. In this new creative era, the power is inevitably going to shift to people who can look at things differently, who can think imaginatively and objectively to deliver new values and ideals. The leaders of the next decade will be those who can deliberately and systematically make fresh connections and discoveries, generate original ideas, solve problems creatively not just logically, and break the rules to overcome sameness. They will be true 'whole brain' thinkers, harnessing

1 Drucker, Peter (1969), *The Age of Discontinuity,* Harper and Row, New York.
2 Pink, Daniel H. (2005), *A Whole New Mind: Moving from the Information Age to the Conceptual Age,* Riverhead Books

both their left (analytical) and right (creative) cortical skills to make optimal decisions.

Information is still important, but unless we make the effort to look at it in different ways we get stuck and stagnate in the same old habits and patterns.[3] It will be this new breed of thinkers who will be able to synthesise, exploit and transform information to find original solutions to contemporary challenges and so forge the way forward. Success is no longer a matter of what we know but **how we think**.

The leaders of the new age will be those who can think differently!

By reading this book, you're fundamentally setting yourself up to be one of these people - to be someone who makes a difference instead of following the crowd. You'll be learning how to equip yourself with strategies and tools to cultivate your thinking and, by doing so, discover how you can add value to your organisation, confidently address problems, and massively boost your chances of reaching pre-eminent levels of productivity and innovation.

"No company can grow and prosper without new ideas. Customer's changing needs, increasing pressure from competitors, and the evolving abilities of suppliers all necessitate a continual source of creative thinking for a company to stay on top."

Henry Chesbrough, Author of 'Open Innovation'

---

3 de Bono, Edward (2009), *Think! Before It's Too Late*, Ebury Publishing

The Most Important Factor...

Here's a question for you. If you wanted to create a successful organisation, whether a business, school or charity, what would be the most important advantage or asset you could have?

Take a few moments to think about this. Would it be the best product, most competitive price, a brilliant sales team, a powerful brand, sound infrastructure and processes, a hungry crowd?

Let's say you believe that brand is the most influential factor. Of course the brand is an incredibly valuable component of a business, but where does it come from in the first place?...

...It comes from **PEOPLE**. People are the driving force of an organisation; they are without doubt the single most important ingredient for success. Seth Godin,[4] entrepreneur, author and public speaker on marketing and change, quotes:

"Carnegie apparently said, 'Take away my people, but leave my factories and soon grass will grow on the factory floors...Take away my factories, but leave my people and soon we will have a new and better factory.' Is there a typical large corporation working today that still believes this? Most organizations now have it backward. The factory, the infrastructure, the systems, the patents, the process, the manual... that's king. In fact, shareholders demand it. It turns out that success is coming from the atypical organizations, the ones that can get back to embracing irreplaceable people, the linchpins, the ones that make a difference. Anything else can be replicated cheaper by someone else."

So with this being the case, what's the most important factor that determines the success of the individual? Again, stop and think about this for a short while.

Perhaps there are a number of qualities and aspects that could be significant here - intelligence, inspiration, communication skills and creativity. But again, where does inspiration come from? Where does intelligence come from? They all funnel down to the ability of people to **THINK** in the correct way. Ultimately, all of the successful elements of a business are devised by individuals who, first and foremost, are able to think fittingly to the task. In simple terms, thought is our most valuable human resource.

---

4 Godin, Seth (2010), 'Losing Andrew Carnegie', *Seth Godin's Blog*, 7th March 2010, http://sethgodin. typepad.com/seths_blog/2010/03/losing-andrew-carnegie.html

People – The most important factor in an organisation

We are what we think, and if we think better we can be more efficient, creative and productive... But how many of us actually stop to think about how we think?

We probably all agree that having adequate systems, processes and procedures in place is instrumental for a business to grow and succeed. A pilot can't fly to his exact destination without a set of monitors and gauges to guide the way and make sure everything is progressing well.[5] Likewise, an organisation benefits from systems and processes to drive its operational efficiency and help optimise end-to-end performance.

McDonald's is an excellent example of how efficient and organised processes can become the basis of a successful business model.

Every activity at McDonald's has a very specific process, enabling the entire organisation to run like a well-oiled machine. Ray Kroc, the man responsible for building McDonald's into a massive-scale fast food operation, even created a 75-page manual detailing the entire 'McDonald's Method' to the letter.[6]

The system is so fine-tuned, it delivers the required end result almost every time.

With such great value brought by systems and processes, surely a chief goal for all organisations should be to implement systems which assist people to **think** in the most focused and effective ways for particular tasks. If thinking is the most fundamental factor for success, doesn't it

5 Peters, Mike (2008), 'The importance of Business Systems & Processes', *Software Projects Inc,* 9th June 2008, http://www.softwareprojects.com/resources/the-basics/-the-importance-of-business-systems-processes-1528. html
6 Roach, Kim (2009), 'The Magic of McDonald's', *Buzz Blogger,* 18th April 2009, http://www.buzzblogger.com/the-magic-of-mcdonalds/

make sense that the best action we could take would be to actually help people **think about thinking?**

> *"The ability to think better will soon become the most significant competitive advantage companies and individuals can claim."*

Tim Hurson, Author of 'Think Better'

Are We Ready For Creativity?

Although most of us have an intuitive understanding of what it means to be creative, there's still a great deal of uncertainty surrounding the nature of this fascinating concept.

I define creativity as *"the incubator and cultivator of new ideas, which are born from existing knowledge and combined to form a new neural pathway in the brain, leading to a personal original thought."*

The key point to take from this definition is that, at its simplest level, creativity relates to the **mental processes** that lead to solutions, ideas, concepts, theories or products that are unique and novel.[7]

Creativity is a fundamental driver for innovation - but what is innovation? It's the *"the marriage of creative thinking and sound logic, which when applied together, create a solution or direction for one to explore and deliver."*

> *"Creativity is thinking up new things. Innovation is doing new things."*

Theodore Levitt, American economist and professor at Harvard Business School

On this basis, we can acknowledge that all progress and advancement is attributable to creativity at the outset. It's the catalyst for change. Without it we remain trapped in the past, rehashing the same out-dated concepts. In business especially, there's a need for creativity to make up for the shortcomings of conventional logical thinking which boxes us in by merely

---

7 Carter, Philip (2007), *IQ and Personality Tests,* Kogan Page Ltd, p. 153

extending what we already know, rather than bringing something entirely new to the table. And critical thinking is just as bad! As the eminent thinker Edward de Bono puts it, "You may be so brilliant at critical thinking that you can destroy any silly idea, even good ones. But no amount of critical thinking can produce good ideas in the first place."[8]

Despite our serious need for creativity, we have a tendency to push it to the side and do very little to facilitate it in the workplace and in our lives. Usually we hope that certain naturally 'gifted' individuals will supply us with new ideas and opportunities, or we hold disorganised 'brainstorming' sessions that are little more than a platform for the more dominant personalities to impress their ideas on others.

The interesting thing is that, as children, we were all far more creative than we are today. Stephen Shapiro[9], author of *24/7 Innovation: A Blueprint for Surviving and Thriving in an Age of Change*, discusses how this premise has been tested over the years. He reports that in a study which began in 1969, 1,600 five-year-olds were given a creativity test used by NASA to select the most innovative engineers and scientists. Of these children a staggering 98% scored in the 'highly creative' range. Five years later, these same children (now 10-years-old) were re-tested and only 30% were still rated 'highly creative'. Another five years later, when the children were 15-years-old, just 12% of them were ranked in this category. More revealing, however, was that 250,000 adults over the age of 25 also took the same test and a paltry 2% of them scored in the highly creative range. So unless you're five-years-old, the chances are your creativity is seriously lacking!

What does this study prove? In the words of Stephen Shapiro, "Creativity is therefore not learned, but rather unlearned." Creativity is a quality that can be universally found in all of us as young children, but it fades rapidly as we progress towards and reach adulthood. We can liken this 'creativity unlearning' process to how elephants are taught not to stray.

An elephant is tethered to a chain when it is still a baby. After pulling at the chain several times, the elephant soon learns that struggling doesn't help it break free. Eventually, when released from its chain, the baby elephant won't attempt to stray further than the length of the original chain! As the elephant gets older, the chain is shortened, and again when it's released, it doesn't go further than the limits originally placed on it. Despite growing into the most powerful land mammal on earth, the chains in the elephant's mind remain deeply ingrained and it doesn't attempt to pull away.

8 de Bono, Edward (2009), *Think! Before It's Too Late*, Ebury Publishing
9 Shapiro, Stephen (2003), '*Unleashing The Inner Innovator*', *Control*, No. 3, p. 19-21

This is so true of children, who during their formative lives have numerous chains put on them. The chains get shorter and shorter as they progress through education and when they're finally released out into the real world, they have difficulty advancing further than the limits that were placed on them in school and by society!

Education systems generally focus on training the mind for storing and analysing information instead of developing its power to generate new ideas and bring them into being. And they stigmatise mistakes! A fear of being 'wrong' frightens a lot of children out of expressing themselves in ways that are even mildly unconventional or different. In preserving such an approach to schooling, Sir Ken Robinson, author of *Out Of Our Minds: Learning To Be Creative*[10] believes that we're actually educating people out of their natural creative capacities. He argues that, in today's world of accelerated change, creativity is as important in education as literacy and, for that reason, we should regard it with the same status and respect.

The idea that many people 'grow out' of their creativity correlates with the results of our own ThinkBuzan Creativity Study,[11] which we devised specifically to measure creativity and its subsets such as flexibility, originality, fluency and association. It's an ongoing study which over 4,500 participants have now completed (you can take part by accessing this weblink: http://www.thinkbuzan.com/creativitytest). Our findings have so far revealed that, while certain skills such as fluency in response are unaffected by maturity, original thinking skills decline dangerously with advancing age.

Research shows that creativity declines in adulthood

10 Robinson, Sir Ken (2001), *Out Of Our Minds: Learning To Be Creative*, Capstone Publishing
11 *ThinkBuzan Creativity Study* (2010), http://www.thinkbuzan.com/creativitytest

But this doesn't mean they're gone forever! My belief is that for the majority of the adult population, creativity is an untapped resource that's withered through lack of use. Young children can generate highly original solutions to problems because they aren't bound by the rigid conventions and methodologies of adulthood. By contrast, adults will try to pull a solution from their repository of knowledge, solving the problem in a way that's been proven to work in the past. A common issue with senior executives is that they'll use their sharp reasoning skills to pick out a tried and tested solution from their wealth of experience and will then impose it onto the problem, forcing it to work no matter what. More often than not, they're trying to fit a round peg into a square hole – the solution just isn't a good match for the problem. We have to understand that an increasing number of today's business problems have few or no precedents, so this line of approach isn't likely to get us very far![12] It's crucial that we start thinking in terms of new possibilities rather than looking for ready-made solutions.

> *"I definitely think people can learn how to be creative, but I think for the most part people unlearn how to do it."*
>
> **Evan Williams, Co-founder and former CEO of Twitter**

We can all be creative, even in the later stages of life. We just have to be very purposeful about it. In writing this book, my aim is to offer a self-contained and systematic guide to reawakening our innate creative abilities and tackling our problems and opportunities innovatively. First we have to free our minds from the shackles of limited thinking that constrain our creativity. We can then apply directed principles, processes and techniques to stimulate the kind of original thinking that brings the best possible answers to our everyday (and not so everyday!) challenges.

Though it may appear otherwise, being creative isn't a process that occurs just by chance. Good ideas usually arise when people are actively engaged in seeking them out; when they're curious, enquiring and on the alert for opportunities.

This notion is reinforced by additional experiments we've conducted using the ThinkBuzan Creativity Test. The pilot group who participated in the original study came from our vast database of contacts and, for this reason, could confidently be said to have a general interest in mental literacy and 'creativity-enhancing' tools such as Mind Maps. When we compare the results of this pilot group with groups of participants who

---

12 Proctor, Tony (1999), *Creative Problem Solving For Managers*, Routledge

have no special interest in the brain or thinking, we gain valuable insight into exactly how much inquisitiveness and directed effort influences levels of creativity. For instance, in the 'Visual Imagination' category, our pilot group scored an average of 7.15 out of a total of 10, compared to a mere 4.3 average within the test groups. In every single category the pilot group consistently demonstrated far greater levels of divergent thinking, idea flexibility and original thought than the test groups. Quite clearly, active interest and pursuit of creativity and mental improvement are important factors in determining our creative ability. It's not just a case of who has the 'natural talent' for it.

This begs the question – how much more creative and innovative can we be if we develop our interest and really start to put a process behind our thinking?...

> *"I have no special gift, I am only passionately curious."*
>
> **Albert Einstein, Nobel Prize winning theoretical physicist**

This brings us to the dual purpose of this book:

1) To help you develop an awareness of your thinking – To be more creatively productive, it's vital that you understand why you think the way you do and how to use your natural thinking abilities to your best advantage.

2) To help you apply a strategy to your thinking – With an understanding of your thinking in place, it becomes possible to apply a process (for problem solving and decision making) that will direct your attention in the most optimal way to bring new and better ideas.

Both of these values are brought to you via the **GRASP The Solution (GTS) System**.

GRASP The Solution (GTS) System

As much as we know that creativity is important to the success of our work or business, it's disheartening how few of us actually understand how it comes about or how to put it into practice. The GTS system was brought into being to provide the know-how and practical strategies that we can all benefit from in striving to think more creatively and productively.

Firstly, it introduces **GRASP** - a concept which paves a way through the maze of established neuroscience and psychological research about how we think, presenting the information in a way that makes it easy for anyone to 'grasp'!

And secondly, it offers a practical and strategic process – the **Solution Finder** – which helps us apply this knowledge of our thinking to generate more options, evaluate them effectively and implement the winning ideas and solutions that will propel us forward.

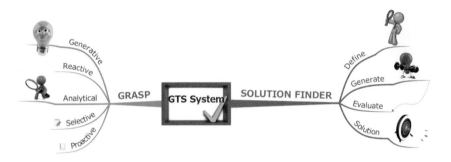

The GTS System

1) GRASP

Definition of 'Grasp' in the Oxford Dictionary:

• Take (an opportunity) eagerly
• Comprehend fully
• A person's power or capacity to attain something
• A person's understanding

In fitting with these descriptions, the aim of **GRASP** is to help you better **understand** your thinking processes so you can ultimately become more productive and creative when making decisions and solving problems. In short, it's there to get you **thinking about your thinking**.

GRASP is an acronym that stands for the various modes of thinking we need to be aware of if we're to take charge of our thinking. These are:

Generative – Generating thoughts and ideas

Reactive – Reacting to existing influences and ideas

Analytical – Analysing ideas to reach a solution

Selective – Validating and implementing a potential solution

Proactive – The strategy of thinking (encompassing all of the above)

The mode of thinking you're in always dictates the way you approach a particular task. When making a decision, you may well draw on all the modes at one point or another to help you find the answer. The problem is that without an underlying awareness of the nature and contribution of each mode of thinking, you're far less likely to apply them in the most constructive and congruent way.

GRASP presents a simple way to become conscious of the independent characteristics of each mode of thinking so you can better understand the mental route you take to reach a solution.

Once this awareness of your thinking is in place, you're in a more advantageous position to approach challenges in ways that deliver more creative and innovative outcomes. At any point during problem solving or decision making, you can use GRASP to discern whether you're in the right frame of mind for the specific task you're working on. It will give you real food for thought!

GRASP helps you become aware of your thinking

Knowing and recognising the modes of thinking is still only half the journey, however. To be successful in business, you need to be able to effectively use systems, processes and tools that harness each mode of thinking, but in ways that are optimally targeted towards your particular situation or desired results. In effect, GRASP gives you the foundation from which to start building a **strategy** for your thinking.

Just like a business creates strategies, systems and processes to facilitate its success, your thinking needs a proactive and purposeful strategy through which you can bring about the results you want. In the GTS System, that strategy comes by way of the **Solution Finder**.

2) The Solution Finder

The Solution Finder is a pragmatic strategy designed to provide focused direction for your thinking. It's a very simple but powerful process, channelling your efforts for 1) defining your challenge, 2) generating ideas, 3) evaluating those ideas and 4) setting your goals and action plans.

When trying to solve problems and make decisions, most of us allow our thoughts to roam haphazardly, hoping that we'll somehow happen upon the right answers. Conversely, the Solution Finder guides us in our mental journey, helping us utilise the modes of thinking optimally to generate and implement successful business ideas. Through making use of the recommended tools and techniques at each stage of the Solution Finder process, we can be sure that our thinking and behaviour will be in line with what we need to achieve.

Importantly, the Solution Finder provides a **proactive** and orderly basis for creative thinking, so it's no longer a matter of waiting for specific people to produce brilliant ideas or forcing teams into ineffectual brainstorming processes. Now everyone has the opportunity to be creative and, instead of being a rarity, innovation can become an everyday practice. If we leave innovation to chance, we may never get around to it. This is because we usually go about our daily lives in a **reactive** state.

What's the first thing you do in the morning when you get into work? Like most of us you probably check your emails. What then? You probably set about immediately responding to the important ones, i.e. you start the day by reacting to what's in front of you![13] While this might seem efficient, you're not actually giving yourself time to think things through, to gather more information, to be innovative or flexible in how you respond. To reach peak levels of performance in today's dynamic world you need to be **proactive**. Success happens on purpose, not by accident. Instead of reacting impulsively to the events in your life, you have to consciously create the opportunities that will bring your desired future and outcomes

---

13 van de Buld, Ronald (2010), 'Measures Individuals Can Apply to Avoid Information Overload', *Nyenrode Business Universiteit*, http://bit.ly/ggg1ir [In Dutch]

into focus. Chapters 4 and 7 will give you the full lowdown on reactive and proactive thinking.

"Once we rid ourselves of traditional thinking we can get on with creating the future."

James Bertrand, Vice President of Delphi and President of Delphi Thermal Systems

In any creative process, it's vital that we begin by DEFINING THE PROBLEM. The way we pose our problem shapes the answers we get and so it's worth taking the time to establish the right 'version' of the problem we want to solve (or goal we want to reach). Chapter 10 outlines how. Understanding the facts and subtleties inherent within a problem sets the scene perfectly for us to find innovative solutions to solve it.

Creativity is essentially about having killer ideas. To get the most out of a situation, we have to learn to use our brain to question, explore, invent, discover and create – in other words we need to be hugely **generative** in our thinking. Whether we're looking to solve a business problem, find new ways of working, change policies or to boost sales, it's through using generative thinking mechanisms such as metaphoric stimulation and reframing that we can produce insights and ideas which we would never have envisaged through conventional problem solving methods. To this end, the Solution Finder employs generative thinking tools to help you tap into your creative abilities at every stage of the process, not just the idea generation phase. Chapter 3 explains all about generative thinking and Chapters 12 to 17 kit you out with a range of creativity enhancing tools and techniques to play with on your problem solving journey.

Work Your Brain!

The GTS system is designed on the basis of understanding the **brain** and how we think. Due to the diligent work of neuroscientists and psychologists over the last three decades, we have a much greater awareness of exactly how the brain works. That's how we know that if we stimulate the brain with the correct thinking tools, it will reward us with brilliant solutions to any kind of problem or challenge. One of the most effective and useful tools for optimising how we use our brain is the **Mind Mapping** technique invented by the world's foremost brain and learning expert, Tony Buzan.

In a Mind Map, we record and present ideas or concepts in a visual format that duplicates the non-linear nature of the human thinking process. Our thoughts, ideas or facts are laid out on branches around a central theme to form an organic, connected structure which 'radiates' outwards. Lines, key words, colour, space and images are all employed according to simple, brain- friendly concepts.

Mind Mapping supports and enhances our creative problem solving efforts by improving the way we take notes and allowing us to consolidate all the information we need in a compact space. Whether it's employed by one person or a team of people, the Mind Map is a positive and constructive way of maximising generative thinking as it puts us in a creative mode for rapidly producing novel ideas and solutions. It can be used comfortably and conveniently alongside other generative tools as an excellent addition to our creative thinking arsenal.

In this book I demonstrate precisely how Mind Mapping can be applied within the Solution Finder process for problem solving, decision making, organising ideas and thinking creatively. Where the Solution Finder helps you set up the best environment and mindset for what you need to achieve, Mind Mapping is the practical device through which you can capture and cultivate your ideas for resolving your specific challenges.

> *"Action is the real measure of intelligence."*
>
> **Napoleon Hill, Author of one of the best selling books of all time 'Think and Grow Rich'**

The overriding goal of this book is to get a balance between intelligence and application to increase your chances of succeeding. After all, it doesn't matter how intelligent you are in the first place, if you can't apply that intelligence, you're not going to get very far. As expressed by Edward de Bono, "Intelligence is a potential. Thinking is an operating skill."[14] Highly intelligent people still need to put their thinking skills into operation if they're to make full use of that intelligence.

You can read all the books you want about improving your golf swing, but in the end it's being able to apply the skills through methodical practice that determines how good you become. Likewise, all the greatest intellectual minds teamed together couldn't produce an idea or a solution without some sort of systematic application. IQ and strong academic results

14 de Bono, Edward (1982), *Thinking Course*, BBC

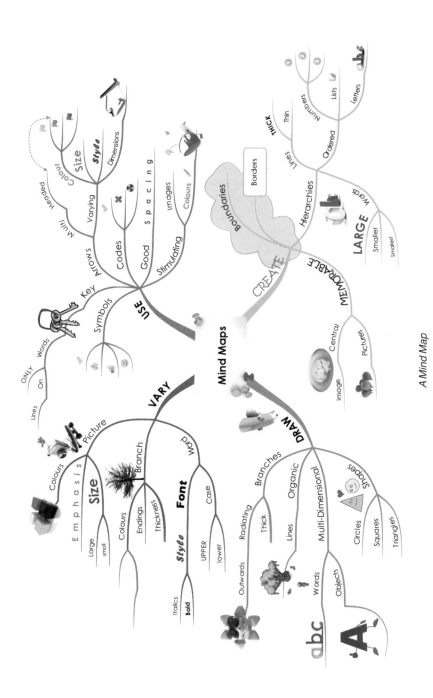

A Mind Map

aren't guaranteed indicators of success in life. Many brilliant students who ace all their school tests go on to perform poorly later in their careers. Psychologist Daniel Goleman argues that this is because cognitive abilities aren't the only ones that count. Self-awareness and the ability to draw on other resources such as emotions to make sound decisions are equally important to success.[15]

The GTS System, in and of itself, is merely an invitation to direct your attention to your thinking. The best it can do is to make you more aware and confident in applying the right thinking modes and tools when you need to. There are no hard and fast rules – your focus on thinking can be as tight or as loose as you want it to be. Though it's fair to say that when you're getting the most out of your thinking, you significantly increase your chances of finding, developing and ultimately implementing novel and creative ideas. To what degree, is all up to you.

Where I'm Coming From...

One thing you'll have gathered by now is that I'm not a neuroscientist or a psychologist. I didn't go to university, so I'm far from being an academically qualified expert. This is certainly not a book by a scientist for a scientist. It's a book for ordinary, everyday people that just want to think better and come up with more ideas. There are thousands of brilliant minds who are specialists in every possible area of neuroscience and applied psychology, and they're discovering more unique facts about our thinking hour by hour and day by day. My goal with this book is to simply bring this knowledge to you in a way that's easy to understand and, most importantly, can be acted upon. I'm simply the translator. It's by interpreting and converting this knowledge that I've been able to design appropriate thinking models such as the GTS system that are easy to grasp, simple to use, very practical and produce synergistic results.

You could say that my expertise is more hands-on and experiential. I've been very fortunate to have kept company with some exceptional people over the last 20 years. I've facilitated brainstorming sessions with over 30 Nobel Prize winners, incredible thinkers who have demonstrated the ability to apply creative thinking to change the world. I've also had the opportunity to spend time with leading experts in science, business, humanitarian concerns and academics. I've worked on developing products with thousands of schools in the UK and across the world. More recently, I've lectured to audiences worldwide on entrepreneurship, the brain, learning and the impact of technology on human thinking. These amazing encounters have furnished me with invaluable knowledge

---

15 Goleman, D (1997), *Emotional Intelligence: Why It Can Matter More Than IQ,* Bantam

and real world experience in how to handle demanding challenges and situations. What I've done with this book is consolidate and repackage that knowledge and experience in a way that makes it easy to apply immediately.

Lately, I've learned that the majority of people are ready for new ways of thinking that are based on sound and solid principles of how the brain works. They want tools that make sense and that are practical for increasing productivity both on a business and personal basis. My wish is to bring this new era of thinking to the fore and demonstrate that, when we target our thinking, we're actually enhancing our most fundamental human resource. In this book the GTS System provides the knowledge and guidance for this to happen.

Many CEOs and entrepreneurs across the globe are now using this system to generate fresh solutions for tough business challenges and lots of individuals rely on it to for their personal issues and goals. Creative thinking is a skill anyone can learn to develop and I'm very proud to say that this material has also been integrated into a nationally accredited qualification to help people maximise their thinking and creative potential.

How much better would your life be if you could truly think creatively and productively? You have a mind and there's nothing stopping you from using it more effectively by way of the material in this book. By all means read about it, think about it, but most importantly apply it!

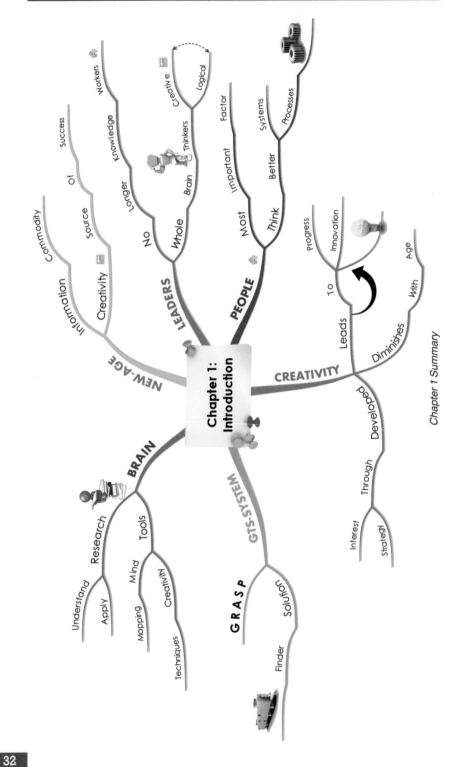

Chapter 1 Summary

Part 1

GTS System: GRASP

GRASP

We live in an age of constant change where we need to be fighting fit if we're to maintain a standing in our market or profession. New knowledge, competition and technological developments are assailing us at every level, so it's becoming virtually impossible to remain on our feet. And as new situations arise, we come face to face with problems, opportunities and challenges that require increasingly novel solutions.

What worked in the past no longer fits the bill so we're being forced to 'up our game' with a new arsenal of creative insights and approaches to stand the best chance of succeeding. In the heat of it all, there's little hope or choice for us other than through continued growth, adaptation, creativity, productivity and innovation.[1]

> *"In today's age of change, as soon as you achieve success, someone is nipping at your heels, learning your unique strengths and planning to take a portion of your market. The only way to succeed is to have the ability to change – rapidly and repeatedly. This requires perpetual innovation from you and your entire staff at all times."*
>
> **Stephen Shapiro, Author of '24/7 Innovation'**

The majority of us have already made a keen start on becoming more creatively productive and we've come to depend on any number of accessible tools and skills to help us. From the latest brainstorming software to the 'hottest' new management techniques, we've embraced anything we believe will provide an effective answer to the multiple challenges we face. We've even gone as far as to adopt different business models to shake up the way we work and help us get ahead. Yet even the most self-aware among us will easily overlook the one primary

1 Treffinger, Donald J. Isaksen, Scott G. and Dorval, Brian K. (2000), *Creative Problem Solving: An Introduction*, Prufrock Press

resource which has the capacity to unleash unparalleled creativity and transformation – the human mind.[2] The climate for successful innovation and productivity doesn't begin with the newest management theory or technological fad, it begins with our thinking. How can we expect to promote serious creative growth without understanding where it comes from in the first place?

Thinking about Thinking

There's nothing more important in your life than your thinking. Whether you're looking to start a new venture, attract more customers or just reorganise your workload, the greatest advantage you can have is the ability to think in the correct way. This may appear to be a bold statement but consider it for a moment...

Q) If you could come up with that one killer idea, that one moment of brilliance, what would it be worth to you?

My guess is that it would be worth a huge deal to your future, and you wouldn't be alone in that regard. Anyone who aspires to excellence in business knows that the generation of ideas – especially creative, high quality ideas - is not only beneficial to their success; it's a vital 'make or break' factor. Indeed, the consulting company Booz Allen and Hamilton Inc concluded from a study of top management that:

"Nowhere inside the business is there any factor as potentially valuable as the 'Big Idea'… At any given time, an outstanding idea can produce more dollars of profits than years of cost reduction programs."[3]

The killer ideas and solutions that drive your business forward don't just simply fall from the sky. They come from using the power of your mind - your thinking.

Thinking is at the heart of everything we do. It encompasses all of the mental activities associated with concept-formation, problem solving, intellectual functioning, creativity, learning memory, symbolic processing and so on.[4] In other words, it's the starting place for every possible pursuit or task. So doesn't it correspond that the more effectively we use our thinking, the more successful we'll be in what we're doing?

---

2 Myatt, Mike (2010), '35 Critical Thinking Strategies', *Blogging Innovation*, 15th April 2010
3 Booz Allen and Hamilton, Inc (1965), *Management and Advertising Problems in the Advertiser-Agency Relationship*, New York, Association of National Advertisers Inc.
4 Dr Shaker Abdel Hamid Soliman (2005), *Systems and Creative Thinking, Pathways to Higher Education Project*, http://www.pathways.cu.edu.eg/subpages/training_courses/Creativity/Chapter2.htm

"If I have any advice to pass on, as a successful man, it is this: if one wants to be successful, one must think; one must think until it hurts."

Roy Thomson, Canadian businessman and author of 'After I was Sixty: A Chapter of Autobiography'

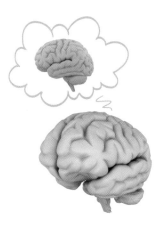

Thinking about Thinking

Unfortunately, most of us never stop to think about **how** we think. At an intellectual level, we can recognise that our thinking is important, but we seldom take the time to understand it or learn how to handle it effectively. However, just as we manage our workload, our staff and our personal lives, we also need to manage our minds. By taking charge of our thinking, we remove the ambiguity out of making business decisions and can move forward to tread new paths clearly and confidently. Good thinking practices also make it much easier to 'see' the most innovative solutions to our pressing challenges and everyday problems – it's akin to working in bright daylight instead of fumbling around in the dark.

Being able to go beyond conventional thinking is particularly crucial if we're to cope in this new 'creative age' where the ability to source and process information is no longer a competitive advantage. As Deborah Gough, a prominent educator and researcher on thinking skills, points out, "Specific knowledge will not be as important to tomorrow's citizens as the ability to learn and make sense of new information".[5] Innovation requires that you use information differently to create unique ideas and convert them quickly into action.

5 Gough, Deborah. (1991), *Thinking about Thinking.* Alexandria, Virginia. National Association of Elementary School Principals

If you consider that all successful endeavours in the fields of engineering, medicine, architecture and business began as just a thought in someone's head, then creativity involves little more than the capacity to apply your mind. The most innovative and useful ideas are the result of good, intentional thinking - the type of thinking that forces you to find opportunities and make things happen. The way you think can therefore propel you to success, or hold you back. Naturally the 'winners' in life are those of us who learn to take charge of and use our thinking so that it serves us in the right ways.[6]

There are countless tools, techniques and systems we could apply to encourage everyday innovation and creative problem solving. But it's only once we've developed a real awareness of our thinking that the introduction of new tools, techniques and systems will make any practical sense. If you understand something, you're better able to control it instead of allowing it to control you. Once you know **how** to think, you can promptly set up an organised approach for identifying problems and opportunities, generating ideas and solutions, evaluating alternatives and deciding on courses of action; and you can guarantee that it will be the most appropriate one for your needs.

How, then, can we understand our thinking? How can we help ourselves and others to practice better thinking and problem solving on a regular basis?...The answer is simple to **GRASP**.

---

6 Borg, James (2010), *Mind Power*, Prentice Hall Life

GRASP – Our Modes of Thinking

As with anything in life, the more you put into it, the more you get out of it. If you want to be more creative and productive, then you have to focus your energy and attention on setting up the most creative and productive environment. And I'm emphatic in saying that this must *always* begin with your thinking.

GRASP is a concept that gets you thinking about your thinking so you can ultimately get more from your thinking. It's an acronym that makes it easy for you and others to recognise the modes of thinking that you can adopt at any one time. With this understanding you're better placed to take charge of a situation and deliver the innovative and useful outcomes you want.

So what does GRASP actually stand for?

It stands for the various modes of thinking that people should be aware of. These are:

Generative – Generating thoughts and ideas

Reactive – Reacting to existing influences and ideas

Analytical – Analysing ideas to reach a solution

Selective – Validating and implementing a potential solution

Proactive – The strategy of thinking (encompassing all of the above)

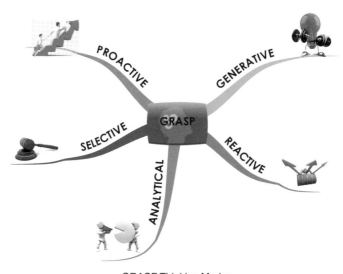

GRASP Thinking Modes

There's nothing radically new or complicated about GRASP. Most people are already somewhat acquainted with these modes of thinking, based as they are on widespread psychology and scientific research. Of course, as human beings we're not limited exclusively to the GRASP modes of thinking, there are other modes we can engage in. However, the GRASP modes are those that I've been able to isolate explicitly in view of their relevance to creative problem solving and innovation.

> "Everything should be made as simple as possible but no simpler."
>
> **Albert Einstein, Nobel Prize winning theoretical physicist**

In my experience and involvement with numerous business people and educators, one thing that's become increasingly evident is that no matter how much we already know about our thinking and the various modes we can adopt, we rarely, if ever, consciously apply them when we're going about a task. Hence this is where GRASP's true power lies – as a simple and credible way to help you become mindful of your thinking so you can ultimately orchestrate the best mental environment for what you need to do or achieve. This method applies whether you're making a huge life changing decision or simply looking to resolve a niggling technical issue.

All the modes of thinking are important to us. In an activity like problem solving, we might apply a number of them concurrently, so they aren't entirely exclusive of each other. The problem is we hardly ever use and combine them in the correct way. One of the most significant discoveries in contemporary psychology is that we choose how we think. In developing GRASP, I wanted to present a means through which we could examine and understand our thinking so that we could do exactly that – choose how to think while tackling certain tasks.

Thinking Proactively

Of all the modes, Proactive Thinking is of central importance in promoting real innovative success. It's the final mode in the GRASP acronym because it's the culmination of all the previous modes of thinking – Generative, Reactive, Analytical and Selective. On an operational level, it determines how we utilise the other modes as we journey through the decision making and problem solving process. We must be able to master it totally and absolutely if we're to think more objectively, creatively and effectively as we work towards our goals.

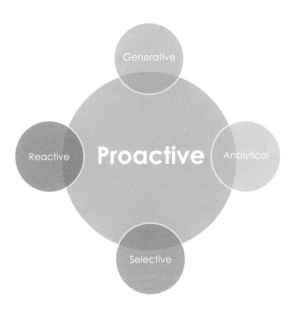

Proactive thinking is central to all the other modes of thinking

Proactive thinking is fundamentally about strategy. If you're aiming for maximum levels of innovation and productivity, you *have* to apply strategy to your thinking. This requires that you pause and assess how you can best employ the modes of thinking to make a difference to your creative performance. In later chapters, I present you with a process called the Solution Finder. This process demonstrates how you can proactively combine the GRASP modes of thinking in the most effective way to:

• Define opportunities, challenges and problems.
• Generate many varied and unique ideas for dealing with a selected problem using appropriate creative tools and strategies.
• Evaluate ideas and determine the most promising solution.
• Strengthen your chosen solution and plan for successful implementation.

Although this approach is highly ordered and might appear overly drawn out, it's also fluid. The power is always with you in choosing how meticulous you wish to be at each stage and in selecting the most appropriate tools and techniques for your own particular situation. What's key about this process, however, is that it helps you deliberately apply certain modes at certain times, making sure that your thinking is aligned precisely to bring your desired results.

With an understanding of GRASP and a proactive drive governing your thinking, you can engage in what Matthew Syed calls 'purposeful practice'.[7] Having explored the territory of sports psychology for his book *Bounce: How Champions are Made,* Matthew presents compelling evidence that 'purposeful practice' is what plays the most crucial role in creating the success of the world's top athletes – it's not just about having an innate talent for their sport. A champion athlete's thinking is perfectly disciplined and they engage in purposeful action which is focused towards skill development, execution and strategy.

Successful athletes use 'purposeful practice'

Similarly, having a high IQ or natural creative ability doesn't translate into good thinking skills without any conscious and purposeful effort to apply the right strategies and tools. For my part the aim of this book is to help you apply a strategy to your thinking, i.e. to become proactive and purposeful so you can create the most fertile climate for innovation and get the most out of your mental efforts. By the time you finish reading you should be at a point where, before you do anything that requires attention, creativity or focus, such as solving a problem, finding a new opportunity or creating a plan, you'll be able to use your awareness of GRASP to make sure that you're ready-placed to be productive and reach more meaningful and innovative decisions.

Remember, your thinking should never be taken for granted – it should be practised purposefully!

7 Syed, Matthew (2010), *Bounce: How Champions are Made,* Fourth Estate

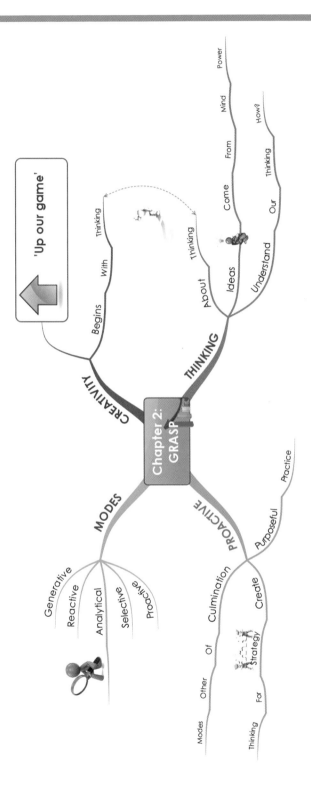

Chapter 2 Summary

GENERATIVE THINKING

With innovation leaping to the top of the list of success factors for companies both large and small, generative thinking is fast becoming an indispensable and obligatory skill. As Tom Kelley, author of *The Art of Innovation* says, "Without creativity a manager may do a good job, but he can't do an outstanding one."[1] Generative thinking is what brings new, fresh ideas to your business practices and leads to breakthrough advances – both much needed if you're to stay ahead of the game.

The basic purpose of generative thinking is to come up with lots of ideas – it's your 'ideas machine'. Thinking generatively involves getting into a frame of mind where you can produce tons of new alternatives, ideas and solutions in relation to your issue, opportunity or problem. You can think inside the box or outside the box, it doesn't matter, the key is that you open your mind into wide focus to consider all possibilities, whether wacky, conventional or impossible. Psychologist J. P. Guilford puts forward evidence that divergent thinking processes such as generative thinking are a major component of creativity.[2] This is because they encourage your thinking to flow freely and stray off in all sorts of different directions, allowing you to explore and engage with multiple aspects of an issue to spark off as many original ideas as possible.

> "*Real, constructive mental power lies in the creative thought that shapes your destiny.*"
>
> **Laurence J. Peter, American educator and writer**

Generative thinking is not only for the obvious applications such as new product development and marketing. It's necessary for all areas of business including strategic planning, operational management and even

---

1 Kelley, Tom and Littman, Jonathan (2001), *The Art of Innovation: Lessons in Creativity from IDEO, America's Leading Design Firm, Harper Collins Business*
2 Guilford, J.P. (1967), The Nature of Human Intelligence, New York: McGraw-Hill

finance. Tantamount with what most people think of as brainstorming, it plays a valuable role during the early stages of problem solving and decision making which call for exploration, insight and inventiveness.

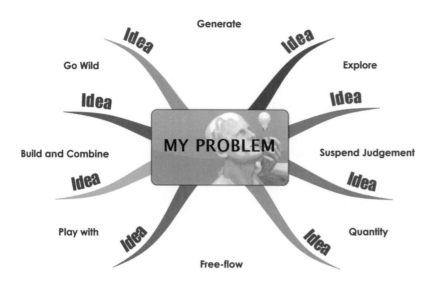

Generative Thinking

How to Promote Generative Thinking

Although there can be no 'rules' for creativity as such, there are four widely-cited principles that serve to encourage high-value generative thinking. These originated from the 'father of brainstorming', Alex Osborn, via his book *Applied Imagination*,[3] and have since evolved through further psychology and management research. The idea is that following these principles will enable us to release our minds to create more energy and deliver greater creative power than we would otherwise. They can be employed when thinking alone, but work even better in a team setting.

> *"The best way to have a good idea is to have a lot of them."*
>
> **Linus Pauling, American theoretical chemist and biologist**

3 Osborn, Alex F. (1953), *Applied Imagination: Principles and Procedures of Creative Problem Solving,* New York: Charles Scribner's Sons

1) Strive For Quantity

The goal of generative thinking is to generate a multitude of ideas and options... but why do we need to generate so many ideas - we only need one to solve our problem? Because innovation is a numbers game. As the saying goes, the greater the number of oysters, the more likely you are to find some pearls in them. By producing as many ideas as possible, we seriously raise our chances of hitting on the one breakthrough idea that surpasses all previously known limits. And so we must aim to take a leaf out of Thomas Edison's book - he conducted around 9,000 experiments before successfully developing a working electric light bulb. Through quantity, we can achieve quality. A high correlation between quantity and quality of ideas has actually been verified by researchers such as Diehl and Stroebe,[4] who in a series of experimental studies found that quantity measures are reliable predictors of total idea quality.

A further example of this principle at play comes from H. J. Heinz in the USA. The company used brainstorming to produce ideas for getting sales promotional material to consumers more quickly. Their efforts resulted in 195 ideas, eight of which they went on to use. A member of Heinz later said, "Brainstorming generated more and better ideas than our special committee produced in 10 meetings."[5]

Aim to generate lots of ideas

While it may be tempting to allow idea generation to be a natural and unaffected process, a substantial body of research indicates that it's more effective to give yourself and other participants a specific target for the number of ideas to be produced.[6] When you're dealing with broad,

4 Diehl, M. and Stroebe, W. (1987), 'Productivity Loss in Brainstorming Groups: Toward the Solution of a Riddle', *Journal of Personality and Social Psychology*, 53 (3), pp. 497-509.
5 Adair, John (2007), *Decision Making and Problem Solving Strategies*, The Sunday Times, Kogan Page
6 Rossiter, John R. and Lilien, Gary L. (1994), 'New "Brainstorming" Principles', *Australian Journal of Management*, June 1994, 19, 1

open-ended challenges such as identifying new product concepts or working out how to improve productivity, 50 is not an unreasonable number to aim for. Yet even for narrower challenges, striving for volume forces you to think more widely to increase your likelihood of striking upon a winner.

A helpful point to remember is that when you compile many alternatives, the first third tend to be obvious, the second third are more ridiculous, and the final third contains the best, most creative ideas – ones that are novel and useful.[7] Unoriginal or unrealistic ideas are easy to come across. To find the practical and original ideas you have to KEEP looking.

2) Encourage Wild and Unusual Ideas

This principle is about assisting yourself and others to open new directions for generating ideas and to express your wilder, madcap notions. There's an old maxim that says, "One doesn't discover new lands without consenting to lose sight of the shore".[8] This is what generative thinking requires of us. It asks us to go beyond conventional thinking and look at things differently by changing perceptions and patterns and playing with new concepts and starting points. It's an approach that has lots in common with Edward de Bono's concept of 'lateral thinking', in which the whole idea is to escape the conventional, obvious, cliché train of thought and draw out more outrageous and unexpected associations.[9] These new associations are what will eventually lead us to new shores.

The important thing is that we stretch our imagination so we don't limit ourselves to just logical ideas and solutions. Take the common paper clip as an example. In just two minutes, you can probably come up with a number of different uses for it if you allow your imagination free rein.[10] For instance, some ideas that people have come up with include: keyring, fishing hook, lock pick, hair clip, pipe cleaner, fuse wire, toothpick, nail cleaner, ornament, catapult missile, picture hook, tie-clip, bookmark, letter opener and many more.

Remember we may need to entertain lots of ridiculous or irrelevant ideas before happening on more feasible options. The more unusual the idea, the better. As Alex Osborn says, "*It's easier to tone down a wild idea than to think up a new one*."[11] For instance, if our problem is to 'reduce the amount of paperwork in the office', then a radical solution could be

---

7 Wheeler, Jim (1998), *The Power of Innovative Thinking: Let New Ideas Lead You To Success*, Career Press
8 Gide, Andre (1926), *The Counterfeiters*, Vintage
9 de Bono, Edward (1990), *Lateral Thinking: A Textbook of Creativity*, Penguin
10 Buzan, Tony (2000), *Head First!: You're Smarter than you Think*, Thorsons
11 Osborn, Alex F. (1953), *Applied Imagination: Principles and Procedures of Creative Problem Solving*, New York: Charles Scribner's Sons

to eradicate all use of paperwork. While this idea might not be viable in reality, you can soften it down to a more practical solution quite easily by, for instance, using email for everything, except where paperwork is absolutely essential.

Breaking the rules is not only ok, it's necessary. Consider how Dell successfully broke the rules of the computer market by selling directly to consumers and building computers to order, while the big companies of the time, Compaq and IBM, relied on a more costly and unwieldy structure of retail and distribution channels. And look at how Amazon made huge bets on its Web Services and Kindle offering to become a dominant player in the book market. When you're looking to make a major innovative decision, breaking the rules is one of the most powerful tactics you can employ as ideas generated in this way can provide the underpinnings of a total transformation.

> "*Daring ideas are like chessmen moved forward; they may be beaten, but they may start a winning game.*"
>
> **Johann Wolfgang von Goethe, German playwright, poet and novelist**

3) Postpone Judgement

For a generative thinking session to run smoothly we have to suspend any judgement of ideas until we've generated a sufficient quantity of alternatives to work with. This means deferring all criticism, analysis, reflection and evaluation - both positive and negative. While all of the four principles are important, 'holding off' on judging your ideas and solutions is fundamental so that the other principles can actually operate.

If you've ever been in a meeting where people are generating ideas and debating them at the same time, you can understand how much it slows down the session, saps the energy of those involved and reduces the production of ideas. In the time it takes to judge, you could instead be creating twice as many ideas! Much of our valuing can be negative, killing off ideas prematurely. When you suspend the critical evaluation of ideas, you give everyone the green light to exercise their imagination freely. A judgement-free atmosphere is a relaxed atmosphere, encouraging a better flow of ideas without fear of rejection.

The previous guideline taught us that, if we want to establish something completely new, we have to take risks with our thinking and break the rules. When we analyse and judge our ideas as soon as we generate them, we lose this risk-taking quality and end up focusing on the known and familiar, hindering our very own efforts to innovate. To get past this, we must learn to treat all ideas as if they contain the seeds of something potentially great. All ideas are good ideas, even the zany ones, because at the moment we conceive them we don't know where they might lead.[12]

> "*Criticism often takes from the tree caterpillars and blossoms together.*"
>
> **Jean-Paul Sartre, French philosopher, novelist and playwright**

4) Build and Combine Ideas

This principle involves creating new offshoot ideas by encouraging participants to improve, link and combine ideas already suggested. Ideas rarely arrive in the world fully formed. Through this principle you can take the buds of success in someone's half-baked idea and, by process of association, develop it to fruition.

> "*The creation of a thousand forests is in one acorn*"
>
> **Ralph Waldo Emerson, American poet and lecturer**

Some of the more wacky and crazy ideas are not solutions at first. This activity is what modifies, expands and transforms them so they can have a better basis in reality. For instance, Art Fry, the 3M company employee who developed a 'useless' super weak glue could have just left things there. Instead he continued to build on what he had invented by looking for a solution for his glue. The result is now the multi-million dollar phenomenon known as the 'post-it' note.

> "*I start where the last man left off.*"
>
> **Thomas Edison, American inventor and scientist**

It's surprising how by elaborating and expanding on just one idea you can

---

12 Mind Gym (2005) , *The Mind Gym: Wake Your Mind Up*, Sphere

give birth to new and unexpected products or ways of doing things. If you want to be really radical then try combining two ideas that aren't closely related and see what happens. The number of combinations you create is limited only by your imagination.

> "It is the function of creative people to perceive the relations between thoughts, or things, or forms of expression that may seem utterly different, and to be able to combine them into some new forms – the power to connect the seemingly unconnected."
>
> **William Plomer, South African novelist and poet**

Capturing and Cultivating Ideas with Mind Maps

We now have the four key principles we need to promote the generation of creative ideas:

• Strive for quantity
• Encourage wild and unusual ideas
• Postpone judgement
• Build and combine ideas

...but what's missing?

We still need something that will help us to capture and store our ideas on paper or on screen for later reflection. This is where the Mind Map comes in. It's one of the most powerful tools you can use to support your idea generation efforts. Besides being a medium for recording your ideas visually, it also works on three levels to enhance and facilitate creativity and innovation:

1) Divergent Thinking

By radiating branches from the centre outwards, a Mind Map encourages your thoughts to behave in the same way so you can explore many possible solutions without limitation or restriction. Entering new ideas or building up existing ones is as easy as connecting another branch to either the central theme or main branch. The key elements of Mind Mapping such as key words, colours and images aid in drawing out novel ideas and perspectives that wouldn't necessarily be revealed using more conventional note-taking techniques.

Divergent Thinking

2) Structured Thinking

Contrary to what some people believe, Mind Mapping is not 'unstructured thinking'. In fact, it's one of the most structured forms of thinking possible, employing a number of organising principles such as a central theme, Basic Ordering Ideas, secondary and tertiary ideas and so on. The central theme, in particular, keeps you focused on your main goal while still allowing you to think freely and expansively as you work around it. What this means is that you can be as generative as you like - letting your thoughts range far and wide - but can refer back to your central theme at any point so that you don't go astray from your task. Essentially the Mind Map stops you 'shooting from the hip' as you always have a clear view of your target.

By another token, your problem may not be that you don't have enough new ideas - you may be drowning in them! In this case the Mind Map gives you the structure in which to organise and categorise your ideas in ways that are most relevant to what you're trying to achieve.

3) Holistic Thinking

A Mind Map allows you to get a 'big picture' view of all your ideas and options so you can clearly see the relationships among them. Just as the branches in a Mind Map are all connected, so are all the ideas in relation to each other. This gives a Mind Map a depth and breadth of scope that a simple list of ideas can't match.[13] From this perspective it becomes easier to springboard off ideas to create new ones more rapidly and thoroughly.

What are the Risks?

Being aware of the guidelines for effective generative thinking and having access to a tool that can help is excellent practice. But it doesn't rule

---

13 Buzan, Tony (2004), *Mind Maps At Work*, Thorsons

out the importance of having to pay conscious attention to our natural leanings in terms of our thinking. For the bulk of us who are mainly analytical and selective thinkers, it can be difficult to be truly divergent in our thinking without making a real concerted effort. When we have a tendency to apply analysis and judgement too early in the problem solving process, it gets in the way of our creativity and causes us to reject ideas that might at first appear ludicrous or off the wall - 'that's silly' or 'that won't work'. What's more, we may exclude certain possibilities due to a biased preference towards a specific idea or pre-existing concept. This is not to discount analytical and selective thinking. They're both highly valuable to the decision making process but they can be awfully obstructive when we use them at the wrong times.

> "Judgment and imagination can help each other if kept apart when they should be kept apart."
>
> **Alex F. Osborn, Originator of brainstorming and author of 'Applied Imagination'**

On the flip side, there are also potential perils for natural generative or creative thinkers. Being creative in our thinking is not about being different for the sake of being different. We've all come across those creative right-brainers who have inborn imagination and artistic talent, but have very little grip on reality. Perhaps they're the misfits, the rebels who have no respect for analytical logic. Yet true creativity and innovation needs some analytical logic behind it. Logic by itself can't be very creative, and creativity without logic has little practical value. So how do we achieve a level of creativity that's actually usable?

The answer is through **strategy**.

Purposeful Creativity

Strategy is what makes creativity purposeful so we can promote unconventional and original thinking, but with practical relevance. Creativity isn't a fluffy or flaky concept as some people think. It requires serious treatment and application. Applying strategy via a good functional process is what turns creativity into planned innovation. The Solution Finder is such a process, illustrating how we can proactively combine the three operative thinking modes - generative, analytical and selective - to set up the most innovative and productive mindset for solving problems. Each of these modes of thinking on its own is nowhere near as powerful as when it's applied in conjunction with the other modes in a clear, staged process:

1. Generative - We generate a wide range of possible options.

2. Analytical - We analyse these options and gather information in order to converge to a single solution.

3. Selective - We strengthen and reinforce our chosen solution and decide how to take it forward.

Generative > Analytical > Selective Thinking Process

> *"If we learn to use our imagination in a guided way it can propel us to success in all areas of life."*
>
> **James Borg, Author of 'Persuasion' and 'Mind Power'**

This process represents what innovative thinking is all about. Productive thinkers know how to facilitate an environment where the modes of thinking actually complement each other. And we can inject something extra into this process to make it even more powerful – an additional dose of **generative thinking.** The power of being creative lies inherently with generative thinking, but most of us stow it aside once a brainstorming session is over and overlook its potential value for other functions.

What I will be demonstrating with the Solution Finder in later chapters is that we can actually conduct the problem solving process using a **GENERATIVE** approach throughout. This means that generative thinking becomes so much more than a simple brainstorming exercise that we perform at the beginning of our problem solving. Integrated into each stage, it becomes a key facilitator for a range of tasks including identifying problems, coming up with ideas, evaluating these ideas, filtering them and implementing them.

Some people suggest that being generative and creative means being free and that the use of strategy and process imposes a structure which impedes creativity. This is far from the case. Edward de Bono explains, "If you are in a locked room, you need a formal key to get out of the room. This key does not determine where you go once you are outside. Structure is your key."[14]

Purposeful Creativity

Strategy and structure is what helps to keep the creative process objective so that you're thinking from the highest vantage point at all times. When you combine structure with the innate ability that we all have to come up with original ideas, you can break barriers and make real transformation. A process also makes it easier to avoid the pitfalls of over-analysis so you don't overlook or reject novel possibilities and alternatives. By deploying a strategy that's based on generative thinking, you provide the directed focus for all participants to tap into their creative potential, meaning that you no longer have to wait for certain people to throw out quality ideas. Everyone, no matter what intellectual level or inclination, has the capacity to become generative in their thinking as long as they find, develop and practice the right skills and tactics.[15]

Employing generative tools and techniques hugely increases the probability of producing a diverse range of ideas. Some of the tools I'll be laying at your disposal later on in the book include provocative techniques such as those which turn the problem on its head, challenge assumptions or use metaphorical thinking to stimulate possibilities. Other approaches are more exploratory. For example, we can change our points of reference to bring new perspectives. These methods aren't new; they've been used successfully in

14 de Bono, Edward (2009), *Think! Before It's Too Late*, Ebury Publishing.
15 Runco, M.A. and Pritzker, S.R. (1999), *Encyclopedia of Creativity*, Academic Press: San Diego, CA

real life and business in a variety of ways and over a number of years. All I've done is simply pull these excellent strategies together within the **Solution Finder** process to equip you with the hands-on approach you need to tackle your future challenges.

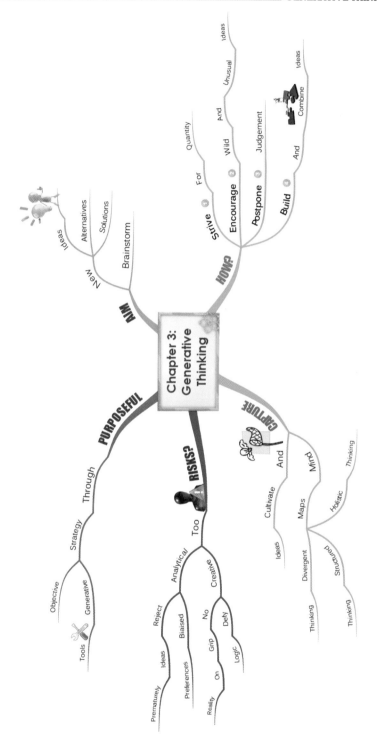

Chapter 3 Summary

REACTIVE THINKING

As human beings, we're biologically, developmentally and socially designed to react – it's what helps us survive in the world. For instance, in traffic we react to what's happening in front of us. If the car ahead is too close, we slow down, if it stops, we stop. It's our ability to react that keeps us alive and safe, rendering it a hugely important mechanism in our lives.

Think about your childhood. Did you grow up hearing repeated messages from parents and teachers about how you should and shouldn't behave; what you should and shouldn't do? For the majority of us this was definitely the case. As children our mistakes are often pounced on quickly, but few of us are told with any regularity that we're smart or creative. Unsurprisingly, once we reach adulthood our normal mode of thinking focuses on avoiding mistakes, solving problems as quickly as possible and being responsive.[1] In other words, we're conditioned to be reactive thinkers.

> "Ninety-nine hundredths or, possibly, nine hundred and ninety-nine thousandths of our activity is automatic and habitual, from our rising in the morning to our lying down each night."

William James, American philosopher and psychologist

We engage in reactive thinking when we react to events, tasks or external influences in pre-programmed ways. Most of the time, this mode of thinking serves a really useful purpose as our 'autopilot', helping us make practical shortcuts as we journey through the patterns of life. Learning a new task such as how to use a new computer system or piece of machinery requires applied focus and concentration. Once we're skilled at the task however, we don't have to rethink the process every time we

---

1 Adams, John D. and Spencer, Sabina (1991), 'Why Strategic Planning Often Fails', *World Business Academy Perspectives*, Summer 1991, http://www.eartheart-ent.com/ docs/ WhyStrategicPlanningOftenFails.pdf

come to do it – it becomes automatic. This makes reactive thinking great for helping us perform the regular and commonplace activities in our lives more quickly, freeing up valuable time for other things.[2]

Reactive thinking helps us perform routine tasks efficiently

How Fast Can You React?

In business today, a huge emphasis is placed on fast reactions i.e. the ability to respond quickly to anything that comes up. When something occurs or is put in front of us - a threat, an opportunity, even an email - we rush to deal with it effectively in a short space of time. In order to respond quickly, we make our decisions intuitively. We'll look to our previous experiences as a pre-conceived set of indicators to determine a course of action without wasting time planning or weighing up alternatives.[3]

> *"Life is 10 percent what happens to you and 90 percent how you respond to it."*
>
> **Lou Holtz, American football coach**

There's nothing wrong with this. This type of reactive functioning is useful, efficient and makes a powerful contribution to our day-to-day productivity. A lawyer thinks in this way while working on a standard case and a doctor will rapidly diagnose and treat a queue of patients with great success. Under predictable conditions, this mode of thinking is extremely valuable, conserving our time and energy and helping us tackle business situations where there's high time pressure.

---

2 Mind Gym (2005) , *The Mind Gym: Wake Your Mind Up*, Sphere
3 Blenko, Marcia (2010), 'How Companies Can Make Better Decisions, Faster', *Harvard Business*, Oct 2010, http://sciencestage.com/v/37283/effective-decision-making-better-and-faster-decisions-how-to-improve-company-and-business-organizati.html

While no one can deny that swift action is very often necessary in business, speed does present some hazards. Consider the following question:

Q) If you were running a marathon, how effective do you think you'd be if you spent most of it sprinting?

Unless you possess incredible, super-athletic powers, you're probably going to burn out pretty quickly! The same applies in business – if you focus all your energy contending with short-term challenges or crises, before too long your productivity will plummet. Speed is important at certain times but at the wrong times it's a massive inhibitor. If at the beginning you don't take the time to strategise where you're going and how you're going to get there, you might even end up heading the wrong way!

Business is a marathon, not a sprint

Business is a marathon, not a sprint. As helpful as it is to take practical and speedy shortcuts, they can obstruct our performance in the long run. Just because a familiar strategy or approach has worked in the past, it doesn't mean it will work in the future! The one constant in business is change. When we're reactive we risk overlooking valuable opportunities to be creative in a fluctuating environment because we're too busy swiftly executing what's always worked before. It makes sense that we would fare far better by pacing ourselves to engage our thinking in activities that will help us evolve and progress, for example:

- To achieve something we haven't done before.
- To do something better than we did it last time.
- To find a more effective way of doing something that we're used to doing routinely.

This latter approach is proactive thinking. When we react we're sprinting, when we're proactive we're running a marathon.

Perception

In Washington DC at a Metro Station, on a cold January morning in 2007, a man with a violin played six Bach pieces for about 45 minutes. During that time, approximately 1,100 people went through the station, most of them on their way to work.

After about 3 minutes, a middle-aged man noticed that there was a musician playing. He slowed his pace and stopped for a few seconds, and then hurried on to meet his schedule.

About 4 minutes later: The violinist received his first dollar. A woman threw money in the Hat and, without stopping, continued to walk.

At 6 minutes: A young man leaned against the wall to listen to him, then looked at his watch and started to walk again.

At 10 minutes: A 3-year-old boy stopped, but his mother tugged him along hurriedly. The kid stopped to look at the violinist again, but the mother pulled hard and the child continued to walk, turning his head the whole time. This action was repeated by several other children, but every parent – without exception – forced their children to move on quickly.

At 45 minutes: The musician played continuously. Only six people stopped and listened for a short while. About 20 gave him money but continued to walk at their normal pace. The man collected a total of $32.

After 1 hour: He finished playing and silence took over. No one noticed and no one applauded. There was no recognition at all.

No one knew this, but the violinist was **Joshua Bell**, one of the greatest musicians in the world. He played one of the most intricate pieces ever written, with a violin worth $3.5 million. Three days earlier, Joshua Bell sold-out a theater in Boston where the seats averaged $100 each to sit and listen to him play the same music.

This is a true story. Joshua Bell, playing incognito in the DC Metro Station, was organised by the Washington Post as part of a social experiment about 'perception, taste and people's priorities'.

This experiment raised several questions:
In a common-place environment, at an inappropriate hour, do we perceive beauty? If so, do we stop to appreciate it? Do we recognise talent in an unexpected context? One possible conclusion from this experiment could be this: If we do not have a moment to stop and listen to one of the best

musicians in the world, playing some of the finest music ever written, with one of the most beautiful instruments ever made…

…How many other things are we missing as we rush through life?

Original article: Weingarten, Gene (2007), 'Pearls Before Breakfast', *The Washington Post*, 8th April 2007

Letting Events Take Control

"There is a time when we must firmly choose the course we will follow, or the relentless drift of events will make the decision."

Franklin D. Roosevelt, 32nd President of the United States

When we react quickly to an event but don't have a clear grasp of the whole picture, we're not necessarily going to reach our destination quicker. In reality, we may end up with a different result than we wanted and have to react quickly again to get back on track. This is because we're operating in crisis-based mode where each new occurrence, opportunity or problem catches us by surprise and ends up setting the agenda for where we're going.

However, if we were to view our situation from a higher perspective *beforehand,* we could consciously engineer our own outcomes by setting our goals and implementing a precise strategy to achieve those goals. Instead of reacting to events and waiting for opportunities, we could create our own events and opportunities.[4] What's more, we might even anticipate any problems or events before they occurred and have contingencies in place to deal with them. In other words, we could be proactive.

When we're predominantly reactive, we spend most of our time trying to fix minor problems and eliminate external threats due to the classic 'fight-or-flight' response. We're also prone to have a short-term, tactical approach and will do things in a predictable way the majority of the time, persistently reinforcing the status quo. This can bring a certain degree of success as business is about managing risks and sustaining good practice. But when we follow this sort of pattern all the time it becomes difficult to implement

---

4 Pavlina, Steve (2004), 'Be Proactive', *StevePavlina.com*, 10th Nov 2004, http://www.stevepavlina.com/blog/2004/11/be-proactive/

innovation in any planned way as our energy and resources are tied up in reacting to what others are doing in a typical 'me too' fashion. From this 'follower' position, we can experience a severe decline in our ability to innovate as we become trapped in a never-ending problem-reaction loop.

Reactive thinking – Reacting to events and crises

"Many organisations and their managers drive toward the future while looking through the rear-view mirror. They manage in relation to events that have already occurred, rather than anticipate and confront the challenges of the future."

Gareth Morgan, Author of 'Riding the Waves of Change'

In contrast, a person who thinks proactively understands that innovation is a force that must be purposefully cultivated and deployed. From this perspective they can be strategic and use careful planning to push the boundaries – looking at additional ideas and applying their energy towards identifying and capitalising on opportunities instead of simply fire fighting. Russell Ackoff, author of *The Art of Problem Solving,* makes a strong point when he says "The effort to get rid of what we do not want is reactive, retrospectively oriented problem solving. The effort to obtain what we want is proactive, prospectively oriented problem solving."[5] These forces also apply at organisational level. Take Amazon for example. For years the company adopted a strategy which targeted growth and expansion over profitability, earning several complaints from its investors. Then it focused on expanding its free shipping program which also caused anger and indignation amongst investors who thought it was costing the company too much at the time.[6] Yet both approaches

5 Ackoff, Russell L. (1978), *The Art of Problem Solving,* John Wiley & Sons
6 Masnick, Mike (2011), 'Jeff Bezos on Innovation: Stubborn on Vision; Flexible On Details', *TechDirt,* 17th June 2011, http://www.techdirt.com/blog/casestudies/articles/20110608/23514814631/jeff-bezos-innovation-stubborn-vision-flexible-details.shtml

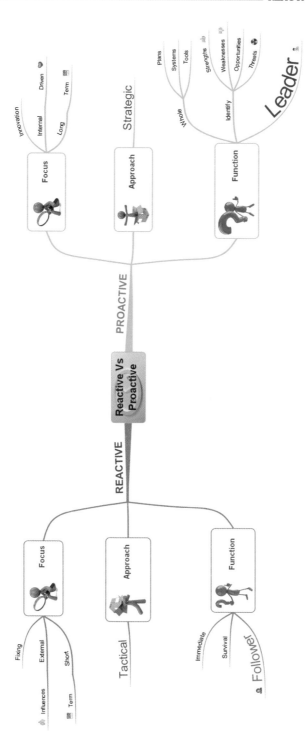

Reactive VS Proactive Thinking

were a huge success because the company sought to proactively open up new inventive opportunities rather than reacting to what other players in the field were doing.

Evidently proactive thinking has an internally driven agenda rather than an external focus.[7] Those who are proactive place control inside of themselves (their own personal decisions and efforts) instead of outside themselves (fate, luck, external circumstances). This is sometimes referred to as having an internal locus of control rather than an external locus of control and can bring lots of benefits as evidenced by Crandall and Crandall's research in 1983.[8] They found that people with an internal locus of control were more likely to display better thinking skills, greater determination and the propensity to choose more challenging tasks. What this suggests is that, by preparing and strategising yourself internally, you develop the faculty to perform better externally. This more or less differentiates you as a leader, rather than a follower.

Are you Reacting or Creating?

In business, people typically start the decision making process by brainstorming in groups – management teams, boards of directors, product development teams and so on. In an Arthur Andersen survey conducted in 2000, more than 70 per cent of business people said they use brainstorming in their organisations.[9] Interestingly, in all the years that I've worked with creative companies and people, I've discovered that many become frustrated by the sheer number of failed brainstorming sessions they have. These sessions fail for a very simple reason – because the participants are not actually brainstorming… they just think they are.

Let's look at the dynamics that take place when a group of people get together to brainstorm for solutions to a particular business challenge.

What usually happens when one person throws out an idea?...

...Almost immediately, the other members of the group analyse and judge it (silently or openly), and the response in their minds will typically be one of the following:

7 Adams, John D. and Spencer, Sabina (1991), 'Why Strategic Planning Often Fails', *World Business Academy Perspectives*, Summer 1991, http://www.eartheart-ent.com/ docs WhyStrategicPlanningOftenFails.pdf
8 Crandall, V.C & Crandall, B.W (1983), 'Material and Childhood Behaviors as Antecedents of Internal-External Control Perceptions in Young Adulthood'. In H.M Lefcourt (Ed) *Research within the locus of control construct Vol 2: Developments and Social Problems*, pp. 53-103, New York: Academic Press
9 Kelley, Tom and Littman, Jonathan (2001), *The Art of Innovation: Lessons in Creativity from IDEO, America's Leading Design Firm, Harper Collins Business*

I agree with the idea and will do everything I can to back it up.

I disagree with the idea so I'm going to do everything I can to make sure it doesn't happen.

Maybe, I'll keep listening and give the idea some thought.

From the outset, these members of the group are being reactive - in their minds, they've already decided and set off down a certain path. They've used analytical thinking to pass judgement on the idea with the result that they accept it, consider it, or reject it. In doing this they've been distracted from their main purpose of idea generation.

People react to ideas during brainstorming

So if being reactive is the predominant thinking mode in the group, can they actually be said to be brainstorming?

Clearly not. By stopping to analyse and evaluate the idea, the group isn't in the right mindset to be generative. They're criticising instead of creating. Their reactive thinking has caused them to fall into a trap. While judgement and analysis play a critical role in decision making, they're hopeless at coming up with creative solutions to problems. As Edward de Bono says, "Six brilliantly trained critical thinkers sitting around a table cannot get going until someone actually puts forward a constructive proposal."[10]

"The possibilities are numerous once we decide to act and not react."

George Bernard Shaw, Irish literary critic and playwright

10 de Bono, Edward (1982), *Thinking Course*, BBC

Brainstorming is a generative exercise and needs to be approached proactively if it's going to be successful in drawing out novel ideas and changes. When we're reactive, we allow ourselves to be influenced by the people and circumstances around us, limiting our ability to participate creatively. By shifting to proactive thinking, we can direct the flow of circumstances and people so that the brainstorming process is guided by our highest intentions. We can think in terms of 'what's possible' instead of focusing on 'what is'. In short, proactive thinking empowers us to be more generative and chip in more ideas.

If we're going to be proactive, however, we need to spot that we're in reactive mode in the first place!

This is the function of the GRASP element of the GTS system – it helps you to recognise the different modes of thinking so you can gradually start taking charge of your thoughts and actions. Being proactive also comes easier when you use a process such as the Solution Finder. The process guides you in uncovering more options, evaluating alternatives and selecting the right solutions so you can escape the inclination to react automatically.

Dealing with Information Overload

We can all agree that having access to information is a positive thing – it's absolutely vital to productivity. There are so many channels and tools that present us with prolific quantities of information, for instance, email, reports, web research, smart phones, online news and social media. As of 2007, humanity's capacity to store the colossal amount of information in the world was calculated by scientists at 295 exabytes (one exabyte is a billion gigabytes). That's the equivalent of 1.2 billion average hard-drives. In the same year, we also broadcast around 1.9 zettabytes of data (a zettabyte is 1000 exabytes). That corresponds to every person on earth reading 174 newspapers every day.[11]

The problem we have here is that an over-abundance of information becomes unmanageable, and gives rise to stress and confusion, hence the term 'information overload'.

Information overload is an escalating problem both in the workplace and in life in general. The more information you receive, the more challenging it is to process it and work out what's credible and useful, and the harder it is to make sensible decisions. Take a look at these statistics:[12]

11 Hilbert, Martin and Lopez, Priscilla (2011), 'The World's Technological Capacity to Store, Communicate, and Compute Information', *Science*, Published online 10th February 2011 [DOI:10.1126/science.1200970]
12 Xerox.com (2010),' Information Overload', http://www.xerox.com/information- overload/enus html

28% The percentage of the typical workday wasted by interruptions caused by unnecessary information.

53% The percentage of people who believe that less than half of the information they receive is valuable.

42% The percentage of people who accidentally use the wrong information at least once per week.

Information overload leads us into reactive thinking mode. When we're bombarded with information, we feel pressure to act on it straight away so we can put the issue to bed quickly. We react to it. The result is that, all too frequently, we end up making the wrong decisions as we haven't taken time to think about the information objectively.

Information Overload

David Allen, best-selling author of *Getting Things Done*, contends that widespread stress from information overload is suppressing a lot of great ideas.[13] Many people have become so used to stress and reactive thinking from information overload that they no longer exist in the relaxed state that encourages constructive thinking and productivity. Moreover, recent psychological and neurological studies confirm that the barrage of information can make it impossible to think deeply or concentrate on one task – a condition that scientists have christened Divided Attention Disorder, or DAD.

Many of us have become so used to short bursts of information such as email, texts or tweets that we've lost the ability to focus on lengthier tasks and think in important ways.[14] It takes time to think seriously and

---

13 Allen, David (2001), *Getting Things Done: The Art of Stress-Free Productivity*, Penguin
14 Carr, Nicholas (2011), 'Why Rich Media Makes Us Poor', *Esquire Magazine*, Jan 2011

cohesively about information, but we've become accustomed to moving on to the next distraction. Unlike our long-term memory, our working memory can only hold a few items at a time. When we take in too much data too quickly, our working memory gets swamped and we struggle to connect the new information into our long-term memory. Our thoughts remain thin and scattered rather than forming solidly into new knowledge. Needless to say, this can have devastating effects on our ability to be creatively productive in any comprehensive or rigorous way.

> *"Information is a source of learning. But unless it is organised, processed, and available to the right people in a format for decision making, it is a burden, not a benefit."*
>
> **C. William Pollard, Chairman of the ServiceMaster Company**

Although there's no simple solution to the problem of information overload, positive action must be taken so that we're able to change crushing quantities of information into something meaningful. If we can extract the most important information, we can be more proactive in our thinking and planning. When we work with inadequate or inappropriate information, it sometimes causes unforeseen problems which lead us into a reactive response to address them. We need a strategy to manage ourselves so that we handle information intelligently, objectively and effectively.

In this book, that strategy is provided by the Mind Map which is a key facilitator of the Solution Finder process. As an information capture and organising tool, the Mind Map has a pivotal role to play in tackling information overload so we can avoid ineffective knee-jerk reactions. It brings clarity to the information available, helping us to focus on quality rather than quantity. We can determine what information we 'need to know' in relation to what information is 'nice to know', reducing the stress that can build up when we try to process inordinate amounts of information. The upshot is that our way of working and conducting business improves dramatically when we're able to filter, assimilate and integrate knowledge at the highest level.

Decision Making Machines

In life and in business you could say that, ultimately, we're all decision making machines. Decision making is at the core of everything we do, whether it's planning, organising, implementing or managing. Even deciding not to decide is a decision!

We make decisions based on our mindset at that particular time. A lot of the time we feel pressure to get things sorted quickly and will adopt a short-term, reactive view to be efficient. This isn't always bad – being reactive can be very positive at times where quick thinking is needed to get us back on track. But when we fall back on it all the time, it's easy to get stuck in a loop of solving the same type of problem over and over again. It then becomes difficult to enact any real innovative change. This is because we're looking at things with a worm's eye view when we need to start with a bird's eye view.

We're all decision making machines

Innovative thinking should be proactive first and reactive second, whenever possible. To be proactive demands a more conscious effort from us as we're habitually ingrained to be reactive. This effort comes through understanding our thinking (GRASP) and applying a strategy to our thinking (Solution Finder). Once a strategy is in place, reactive thinking can become more meaningful and rational when put into service to help us on the day-to-day journey to reach our goals. It provides the backbone for our actions so we can be confident that we're reacting in the right way.

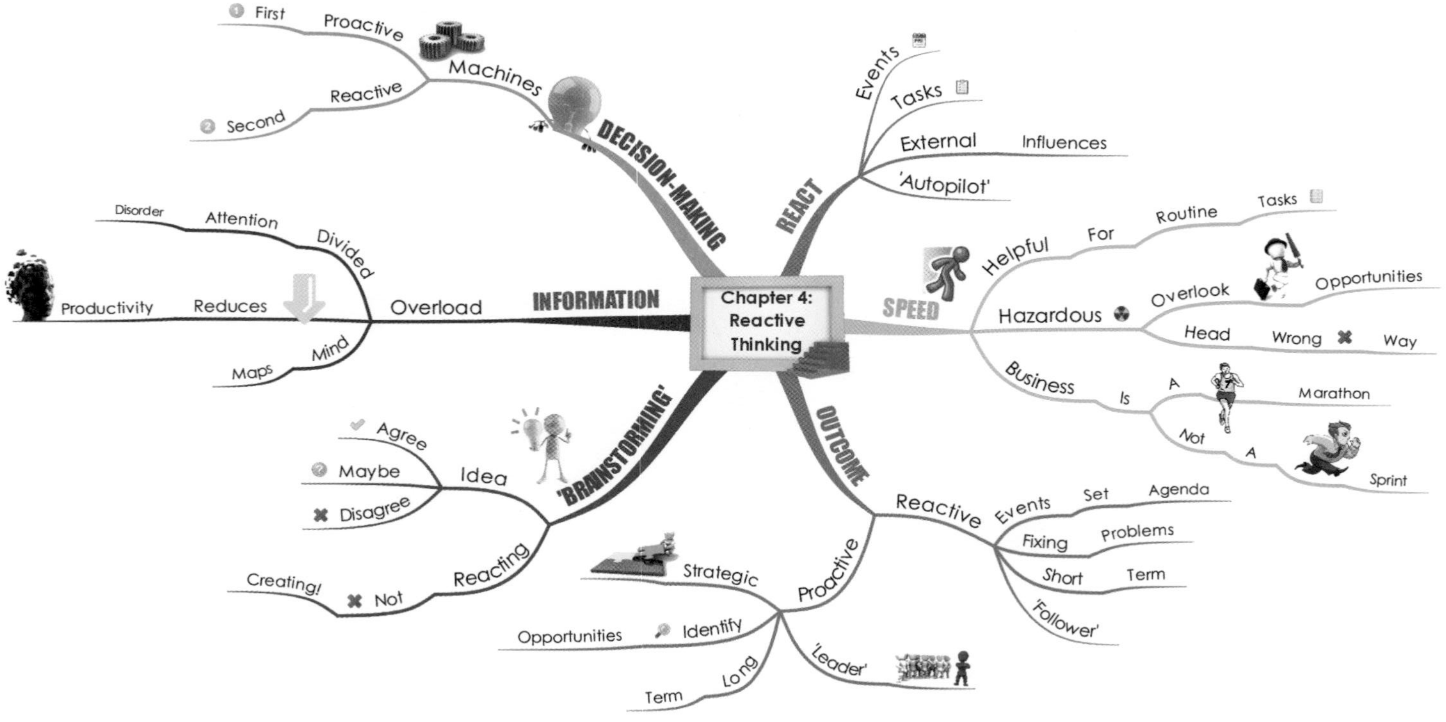

Chapter 4 Summary

Central topic: Chapter 4: Reactive Thinking

REACT
- Events
- Tasks
- External Influences
- 'Autopilot'
- Helpful
  - For Routine Tasks
  - Overlook Opportunities
- Hazardous
  - Head A Wrong Way
  - Business Is Not A Marathon / Sprint

SPEED

OUTCOME
- Reactive
  - Events
  - Set Agenda
  - Fixing Problems
  - Short Term
  - 'Follower'
- Proactive
  - Strategic
  - Identify Opportunities
  - Long Term
  - 'Leader'

DECISION-MAKING
- Machines
  - Proactive — First
  - Reactive — Second

INFORMATION
- Overload
  - Divided Attention
    - Disorder
  - Reduces Productivity
- Mind Maps

'BRAINSTORMING'
- Idea
  - Agree
  - Maybe
  - Disagree
- Reacting
  - Not Creating!

ANALYTICAL THINKING

Analytical thinking is the mental activity that leads us towards making a correct and informed decision. With generative thinking we can come up with tons of ideas for our problem, but we need analytical thinking to help us, sort, screen and select from them to make the transition from idea to solution.

As we saw in Chapter 3, we risk throwing away a good chunk of our most fruitful ideas by analysing them prematurely and this is why we should 'put off' analytical thinking until after we've generated a sizeable pool of potential solutions to our problem. Once we've done this, we can switch from suspending judgement to critical evaluation to whittle down our options and ultimately select the best one to carry through to implementation.

> *"Get the habit of analysis – analysis will in time enable synthesis to become your habit of mind."*
>
> **Frank Lloyd Wright, American architect and writer**

A widely held view of this process refers to Divergent-Convergent thinking. When we apply generative thinking we're 'diverging' our thoughts broadly to generate more ideas. With analytical thinking we're 'converging' our thoughts to a single point – the solution. Analytical thinking is therefore a logical follow-on to generative thinking, bringing a healthy dose of reality to the creative process.

Analytical Thinking in Action

The basic challenge for analytical thinking is how to manage and make practical use of the output of creative ideas from the generative thinking stage.[1] How can we filter out the bum ideas without hastily killing off those

---

1 Jones, Sue and Sims, David (1985) 'Mapping as an Aid to Creativity', *Journal of Management Development,* 4,1 pp. 47-60

which could be made to work with a little adjustment? And how can we make positive, objective and explicit judgements on our ideas? These questions are important because it's the effectiveness of our analytical thinking that determines how well we make use of our creativity.

Generative (Divergent) and Analytical (Convergent) Thinking

The analytical process typically involves breaking down options and ideas into smaller elements. We then make reasoned assessments about how valid, effective, important, relevant, useful and worthwhile they are in order to arrive at our final solution. All in all analytical thinking follows a methodical and scientific approach to problem solving and decision making. A lot of people believe that analytical thinking and critical thinking are one and the same. For others (including me) critical thinking appears to encompass lots of different strategies of thinking under one banner and, as a result, makes very little sense at all. To me, critical thinking implies bearing down on a problem or issue and picking holes in it i.e. being critical about it. There's an underlying assumption of unearthing errors, defects or incorrect conclusions. Being critical is a necessary skill - it helps us to reason things out and identify the main contentions in issues, but it needs to be handled properly so our thinking doesn't become discoloured by invalid reasoning.[2] What people really need for the problem solving process is well-managed analytical thinking. Rather than focusing on finding flaws, we analyse knowledge and possibilities *positively* to better understand them and come to a sound and workable solution.

---

2 Vallee, Virginia (2010), *The Roots of Sound Rational Thinking*, http://plusroot.com/dbook/07Critical.html

Thinking analytically to reach a solution

I recommend the following three guidelines to smoothly facilitate the way you carry out analytical thinking:

1) Narrow down ideas using positive judgement

Immediately after the generative thinking phase, you're left with a bunch of random ideas that you now need to reduce down to a meaningful quantity before you can conduct a successful analysis. Considering general practicalities, feasibilities and costs will help in eliminating the bulk of ideas to a shortlist of approximately three to six viable contenders.

> *"Replace 'either/or' thinking with 'plus' thinking"*
>
> **Craig R. Hickman, Author of 'Creating Excellence' and 'An Innovator's Tale'**

During this period it's crucial to remain completely open minded as it's all too easy to fall back on the safe ideas that you've tried before or have heard to work for others. Remember, innovation doesn't come from the same old ideas; it comes from bold, fresh and novel ideas. Judgements starting with "no, because..." should be avoided. These negative openings discourage discussion by closing the door to further evaluation on an oddball idea that could possibly be made to work if modified in some way. If you begin a judgement with "yes, if..." this invites further speculation on the idea. It gives it a chance to breathe and may eventually materialise a very practical solution that would otherwise have been rejected as being unrealistic.[3]

---

3 Kaufman, J.J. and Carter, J.L. (1994), 'Evaluating Brainstorming Ideas: The Making or Breaking of the VE Workshop', *International Conference of the Society of American Value Engineers (SAVE)*, New Orleans, LA

Researchers at Cornell University found that people with limited knowledge in a certain domain automatically overestimate their ability and performance. Because of this, not only do they reach erroneous conclusions and make unfortunate choices but they fail to realise it.[4] This is a hazard we must all be alert to when thinking analytically. Recognising our limitations helps us become more accurate in our judgements about the ideas that are most meaningful to our problem, and those we should set aside. When working in a group, any idea that has the support or interest of even just one member of the team should stay and those without any backing can be eliminated.

> *"If a man will begin with certainties, he shall end in doubts. But if he will be content to begin with doubts he shall end in certainties."*
>
> **Sir Francis Bacon, British author and philosopher**

This stage can be tricky as there's a delicate balance between eliminating too many or too few alternatives which can impact on later evaluation. Being ruthless and purging all but the 'best' options will make the following evaluation stage easier and faster, but it also increases the possibility of getting rid of an option that, when all factors have been counted, might have turned out to be the best choice.[5]

2) Evaluate ideas using appropriate criteria and techniques

How do you decide which ideas are better than others?

Once you've whittled down your ideas to a shortlist of three to six possible solutions, it's time to begin a more precise and systematic analysis. This involves applying evaluation techniques and criteria to determine the worth of your selected ideas. The techniques you can employ at this stage range from simple rating systems (e.g. rating ideas on a scale of 1 to 10) to specialised methods for weighing pros and cons (e.g. Force Field analysis[6]), to full blown measurement systems for complex decisions (e.g. Analytic Hierarchy Process, AHP[7]).

---

4 Kruger, Justin and Dunning, David (1999), 'Unskilled and Unaware of It: How Difficulties in Recognizing One's Own Incompetence Lead to Inflated Self-Assessments', *Journal of Personality and Social Psychology*, Vol. 77, No. 6, pp. 1121-1134
5 Forman, Ernest and Selly, Mary Ann (2001), *Decision by Objectives (How to convince others that you are right)*, World Scientific Publishing.
6 Force Field Analysis, http://en.wikipedia.org/wiki/Force_field_analysis
7 Analytic Hierarchy Process (AHP), http://en.wikipedia.org/wiki/Analytic_Hierarchy_Proces

It's important to be aware that some rote-step analytical approaches are too demanding and complicated to be effective for what most circumstances demand. Many individuals and groups are put off by highly complex and formal tools as maintaining the discipline to apply them to problems other than the most extreme issues can be difficult. Ideally your methods and criteria should be somewhat broad and flexible, but not too hazy. The key thing is that they keep you organised while in search of the right solution. For instance, UK retail giant Tesco uses the following simple but constructive criteria for approving ideas.[8]

• Is it better? (For customers)
• Is it simpler? (For staff)
• Is it cheaper? (For Tesco)

So the ideas that are better, cheaper and easier are the ones most likely to be taken forward.

In the Solution Finder, I recommend a straightforward process for evaluating ideas based on two main considerations:

a) **Heart Rating and Head Rating** – Each idea is scored on the basis of how you feel about it instinctively (heart) and whether it makes sense logically (head). So you're actually combining emotion and logic to evaluate the idea. Good analytical thinking doesn't ignore or deny emotions. As I'll explain later on, positive analysis actually recognises and manages emotions to support decision making.

b) **Greens (Pros) and Reds (Cons)** – Each possible solution is broken down into its positive and negative aspects. These can relate to any factor such as cost, time, reliability, quality, morale, customers, legality, safety, company practices and approvals, feasibility, timeliness and ease of implementation. Additional research and gathering of information may be necessary here to furnish the analysis. For instance, if you're evaluating the idea to introduce a new advertising strategy to counteract declining sales, some possible Greens could be that it allows you to reach a huge number of people in a given area and to develop brand recognition. Likely Reds could be that it's costly and cannot target specific potential buyers.

Sometimes pure facts and figures dictate which ideas will work and which won't. In other situations, feelings and intuition have a stronger input. Good evaluative criteria and techniques are what will help you look at each option as a whole and apply your judgement effectively.

---

8 BQF Innovation (2010), 'How to Evaluate Ideas', *BQF Innovation Unit Blog*, 31st March 2010, http://www.bqf.org.uk/innovation/2010/03/31/how-to-evaluate-ideas/

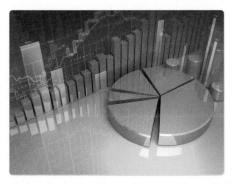

Analysis – Evaluating ideas using appropriate criteria

3) Choose the best solution(s)

Lastly, having gone through the evaluative process, you'll end up with one or two viable solutions to carry forward to implementation. Before you make a decision to implement a solution ask yourself:

a) Will the solution achieve what you want?
The solution has to be significantly workable in addressing the problem. It must have the optimal combination of benefits to most successfully resolve the problem, rather than just being 'good enough' for now.

b) Is the solution in line with your ultimate goals and objectives (individual or organisational)?
Keeping the big picture in mind is vital to make sure your solution addresses the problem in a comprehensive and integrated way.

c) What are the possibilities it will fail and in what way?
Often the solutions with the greatest potential also carry the greatest risk. You'll need to consider how much risk you're willing to take in your particular situation.

Asking these questions expands your analytical thinking and fuses your final decision with objectivity and positive reasoning.

'Whole Brain' Analytical Thinking

The general view of analysis is that it's a predominantly left brain cortical skill. However, recent scientific research is shedding new light on this soon to be outdated supposition. Most people perceive chess to be an entirely analytical sport and science supports this to a point - fMRI scanning shows that amateur chess players typically apply left brain analytical processing to work out a chess problem. But with chess grandmasters, who are quicker in tackling the same problem, the picture is somewhat different. While still engaging similar left brain structures to the amateurs, these expert players also go on to employ additional structures in the *other half* of their brain.[9]

From this evidence, we can deduce that the difference between being good and being great at something is the ability to use whole brain skills, even during what we might consider 'left brain' tasks. Hence, to excel at analytical thinking, you have to be more than just analytical – you have to use additional resources.

What's unique about the Solution Finder process is that it helps you apply a whole brain approach to analysis, utilising techniques which stimulate both your left cortical skills (words, numbers, analysis, listing, language and logic) and right cortical skills (rhythm, colour, shape, maps, imagination and daydreaming).

The best chess players use both left and right brain skills

"Your illogical approach to chess does have its advantages on occasion, Captain."

Ambassador Spock, 'Star Trek' TV series character

---

9 Schultz, Nora (2011), 'Chess grandmasters use twice the brain', *NewScientist*, 11th January 2011, Issue 2795

This latest research dispels the myth that analytical thinking is all about reasoning and logical deduction. It can also embrace mental tasks that we would consider more 'creative'. Amusingly, in the early days of my relationship with my wife, she gave me the nickname 'Spock' after the well-known character of the *Star Trek* TV series because I was so logical. Yet my inherent nature was creative as well as analytical. Of course, I've since become aware that these skills aren't exclusive of each other. We can all bring both aspects into parallel and cooperative use with the aid of whole brain thinking tactics quite effortlessly.

Connected to this is the relationship between logic and emotion, which coincidentally *Star Trek* has touched upon numerous times in its long running TV history. Unlike many people are prone to believe, emotion and logic aren't conflicting ideas at war - they're attributes that can work harmoniously in partnership. While analytical thinking may be fact-based and rational, it can also encompass emotion and intuition. The whole notion of having to 'leave emotion out of it' during analysis is misplaced. It's impossible because emotions and feelings are part of everything we do and think – we can't just turn them off!

Emotion plays a role in analytical thinking

Gut feelings and intuition can provide valuable input into our decision making, helping us screen and sort our options through another lens. Sometimes an idea will just 'feel right'. Prior to launching the online social networking tool Twitter, former CEO Evan Williams introduced a blog publishing system called Blogger. While it wasn't what the company had set out to do, he couldn't let go of the idea as his gut instinct kept nagging him. Instead of sidelining it, Evan decided to pursue the idea and it eventually became a massive success.[10]

It's true that emotions can be irrational and can sometimes mislead us, making us feel that we're right even when we're not, but it's possible to use them constructively, wisely and intelligently as part of a well-rounded

10 Steward, D. and Simmons, M. (2010), *The Business Playground: Where Creativity and Commerce Collide*, Financial Times / Prentice Hall

analytical process. The instinctive response of emotions and feelings can be tempered and directed so that logic and emotion can interface successfully. As a matter of fact, modern neuroscience embraces the idea that emotions are a key support of intellectual performance.[11] When we analyse properly we can engage a positive dialogue between intuition and reason without being controlled by either, giving us a steady and balanced mindset.

An Aid to Creativity.....

What should be clear by now is that analytical thinking is an indispensable part of a well thought out problem solving process. Still, if we were to use it on its own it would be totally insufficient for our needs. Analysis and judgement are great for avoiding the errors of erratic and unrestrained thinking but, as Edward de Bono tells us, they can't replace the "generative, productive, creative and design aspects of thinking" that are so vital to the problem solving and decision making process.[12]

Traditional analysis is only concerned with what we already know about something, not what we can discover. If we're going to get the best out of a situation we need to employ generative qualities to explore and source new aspects and outlooks. We've already discussed the danger of using analysis at the wrong stage of the creative problem solving process in Chapter 3. Although it seems to make sense to eliminate illogical ideas as they come along during the generative phase of thinking, you're effectively killing off some of your best, most creative ideas from the outset. Despite this, it's a mistake to view analytical thinking as the death of creativity.[13] Performed properly and at the correct times, analytical thinking can be a brilliant aid to creative thinking. It might be an inefficient and dangerous way to explore new ideas but it's perfect when you're trying to decide between different alternatives! Where generative thinking gives birth to ideas, analytical thinking raises and develops solutions.

In Chapter 3, I introduced the idea of applying generative thinking strategies and techniques throughout the problem solving process to help us deal with our challenges in the most creative way possible. What many people find surprising is that you can actually be very generative and divergent in your thinking during the analytical phase of the problem solving process. Frankly, this is what will keep your thinking open and inspired and steer you away from the temptation to adopt boring, mediocre ideas simply because they 'make sense'.

11 Stevens, Tom (2006), 'EQ Meets Critical Thinking', *Think Leadership Ideas*, 26th August 2006, http://www.thinkleadershipideas.com/files/EQ_Meets_Critical_Thinking.php
12 de Bono, Edward (1982), *Thinking Course*, BBC
13 Dr Ayman Amer (2005), 'Analytical Thinking', *Pathways to Higher Education Project*, http://www.pathways.cu.edu.eg/subpages/training_courses/C10-1%20Analytical%20Thinking.pdf

Mind Mapping is clearly a divergent thinking process – we expand outwards from the centre to generate ideas and explore new associations. One of the comments I typically get in relation to Mind Mapping is along the lines of "I really like it but it's a very generative tool – ideas shoot off in all directions – what I really need is a convergent tool to get to a solution." What's worthy of understanding is that a generative thinking tool like the Mind Map can be helpful during both the divergent (generative) AND convergent (analytical) stages of the problem solving process. It can actually assist you in reaching a winning solution much more actively than your bog-standard analytical process. As psychologist J. P. Guilford points out, divergent and convergent modes don't have to be isolated from each other - they can be merged in so far as a divergent approach can be used on the journey to a convergent solution.[14]

Once you've built up a huge pool of ideas during the generative phase of problem solving, you simply use the divergent form and structure of the Mind Map to converge to the most appropriate and useful solution. When you Mind Map, you're naturally pulled into a generative frame of mind so you can evaluate a limitless number of angles in relation to each possibility. This helps you separate the wheat from the chaff without all the stress that usually comes with this process.

During analysis you break things down into smaller components and this can often mean that you lose sight of the interactions between them, decreasing your comprehension and insight.[15] When this occurs you risk overanalysing things and becoming muddled up. With a Mind Map, you can visually see the 'big picture' in addition to all the smaller facts and details – your vision is no longer narrow and you have full control of the situation. This control leads you more directly to your solution than any complex or convoluted process could.

The Mind Mapping process also adds lots of extra vigour to your analytical thinking because you're able to apply 'whole brain analysis'. You can tap into a wide range of cortical skills, both rational and imaginative, to evaluate each idea in a more productive and cohesive way. What's more,

14 Guilford, J.P. (1975), *'Creativity: a quarter century of progress'*, in I. A. Taylor and J. W. Getzels (ed), Perspectives in Creativity, Chicago, III: Aldine.
15 Dr Ayman Amer (2005), 'Analytical Thinking', *Pathways to Higher Education Project*, http://www.pathways.cu.edu.eg/subpages/training_courses/C10-1%20Analytical%20Thinking.pdf

your attention is constantly drawn to the heart of the matter (centre of the map) so you remain in an objective and focused frame of mind when selecting a solution. This is critical! You must always stay in tune with your objective when analysing alternatives. While novel and original factors are important for producing a creative solution, when it comes to the crunch your choices and decisions must always apply to the problem. Originality without focus is of little use in the real world.

You can be generative while converging to a solution

Analytical thinking is, by its very nature, a scientific approach. The Solution Finder process that I recommend in the GTS System is not only scientific and practical, it also broadens and amplifies your reasoning capacity by inspiring you to be generative in your thinking, even during the analytical phase of problem solving. Through a systematic set-up, it helps you apply generative, whole brain thinking to your situation so you can analyse the pros/cons and emotional/logical factors of each potential idea.

> *"I always had a different vision than my father, the ability to see beyond pure logic. He considered it weak. But I have discovered it to be a source of extraordinary strength."*
>
> **Ambassador Spock, 'Star Trek' TV series character**

In testing and applying the Solution Finder with various groups and individuals, I've learned that you're liable to get totally different results than if you were to employ a wholly logical/analytical approach. For example, at ThinkBuzan we wanted to explore the prospect of improving the audio notes feature in our iMindMap software. We used the Solution Finder process to evaluate our various options in Mind Map form. Now if we had selected our solution purely on the basis of highest ratings, we would have overlooked the final route that we decided to take as it had scored low in both head and heart categories. However, one of our key pros (Greens) was that it was an easy option and would take little time to try out. The fact that this particular solution could be put into action with little expenditure of time, energy and money meant that we could bypass its low ratings. The result – it worked!

I believe this is a good example of the risks of applying only factual and numerical reasoning when making decisions. Other balancing elements must come into play if we're to make a well-rounded and well-informed decision. In our case, we used a generative tool (Mind Map) within an ordered environment (Solution Finder) and it proved to be very powerful in illuminating the correct path.

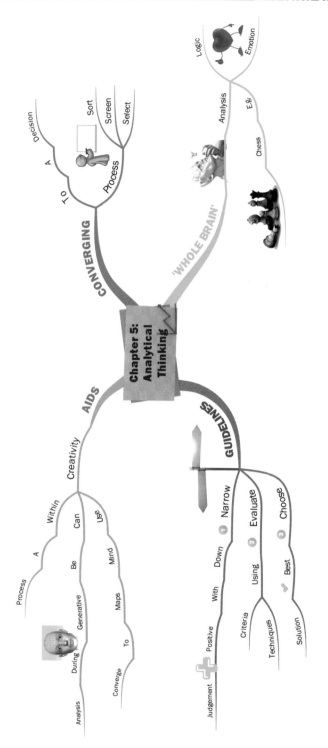

Chapter 5 Summary

SELECTIVE THINKING

The eminent philosopher, Sir Francis Bacon, is quoted as saying, "The human understanding when it has once adopted an opinion draws all things else to support and agree with it."

This quote does a terrific job of summing up selective thinking. Generally speaking, it's our tendency to favour information that confirms an existing belief or preconception, regardless of whether the information is true. For instance, we might have long ago reached an opinion that a particular colleague is lazy. If we see them miss a project deadline or come in late, we'll be quick to take this as validation of our belief. And on the same lines, if we were to see them perform outstandingly at a certain task, we may well ignore it or discredit it as a 'one off'. In both cases, we're being selective in what we pay attention to whenever we come to think of this colleague.[1]

> *"A man sees what he wants to see, and disregards the rest."*
>
> **Paul Simon, American singer and songwriter**

What's remarkable about selective thinking is that it has the potential to be both extremely dangerous and tremendously fantastic. To this end, you have to be mindful of how it works as the consequences of not knowing can be disastrous when solving problems and making decisions.

Theories, beliefs and opinions are useful to us in our everyday lives. They help us to sort information, define patterns that we can take for granted and operate efficiently in a constantly changing world.[2] The problem is that theories and opinions, once formed, can be infuriatingly obstinate and resistant to change, closing off our minds instead of opening them up to consider new opportunities. Let's look at an example. A belief in thrift

---

1 Haskins, Greg R. 'A Practical Guide to Critical Thinking', http://www.skepdic.com/essays/Haskins.html
2 Butler, Gillian and Hope, Tony (2007), *Manage your Mind: The Mental Fitness Guide,* 2nd Edition, Oxford University Press

and economic prudence can be a valuable asset at times as it helps you practise caution in how your organisation's resources are used. On some occasions however, it can be a major impediment. If you're exploring investment in research and development or new marketing strategies you'll be inclined to go for the least costly approach almost every time, excluding other potential outcomes or possibilities. By sticking to this belief religiously, you mentally imprison yourself whenever you need to make a decision that might involve financial risk.

Selective thinking – Preoccupation with one idea

Unsurprisingly, this type of thinking can be potentially ruinous during the creative problem solving process, especially when applied at the wrong times. If you're selective at the generative or analytical stage of the process, you risk becoming narrow-minded and self-righteous, and might even refuse to confront the facts before you – all damaging thought behaviours for what you're trying to achieve. This is because you haven't followed enough of the process to gather and objectively evaluate all relevant information and aspects of an issue before deciding which side to take. At the beginning of a problem solving process, it's important to open up new pathways and consider alternate options instead of charging forward with the first decent idea. Instead of getting mentally involved, you need to be playing the field! Similarly, when evaluating ideas, it's critical that you don't shut out seemingly irrelevant facts or data as they may turn out to be pivotal to the final decision.

> *"The profit of great ideas comes when you turn them into reality."*
>
> **Tom Hopkins, Author of 'How to Master the Art of Selling'**

Despite these dangers, selective thinking is definitely not something you should completely reject. Used positively, it can be an immense and powerful force for turning your ideas into reality. Strong belief and conviction are vital for driving an idea forward to successful implementation and for motivating yourself to do what it takes to reach your desired goals. Selective thinking can play a momentous role at the end of a well-managed and objective decision making process in actually making things happen. In other words, it's what makes you switch from thinking into doing.

Selective thinking is a bit like power. Power has the potential to be used in a positive or negative way. When we abuse power, it can be harmful and damaging, but when we use power to turn a vision into reality, it's a good thing.

Do tools drive creativity?

An example of how modern technology leads us into selective thinking

A good software tool is an extension of the brain. It helps us structure our thoughts and externalise our creativity simply and effectively. As technology advances, software tools are becoming more and more powerful and complex. While these developments are great for increasing our productivity, they don't always spell good news for our creativity. What we see happening today is that, instead of our brains driving the tools, the tools are driving our brains!

Frédéric Vève, CEO of French communications agency Communiquons. Biz, got wise to this several years ago. He noticed that in creative tasks such as video editing, it was possible to recognise the software that the editor had used by the way the film was set up. It became clear that editors were falling into habits while using some of the more complex tools. To avoid this predictability, he developed a practice of switching the software the editing team used on a regular basis, bringing on board non-mainstream, less well-known tools. The impact of this? Changing the software altered the way the editor approached the task and opened their mind to be more creative.

The same pattern occurs when we allow our beliefs and opinions to drive our decisions i.e. when we're being selective. All too often we get stuck in habitual thinking and end up running along the same old lines. By taking control of our selective beliefs, we allow our creative genius to be unleashed and directed to exactly where we want it to be.

Source:
Frédéric Vève, CEO of Communiquons.Biz, France,
http://www.communiquons.biz/

VIDEO EDITING

Changing — Soft — Implicates — Effects — Thinking
Effects — Editing
Soft — Changes — Thinking
Changes — Mind
Approach

Tools drive creativity

WHY

Use functions — Power
In — Programmer Mind
The — Software
Automatisms
Simple tool — Function — On
Continuity — Of
Complex tool — Functions — Lots
The Drive — The Brain
Brain

The power of simple software boosts creativity. Complex software drives the brain to habits.

Mind Mapping — Fred's Experience

7 Years — Mind Manager — MAPS — Straight — Blue — Schematic
Use — Organize — Ideas — Planning — Document — Finding
Software

Self learning Mind Mapping
Without reading Tony's Book

1 month — Fun — Ideas — More
iMindMap — MAPS — Colours — Images — Organic
Use — Ideas — Brainstorming

Frederic Veve's Mind Map

A Natural Impulse...

The occurrence of selective thinking during problem solving isn't a sign that a person lacks intelligence; it's simply a natural bias reaction of the human mind. Once you have a theory or belief, your mind works very cleverly to seek confirming evidence. The problem is that beliefs can easily slip into prejudices and you can become overconfident (or pig-headed!) in what you perceive to be true. This results in 'tunnel vision' as your conceptual framework limits what you see around you.

> "Smart people believe weird things because they are skilled at defending beliefs they arrived at for non-smart reasons."

Michael Shermer, Scientific American, Sept 2002

Sociologist Paul Lazarsfeld highlights the failings of our selective reasoning by demonstrating how we can rationalise both one particular point *AND* it's opposite[3]. In writing about '*The American Soldier*', a study of over 600,000 servicemen, he listed the finding that 'men from rural backgrounds were usually in better spirits during their Army life than soldiers from city backgrounds'. He then illustrated how the reader might reconcile this in their minds by reasoning that the rural men were accustomed to harsher living standards and more physical labour than city men, so naturally they would have an easier time adjusting. Why would we need such a vast and expensive study to tell us something so obvious? But then, Lazarsfeld reveals that the true findings of the study were the exact opposite. It was city men, not rural men, who were happier during their army life. Of course, had the reader been told the answer in the first place, they could just as easily have rationalised it another way. For instance, city men are more used to working in corporations, with chains of command, strict standards, etiquette and so on.[4]

This proves how our selective thinking can mislead us, even when it comes to something we feel is an obvious fact or common sense. If you're planning a marketing campaign, you may already feel you have a decent sense of what consumers want and how to make them want more of it. In all likelihood, this 'knowledge' could be undermining your ability to think differently and innovatively while organising your campaign.

If you're at a stage where you need to generate or evaluate ideas, being selective in your thinking can lead to a major failure to consider what the

---

3 Lazarsfeld, Paul F (1949), 'The American Soldier – An Expository Review', *The Public Opinion Quarterly*, Vol. 13, No 3, pp. 377-404
4 Watts, Duncan (2011), 'Un-common sense', *New Scientist*, 16th July 2011

philosopher and mathematical trader, Nassim Nicholas Taleb calls 'Black Swans'[5] – a term introduced in his best-selling book *The Black Swan*. These are the highly important but unexpected events that catch you by surprise because they render standard predictions and explanations worthless. Biased thinking and closed-mindedness leave you exposed to unpredictable forces which can end up yanking you away from where you want to be. Under these circumstances you're apt to make snap judgements which are more likely to be influenced by silly details rather than well thought out considerations. In short, you end up being reactive instead of proactive and, consequently, risk losing control of your entire situation. These deadly perils all stem from rushing into selective thinking and neglecting to apply a careful and comprehensive process to how you solve problems.

Selective thinking leads to failure to consider black swans

"Minds are like parachutes, they operate only when open."

Sir Thomas Dewar, Scottish whisky distiller and salesman

During a typical discussion or meeting, it's natural that you'll want to put forward your point of view on a particular matter. Once you've done this however, your brain will instinctively look for ways to strengthen and build upon this viewpoint for the remainder of the discussion. Unless someone has a fantastically strong counter-argument that changes how you see things, your selective thinking will have set you down a certain path that can be difficult to retract.

To use an example, let's say you're embarking on a flight around the world and, in your eagerness to set off, you happen to be one degree off target – just slightly out of line with your final destination. While this deviation might not seem very much when you first set out, by the time you've travelled 1,000 miles, you would be approximately 17 miles off course. And by the

5 Taleb, Nassim Nicholas (2007), *The Black Swan: The Impact of the Highly Improbable,* Allen Lane

end of the journey, you would land almost 500 miles off target. That's if you don't run out of fuel before then! By failing to establish the correct path before setting off, you've allowed yourself to end up a huge distance from where you want to be.

This is the exact risk you take with your thinking if you're selective too early during a problem solving situation. When you apply strong belief, conviction and commitment without having gone through the necessary prep work, you can very easily end up miles off course.

It's for this reason that you need a process to help you work through problems and decisions systematically and objectively to reach the best possible solution or outcome (which may or may not be the one you initially favoured!). The process that I recommend (the Solution Finder) can't be said to be anything but simple, however, to some people it could seem a little excessive or unnecessary - "Why do we have to define, generate, analyse, select, set goals etc?"...

...Because it's far better to have an idea of the journey you need to take before you actually take it, as the flight journey example above proves. Going through the Solution Finder process could take you only minutes but potentially saves you hours, days, weeks and even years. It's proactive and forces you to think things through, helping to control your selective preferences so that they don't bias your idea generation and analytical reasoning skills.

As we've seen, most of us are inclined to jump straight into selective thinking mode – we make up our minds before all options are on the table. It takes a concerted effort to control this natural impulse by using a careful process. The Solution Finder doesn't have to be followed exhaustively for every single decision, but for key issues that dictate a significant change in direction or use of someone's time, it's important to go through all the stages to maintain clarity of thought and objectivity. What you'll find is that, far from being a negative thing, selective thinking becomes a powerful and motivational instrument in the final part of the process when you need to craft your solution and put it into action.

"Ideas won't keep. Something must be done about them."

Alfred North Whitehead, British mathematician and philosopher

The Power of Selective Belief

Exceptional people who achieve amazing things in life do so because they have belief and conviction in their ideas. Through material such as *The Secret* by Rhonda Byrne[6] (the author and television producer best known for her work in the self-help arena), we can understand the power of faith and belief in materialising what we desire in our lives. This is based on the 'Law of Attraction' which works on the premise that whatever you deeply believe at the subconscious level, you attract. And Norman Vincent Peale's *The Power of Positive Thinking*[7] demonstrates how positivity and faith in ourselves can make good things happen.

Research on the thinking patterns of some of our most successful business people, scientists and artists is inclined to support this new brand of 'scientific thought'. Contrary to conventional science which stresses that claims should be independent of personal bias, this 'new science' actually demands a high level of bias as only true believers will discover the evidence to support their claims. It's when we believe in something utterly and passionately that we engineer things, consciously and subconsciously, to draw it into our lives. One of my favourite quotes of all time is:

"Until one is committed, there is hesitancy, the chance to draw back. Concerning all acts of initiative (and creation), there is one elementary truth that ignorance of which kills countless ideas and splendid plans: that the moment one definitely commits oneself, then Providence moves too. All sorts of things occur to help one that would never otherwise have occurred. A whole stream of events issues from the decision, raising in one's favor all manner of unforeseen incidents and meetings and material assistance, which no man could have dreamed would have come his way. Whatever you can do, or dream you can do, begin it. Boldness has genius, power, and magic in it. Begin it now."
Johann Wolfgang Von Goethe, Faust - paraphrased by W.H Murray, The Scottish Himalaya Expedition

This quote is a perfect illustration of the positive power of selective thinking – you see every opportunity as another way of getting you closer to that one idea that you believe in and in the end, incredible things happen! Of course that's how lots of our much-admired business personalities have become tremendously successful. We've all heard the story of Colonel Sanders who's said to have been turned down by no less than 1,009 restaurant owners before he sold his first KFC franchise in 1952.[8] By 1964 he had 600

---

6 Byrne, Rhonda (2006), *The Secret*, Atria Books/Beyond Words
7 Peale, Norman Vincent (1996), *The Power of Positive Thinking*, Ballantine Books
8 From Bottom Up (2009), 'Success Story #3: Harland Sanders', *From Bottom Up Blog,* 29th Sept 2009, http://frombottomup.com/success-story-3-harland-sanders/

franchised outlets for his chicken recipe and later sold his business for a huge sum of money. If there's one thing that Colonel Sanders can teach us it's that if one is passionate enough in what they do, they can counter all obstacles to become a success. Colonel Sanders was a persistent and committed man who never stopped believing in his chicken recipe, even when no one else would give it a chance. Today the KFC empire lives on because of his remarkable conviction.

The power of belief – Faith can move mountains

The iconic Donald Trump gives us another excellent example of constructive selective thinking. No matter what project he chooses to get involved in, he makes up his mind to succeed. Even when he faced catastrophic failure, he was able to come back stronger than before. His vision and belief catapulted him from being $900 million dollars in debt to a net worth of over a billion dollars in a relatively short period of time. In his book, *Think BIG and Kick Ass in Business and Life* (co-authored by Bill Zanker),[9] he talks about the importance of managing your mind and achieving a state of total and absolute certainty in success, without ever entertaining even the tiniest thought of failure. According to Donald, achieving unbelievable success has nothing to do with having the right amount of knowledge; it's about having the right mindset from the beginning. Knowledge comes easily after that. He's a living example of how knowing when to back up your beliefs regardless of what others think, can help you maximise your achievements.

Donald Trump – A positive selective thinker

9 Trump, Donald J. and Zanker, Bill (2007), *Think BIG and Kick Ass In Business and Life*, Harper Business

Yet another case of positive selectivity and determination is provided by James Dyson. An industrial designer by training, Dyson persevered through more than 5,000 prototypes of his first bagless, cyclone-technology vacuum cleaner over a period of 15 years. He then launched Dyson Limited to produce his design when no other manufacturer would take it on. His main lesson is one we can all learn from in employing selective thinking correctly:

"It can take a very long time to develop interesting products and get them right. But our society has an instant-gratification thing. We admire instant brilliance, effortless brilliance. I think quite the reverse. You should admire the person who perseveres and slogs through and gets there in the end."[10]

Instead of pouncing on the first idea we like, we have to take time going through an adequate process of creative development. Dyson was generative and analytical to a high degree before he landed on his final prototype. Only then did total selective belief come into play – he got behind his idea 100 per cent and took the steps he needed to make his product a success.

This is a key point - being selective is the final stage of the problem solving process. It's not an exaggeration to say that most people end up pursuing the wrong goals because they get caught up in selective thoughts far too early. You have to be vigilant in how you use selective thinking because it's such a remarkable and formidable force. The positive value of selective thinking is experienced only at the end of the process when everything culminates so that the power of our beliefs can propel us forward to achieve what we want.

Selective Thinking in its Rightful Place

What should have become clear by now is that selective thinking has excellent merits when used correctly as part of a process. Generative thinking produces piles of ideas for us to consider at the beginning of the problem solving process but, if we were to use it all the time, we would be constantly broadening and exploring and would never get anywhere! Through analytical thinking we can get as far as deciding on a solution, but this is still not enough. Finding the solution doesn't mean the problem is solved. A creative idea needs to be actioned effectively if it's to succeed and this is best achieved if you believe in it passionately and conclusively. You have to have conviction and commitment to make the solution work. Selective thinking is a decidedly useful feature for helping us put together

10 Dyson, James (2007), 'Failure Doesn't Suck', Interview by Chuck Salter, *Fast Company Magazine*, 1st May 2007, http://www.fastcompany.com/magazine/115/ open_next-design.html

our goals and plan of action to carry the solution forward to fruition. It's what allows our minds to concentrate wholly on what we need to do without getting overwhelmed or distracted by other people, data and events.

Within the **Solution Finder** we include the power of selective thinking - of belief, conviction and passion - in a positive and affirmative way. Utilising the other modes of thinking progressively puts you in an objective state as you work towards a decision. Selective thinking comes into play after you've gone through the analytical stage and converged to a solution. Only at this cumulative point can you be totally congruent in the actions you have to take to reinforce your solution and implement it. As a result, belief and confidence will come naturally because you've done all the preparation and can be sure that you're heading in the right direction.

Selective thinking also has a positive influence on your motivation. If you believe in something wholeheartedly, it's much easier to motivate yourself to get up and do what needs to be done to make it happen. Have you ever noticed that if you're implementing something you're not quite sure about, you're much less motivated to do it? This uncertainty is the result of rushing into a decision without exploring the situation thoroughly. When you pause to view a situation from all angles and perspectives, you can, in due course, form the right conclusions about it. This is why having a good, functional process like the Solution Finder is so important. It confirms that you're on the right path so you can be confident that your belief, motivation and commitment will be well-placed as you go about strengthening your solution and putting it into action.

"An idea that is developed and put into action is more important than an idea that exists only as an idea."

Edward de Bono, Author, consultant and inventor of 'Lateral Thinking'

In the Solution Finder, we conduct selective thinking using the following steps:

1. Strengthen your solution – Use a divergent tool like Mind Mapping to generate ideas for reinforcing and honing your solution. This is necessary so that you have all the back-up you need to gain maximum acceptance for your idea.

2. Goal setting – Once you've strengthened your solution from all angles, you can then identify your goals. What exactly do you want the solution to achieve?

3. Action plan – Prepare yourself to implement the solution by creating a plan that defines what's to be done, where, by when and by whom. Take note – the best solution can easily fail because it isn't executed correctly.

4. Implement the plan! – This is the point where you make things happen through commitment and applied focus. Selective thinking is related to positive thinking and self-esteem because you can be confident in being able to reach your goals.

Selective thinking gives you the drive to implement your solution

Applying selective thinking correctly in line with a sound and careful process helps you set up a productive climate for achieving a first-rate performance. Keep in mind that this doesn't mean you can't change your solution later on. It's still important that you revise your beliefs and ideas when confronted with conflicting evidence. It's one thing to have belief, but another to be dogmatic in the face of undeniable signals for a different course of action.

> *"If you expect the worst, you'll get the worst, and if you expect the best, you'll get the best."*
>
> **Norman Vincent Peale, Author of 'The Power of Positive Thinking'**

Out of all the modes of thinking, selective thinking is the mode I believe people have to be most wary of when working through the decision making process. It's the mode that most of us automatically switch into when we have an idea – we immediately try to back it up. If we're selective too early, we risk reinforcing the wrong initial ideas. By understanding the modes of thinking, we can be mindful of this happening and avert ourselves from getting caught up in a vortex of selective thoughts at the wrong times. On a positive note, selective thinking is absolutely vital once we've reached our decision so that we can follow our vision to the end. It's what ultimately helps us reach our dreams.

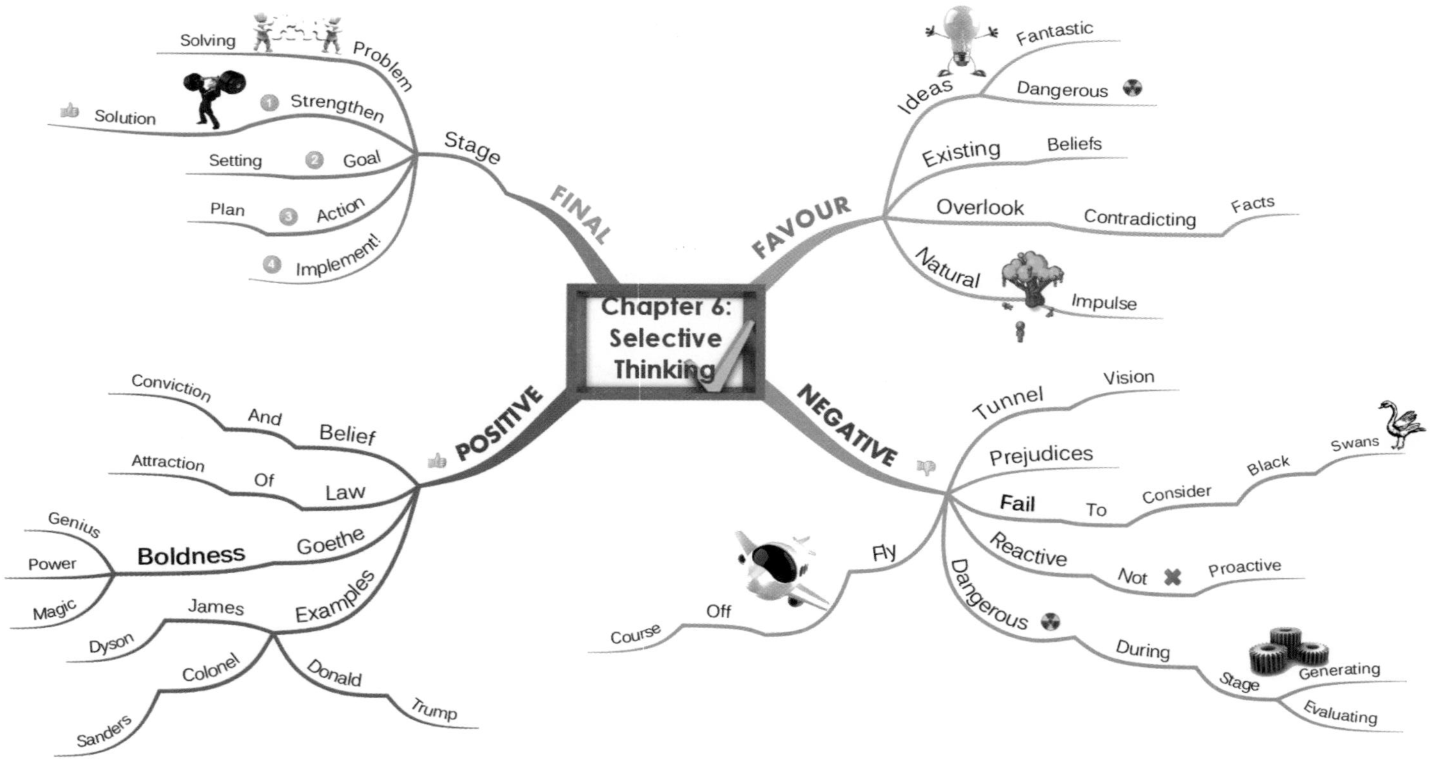

Chapter 6 summary

Chapter 6: Selective Thinking

FAVOUR
- Ideas
  - Existing
  - Dangerous
  - Fantastic
- Overlook
  - Beliefs
  - Contradicting
  - Facts
- Natural
  - Impulse

NEGATIVE
- Tunnel
  - Vision
- Prejudices
- Fail
  - To
    - Consider
      - Black
        - Swans
- Reactive
  - Not
    - Proactive
- Dangerous
  - During
    - Stage
      - Generating
      - Evaluating
- Fly
  - Off
    - Course

POSITIVE
- Boldness
  - Conviction
  - And
  - Belief
  - Attraction
  - Of
  - Law
  - Goethe
  - Genius
  - Power
  - Magic
  - Examples
    - James
    - Dyson
    - Donald
    - Colonel
    - Sanders
    - Trump

FINAL
- Stage
  - Problem
    - Solving
    - Solution
  - Strengthen
    - Setting
    - Goal
  - Plan
    - Action
  - Implement!

PROACTIVE THINKING

Henry Ford is known to have said, "Thinking is the hardest work there is, which is probably the reason why so few engage in it."[1]

This quote communicates a crucial point. Most of us go through our lives without being aware of the thinking processes behind the decisions we make or activities we perform. We operate on 'autopilot' - we wake up in the morning, get dressed, journey to work and go about our daily tasks without giving it much thought.

This automatic (i.e. reactive) thinking and behaviour is ideal for routine tasks as it puts us in the right frame to tackle things quickly and efficiently. For instance, we might have found an approach that works particularly well for dealing with difficult customers and will use it time and time again with great success. We don't have to waste our energy reinventing the wheel each time we encounter that same problem.[2] But while this approach saves us valuable time and effort, it can also lead us to miss opportunities. As our work climate changes rapidly and we encounter new kinds of challenges, we need our thinking to become more 'switched on' so that we can seek out different ways to get results. In other words, we need to be able to think proactively.

This draws us back to Matthew Syed's theory of 'purposeful practice'[3] (see Chapter 2). We're all capable of running, but a professional sprinter will run in a disciplined and deliberate way to reach optimal performance. It's the same with our thinking. If a sprinter can be trained to run better with the help of appropriate methodologies, then people who need to solve problems and make decisions can be taught to think better along the same lines. To this end, Proactive Thinking plays a governing role in creating successful innovation. It helps us initiate a conscious and focused approach to problem solving and decision making so that we can think more objectively, work more creatively and plan more effectively.

---

1 Ford, Henry, American industrialist and pioneer of the assembly-line production method, 1863-1947
2 Proctor, Tony (1999), *Creative Problem Solving For Managers*, Routledge
3 Syed, Matthew (2010), *Bounce: How Champions are Made*, Fourth Estate

Pointedly, proactive thinking is the final thinking mode in the GRASP acronym because it's the culmination of all the previous modes of thinking – Generative, Reactive, Analytical and Selective. It's what connects them all together in a strategic and purposeful way. This transpires because proactive thinking gets us thinking about how we think, rather than simply what we think. Doesn't it make sense that we have to know how to think before we can decide what to think?

Consider the following two questions:

Q) Would you go swimming in a business suit?

Q) Would you go the gym after eating a three course meal?

These aren't trick questions...

...And I assume I'm correct in guessing that your answer to both would be "No".

The reason for this is obvious in both cases. It doesn't make sense to go swimming in a business suit because you wouldn't be able to swim effectively. Your clothing would be completely inappropriate for the task and would restrict you from swimming freely.

Would you go swimming in a business suit?

Likewise, you're unlikely to go to the gym after eating a three course meal because you wouldn't be able to train effectively. You would probably feel too heavy and sluggish to make any real effort.

Would you go to the gym after eating a three course meal?

These responses are common sense. You're not going to perform brilliantly in those tasks by carrying them out in that way. This might be a simple point to make, yet when we have to solve a problem or devise a new idea or concept, most of us fail to treat our thinking in the same fashion. Often we allow our minds to work in a disorderly way without considering what's most effective for the task we're embarking on. Thinking isn't a tidy process, but it should be done with a sense of order.[4] When we understand the architecture of our thinking, we can establish better ways of applying it so that our choices and decisions are made using prime mental processes. Proactive thinking assists us in gaining this sort of active control over our thinking, effectively engaging us in metacognition.

What is Metacognition?

Metacognition is commonly understood to mean the act of 'thinking about thinking', but in reality it goes far beyond this. More than anything, it's the act of applying a strategy around your thinking to get the results you want. In this sense it represents the highest order of thinking possible.

---

4 Adair, John (2007), *Decision Making and Problem Solving Strategies*, The Sunday Times, Kogan Page

The following are questions that I often pose to my audiences during seminars or conferences. What would your answer be to each question?

Q. Do you think about your *diet*?

Q. Do you think about your *fitness*?

Q. Do you think about your *appearance*?

Q. Do you think about your *thinking*?

If you're like most people, your answer to the first three questions is likely to be an immediate 'Yes'. It's only when we reach the last question that the response tends to be quite different! At best the answer is 'Sometimes'. More often than not, it's a straight 'No'. This is precisely the problem – we rarely, if ever, think about our thinking.

Thinking about thinking

Thinking is something that concerns all of us. It's an essential component of who we are and part of everything we do, yet we hardly ever examine it on any deep level or strategise how we use it. When it comes to other areas of our life such as our health and appearance, most of us will apply strategies and processes to manage them. For instance, we might design a meal plan or exercise programme to help us reach our ideal weight and fitness level. Becoming fitter and healthier isn't something that happens by chance. You don't become healthy by wanting to be healthy, you have to do something to make it happen – you have to use strategy.

The same applies to your mind. Surely it makes sense to manage your thinking through strategy as you would other areas of your life such as your health. A good strategy provides you with the systems and processes that can dramatically improve your ability to find new opportunities, think with greater clarity and problem solve more effectively.

We design strategies for our fitness, but not for our thinking

The first step towards applying a strategy to your thinking comes through awareness. Self awareness promotes self regulation.[5] Being proactive demands that you first understand the modes of thinking and how their usage influences your working environment. You wouldn't risk building a house without a foundation as it would be highly unstable. So why do so many of us rush into problem solving and decision making without a solid grounding in the modes of thinking?

GRASP is a helpful way of identifying the principal thinking modes that we're apt to use: Generative; Reactive; Analytical; Selective and Proactive. Most people are more or less familiar with each of the modes of thinking, but they rarely use them in the right way. Each mode of thinking has merit and all are useful for problem solving and decision making in various ways. Nonetheless proactive thinking is the ultimate and all-encompassing goal. It's what helps us stop to recognise what mode of thinking we need to be in for the task at hand - "Do I need to be generative here?" or "Should I be analytical at this stage?" Proactive thinking is what puts all the distinct modes of thinking into context. And by applying proactive thinking, you put yourself in a better position to create peak conditions for innovation.

If you take just one thing away from this book, it would be to think about the strategies you employ for your thinking. Setting up the most fertile climate for your thinking involves a good deal more than saying "I need new ideas for the promotional mix, so I'll use generative thinking". While still helpful, utilising the modes individually is far less effective than structuring them together in a careful and considered process. There's always the danger that your thinking might become wasteful

5 Pierce, William (2003), 'Metacognition: Study Strategies, Monitoring and Motivation', presented at Prince George's Community College Workshop, 17th Nov 2004, http://academic.pgcc.edu/~wpeirce/MCCCTR/metacognition.htm

and unproductive when you apply it ad hoc. For instance, you can risk simultaneously generating and judging ideas when there's no clear process to separate the tasks. The best results can only be achieved using the best processes. Consequently, you need to be proactive in controlling how you direct your mental path.

Applying a 'Thoughtful' Process

A successful business relies on a clear strategic process to give it direction and drive its resources (money, time, people, equipment) towards its goals. It's all too easy for a business to go astray without one. Similarly, those who have to solve problems and make decisions can benefit tremendously from a formal process that guides their thinking towards innovative results. Shelley Carson, author of *Your Creative Brain* argues that the key to being creative is to approach it as a step-by-step process similar to how you would prove a mathematical theorem. Leave out a step and you risk missing out on the stroke of genius that could illuminate the right answer.[6]

The chief advantage of having a process for approaching challenges is that it makes your thinking conscious. It becomes much easier for you to recognise whether you're performing a task with the appropriate understanding and intention. What's more, you can be more purposefully innovative as the process gives you a disciplined, repeatable way to generate more high quality ideas, more of the time.[7]

"Success is not 'reaching a goal' – it is the pathway to the goal."

Jim Wheeler, Author of 'The Power of Innovative Thinking'

When faced with a challenge, most executives will turn to their past experience and favoured patterns to solve it. This can be a harmful approach as far as problems that have never been encountered before are concerned. Thankfully, a process which employs the right thinking tools and techniques at the right times can help to tone down reactive propensities and selective biases, keeping us in check to work through the problem comprehensively.

The process described in this book – the Solution Finder – illustrates how we can systematically combine generative, analytical, selective and reactive

6 Carson, Shelley (2010), *Your Creative Brain: Seven Steps to Maximize Imagination, Productivity and Innovation in Your Life*, Jossey Bass
7 Hurson, Tim (2008), *Think Better: An Innovator's Guide to Productive Thinking*, McGraw-Hill

thinking modes to set up the most productive mindset for solving problems. Each step of the process becomes an anchor for one of the operational modes of thinking, forcing you to stop and work through the right thinking activity at the right time. As you move through the process, a new mode with its family of specific skills comes into play. On the whole, the process helps us to get the right balance of divergent and convergent thinking to produce solutions that are both brilliantly creative and practically workable.

A process leads you step by step to innovative solutions

While the Solution Finder process is a sound and sensible approach to utilise when you're making a decision by yourself, you might be curious as to how successfully it can translate to a group setting. The way people work together in groups can be fairly difficult to manage as there are additional variables presented by the dynamics between different members. Individuals bring their own needs and biases into the fold and there's often incompatibility in how people work. For instance, a highly selective thinker may pick an idea and run with it, ceasing to be part of the generative process. Another individual may be able to generate a huge volume of ideas but never progresses to analysis of those ideas.

The advantage of using a process such as the Solution Finder, however, is that it promotes unity and maintains the cohesiveness of the group. Everyone falls into step with respect to the thinking mode they should be using at any one point i.e. they are all singing from the same hymn sheet. During the generative stage of the process, each member of the group understands that they must employ generative thinking strategies and techniques for stimulus and fresh perspectives. Once that activity is complete, each individual becomes aware of the need to begin thinking analytically as a group to ascertain solutions and start taking them forward.

There's nothing ground-breaking about this approach and, for many people, it might seem absurdly obvious - common sense in fact. Yet common sense is often not common. The majority of us know that using a process or framework for decision making is useful for making sure our thinking is relevant to the task we're working on, but few of us actually do it in practice.

While the Solution Finder is built on established research and effective creative and problem solving methodologies, it's certainly not the only way to apply a strategic process to your thinking. There are several other examples of deliberate strategies which have been proven to work. A notable one is Edward de Bono's *Six Thinking Hats*[8], which is a decision making framework that enables group members to think in parallel by rotating through six thinking perspectives (hats).

The actual strategies and processes you employ are less important than the recognition of where, why and how you're using them. As Jim Wheeler states in his book *The Power of Innovative Thinking* - "When you know where you're going, why you're going and how you're going to get there, you will get there, successfully."[9]

What's particularly unique about the Solution Finder is that it makes considerable use of generative tools and techniques at every single stage, not just during the idea generation phase. The reason for this is that the majority of us aren't inclined to be generative when we're solving problems; most typically we will be reactive, analytical or selective. But generative thinking is where our true creativity originates. The Solution Finder overcomes this liability by putting generative thinking into service extensively within its entire process.

It's important to remember that innovation doesn't happen by accident. We could have the right people, the right place and the right timing, but we would still need a strategy to use them to the best advantage. The power of proactive thinking lies in its potential to increase your chances of finding, developing and implementing novel and sound solutions through strategy. The GTS System provides the two elements you need to be proactive. Once you have a basic knowledge and awareness of your thinking (GRASP), it becomes easier to balance and orchestrate when you need to be generative, reactive, analytical and selective (The Solution Finder) to create the best momentum for your thinking. The overall result is that you stop thinking along the same old lines and can differentiate in relevant and fruitful ways.

8 de Bono, Edward (2000), *Six Thinking Hats*, 2nd Edition, Penguin 8Wheeler
9 Wheeler, Jim (1998), *The Power of Innovative Thinking: Let New Ideas Lead You to Success*, Career Press

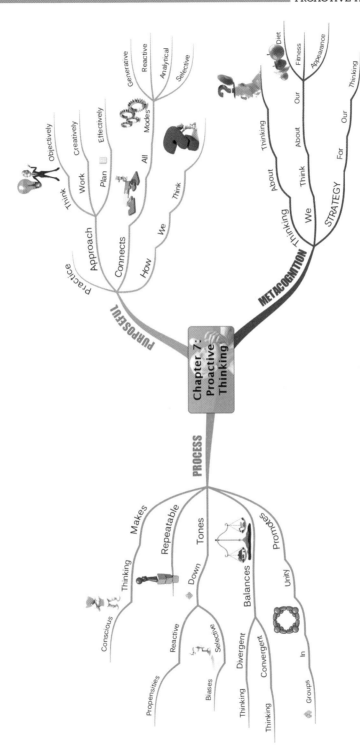

Chapter 7 Summary

Part 2

GTS System:
SOLUTION FINDER

SOLUTION FINDER

Problem solving and decision making are integral to organisational life. Regardless of the profession or market we're in, much of what we do on a daily, weekly and monthly basis is solve problems and make decisions. Most problems or challenges we face are relatively trivial, some are large and complex, but ultimately they all need to be solved in a favourable way. After all, the quality of our solutions and decisions is what determines our outcomes. Successful organisations and individuals recognise that being able to find **creative solutions** to challenges dramatically enhances business potential and results. Though as we've seen, rather than adopting an organised and proactive approach, people often solve challenges by 'reacting' to them, hampering their ability to think and perform creatively.

> *"Real freedom is creative, proactive, and will take me into new territories. I am not free if my freedom is predicated on reacting to my past."*
>
> **Kenny Loggins, American singer and songwriter**

Why is it Important to Solve Problems Creatively?

In the world of business, we all face similar problems and challenges as everything tends to revolve around a few essential elements - resources, deals and people.[1] For instance, the following are typical of the kinds of problems we have to contend with at one time or another:[2]

• How to make more effective use of a manager's time
• How to improve a product's appeal to customers
• How to improve motivation amongst staff

1 Foerster, Anja and Kreuz, Peter (2007), *Different Thinking: Creative strategies for developing the innovative business,* Kogan Page Limited
2 Proctor, Tony (1999), *Creative Problem Solving For Managers,* Routledge

- How to appeal to customers' wants and needs
- How to cut costs through more efficient/effective production methods
- How to identify new and profitable product-market opportunities
- How to get skilled and experienced staff to stay with the company without paying them excessively high salaries

We all have to solve problems

Notice how these problems are 'open-ended' - they have more than one solution. Such problems benefit tremendously from a creative approach to bring in ideas and options that we wouldn't normally contemplate. These 'unique' ideas and options are what will separate us from the competition and allow us to perform in more exceptional ways.

It's precisely because competitive problems and decisions are generic that we should do all we can to differentiate our solutions. According to Clay Carr, author of *The Competitive Power of Constant Creativity*, the only way to gain a sustainable competitive advantage is through the generation and use of creative knowledge.[3] This knowledge can be used to develop new products or services, generate new strategies and opportunities, or solve complex problems. It follows therefore, that companies can only be successful if the people in them are capable of thinking differently.[4] If we don't make the effort to look for novel ideas on how to work more efficiently and achieve more, we stagnate and inevitably get left behind.

We must always remember that a solution that's adequate for solving our problem is not necessarily the 'best' solution for it. Too often, once we have a passable solution we give up on further idea generation, potentially blocking better options.[5] We're then left to move forward with a 'so-so'

3 Carr, Clay. (1994), *The Competitive Power of Constant Creativity*, AMACOM, New York.
4 Nordstrom, Kjell and Ridderstrale, Jonas (2001), *Funky Business,* Financial Times Prentice Hall
5 de Bono, Edward (2008), 'Creative Solutions: How Creativity Can Help With Decision Making and Analysis', *Thinking Managers*, 19th Dec 2008

solution that's only likely to lead to second-rate competitive performance. Instead of competing on a mediocre standpoint, however, we have to aim to compete with imagination, ingenuity and initiative if we're to pull away from the pack. This requires conscious and systematic application of our thinking to a particular situation.

When we react, we become far too complacent about the thinking methods we use. It's this sort of complacency that leads us to take our problem solving for granted and lose our creative effectiveness. The challenge to us all, therefore, is not the problems themselves, it's achieving the differentiation that defines and accomplishes more spectacular results.[6]

> "When I am working on a problem, I never think about beauty. I only think about how to solve the problem. But when I have finished, if the solution is not beautiful, I know it is wrong."
>
> **Buckminster Fuller, American engineer and architect**

What implications does this have for our problem solving efforts? By and large it means that we have to be consciously aware of how we apply our thinking modes (GRASP) in dealing with problems and opportunities so that we can proactively direct our minds towards a path of optimal innovative thinking. And in directing our thinking, we must aim to be heavily generative as this is the key requisite to mobilising and harnessing our creative energies.

Having familiarised yourself with the architecture of the mind in the previous chapters via the GRASP element of the GTS System, you now need a systematic process within which to express the thinking modes to the best advantage. The Solution Finder is that process. The remainder of this chapter outlines how the Solution Finder provides individuals and groups with a course of action for problem solving and decision making that engages mental precision and natural creativity step-by-step.

The Solution Finder Process

As its name suggests, the Solution Finder is a method for finding solutions to problems or challenges. People often talk of the brain as a 'problem-solving organ', but in truth it's a 'solution-finding organ'.[7] Human beings

---

6 Rao, C.B. (2010), 'Decision Making: Perspectives and Platforms', *Strategy Musings,* 11th July 2010, http://cbrao2008.blogspot.com/2010/07/decision-makingperspectives-and.html
7 Buzan, Tony and Griffiths, Chris (2010), *Mind Maps for Business*, BBC Active

are designed to find solutions, not solve problems. Taking on board the fundamental principles of human effectiveness, the Solution Finder is a four-step process which is set out to prepare appropriate conditions for directing your thinking in the correct way.

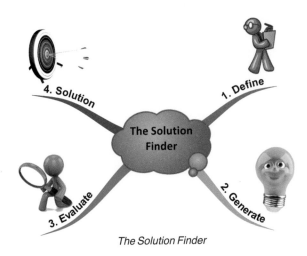

The Solution Finder

The following four steps represent the journey you take to find creative solutions for any type of business problem, opportunity or challenge:

1) Define - The first stage of creative solution finding is to develop a thorough understanding of the problem or challenge you're facing. This uses the Five W's and One H technique to help you explore the issue fully and define precisely what you need to deal with.

2) Generate - This stage is devoted solely to finding plentiful ideas to potentially solve your problem with the aid of a wide range of generative thinking tools and techniques. These include metaphoric stimulation, reversing the challenge, thought experiments and so on.

3) Evaluate - This stage focuses on evaluating the effectiveness of the collection of ideas using appropriate measures. It involves assessing the more promising ideas based on 1) Head and Heart and 2) Greens (Pros) and Reds (Cons) and ultimately selecting one or more potential solutions to implement.

4) Solution - The final stage is where you strengthen, improve and refine your potential solution as far as possible and subsequently devise a sequential plan of action for its implementation.

Most people have partial strategies or processes that they turn to for making decisions - certain analytical methods or brainstorming tools they always find helpful. For the most part, this is a good thing. But imagine you are a world class chef about to prepare a delicious meal. You've got a fantastic kitchen and all the best utensils money can buy - but you don't have all the ingredients. It's highly unlikely you'll be able to create something magnificent. In the context of problem solving and decision making, the purpose of the Solution Finder is to give you all the mental tools and ingredients you need to create something truly special.

The Solution Finder steps are clearly designed to help you diverge and converge fluidly in your thinking. You begin with a single question or problem, and extend your search in many different directions, generating a wide range of new and varied possibilities (Diverge). Then, you take the many different ideas and draw them together towards a single solution, goal or result which is reinforced and finally acted upon (Converge).

We at ThinkBuzan have found the Solution Finder process to be consistently effective and highly dependable in situations that call for defining or understanding a problem, thinking up new ideas or designing and implementing an action plan. Why? Because it allows us to instruct our minds to work in exactly the way we want them to, using generative, analytical, selective, reactive and proactive thinking in the correct form and order. Predominantly, it's a **proactive**, metacognitive process which puts a strategy around our thinking – a strategy which helps us gain maximum benefit from how we use our mental energy. Second to this, it kits us out with a powerful set of tools for **generative** thinking which increases the divergence of ideas and perspectives that we bring to bear on an issue.

The Solution Finder is... 1) PROACTIVE

Without a practical and purposeful means for using our thinking, it's tempting to adopt tried and tested or 'off-the-shelf' solutions to problems instead of seeking out more creative options. As a result, we can easily become lazy problem solvers who remain trapped in old patterns.

Thinking creatively requires a **strategic approach** which counteracts our natural tendency to react. Our mind wants to be reactive because we're eager to crack on with things, and having too many options often means that we dilly-dally in making decisions. A conscious and deliberate process for thinking is therefore paramount. It's what provides us with solid instruction in situations where it's necessary to seek new options and determine the best way forward. The Solution Finder is a perfect example of such a process. By offering us a purposeful and constructive means for applying and integrating the GRASP modes of thinking, it allows us to escape our usual knee-jerk reactions and come up with more creative and robust solutions.

> *"Most people spend more time and energy going around problems than in trying to solve them."*
>
> **Henry Ford, American industrialist, founder of Ford Motor Company**

Problem solving requires a strategic approach

In conventional problem solving it's tempting to wander off along avenues we find particularly interesting or become distracted by themes that aggravate us. A process like the Solution Finder prevents us becoming side-tracked like this by helping us uphold our objectivity and focus. The key word here is focus – because the Solution Finder is focused and outcome driven, we can be confident that we're always heading in the right direction and that our results will be outstanding. And, in directing our minds, it also helps to take the burden and stress out of thinking.

Those of you who've been doing very well with your existing problem solving approaches may well question why you would need to follow a process such as the Solution Finder. It's important to understand that if you want to undertake problem solving that's truly **creative**, then you need to take it seriously.[8] Creativity is a massive factor in determining progress during times of rapid change, so you have little choice but to approach it in an official and formal way. In reality, a good process serves to boost rather than constrict your mental freedom and provides a working environment where you can really excel. Researchers David Oliver and Johan Roos found that companies that have demonstrated the ability to sustain good performance in high velocity environments all have

---

8 de Bono, Edward (1982), *Thinking Course*, BBC

established sets of guiding principles to help them make decisions.[9] This is because principles and processes provide a framework for thinking better so you can repeatedly reach the right answers and achieve fantastic results.

The Solution Finder is... 2) GENERATIVE

The entire Solution Finder process is heavily reliant on generative thinking tools and techniques that empower you to explore and manifest extensively, applying as much of your innate creative ability as possible. In conventional problem solving, the difficulty in reaching a solution usually stems from a failure to produce a sufficient volume of ideas at the outset. Most of the time there are 'obvious' solutions, but these don't always represent the 'best' course of action. A situation can always be improved by expanding the range of options available to you through generative thinking. If you aren't generative, you're much more limited in your choices and possibilities. The more options you have, the more your world opens up.

Every profession uses specialised tools and techniques to accomplish specific tasks – the doctor has his medical kit, the carpenter has his tools. Similarly, problem solvers must also utilise the appropriate techniques to be creative in their efforts. It's widely understood that using 'proper' creative problem solving techniques can help teams and individuals develop more innovative and novel ideas.[10]

Generative Thinking Techniques – A toolset for creativity

The Solution Finder offers a fresh way to apply some of the most time honoured creative techniques. These include techniques such as reframing a problem, metaphoric stimulation, thought experiments, challenging assumptions, changing points of reference and reversing the challenge. All of these 'tools for the mind' have been used successfully in real life for

9 Oliver, David and Roos, Johan (2005), 'Decision-making in high-velocity environments: The importance of guiding principles', *Organization Studies*, 26/6: 889-913
10 McFadzean, Elspeth (1998), 'Enhancing Creative Thinking Within Organisations', *Management Decision*, Vol. 36, Issue 5, pp. 309-315

creative purposes. Pooled together in the Solution Finder process, they provide an incredibly useful toolset that will magnify your ability to solve problems and make decisions creatively.

> *"Creativity methods provide senior management with a unique tool to tap into a massive organizational resource. Learning to leverage the creative thinking skills of every individual, regardless of their level, creates the sustainable competitive advantage every corporation is striving for."*
>
> **Jim O'Neal, Retired President and Chief Executive Officer, Frito-Lay International**

The Role of Mind Mapping

Mind Mapping is the medium that I advocate for recording your efforts at each stage of the solution finding journey, from capturing your ideas to setting your plan of action. It provides order and structure to your thinking as you work through each stage. Currently, most problem solving and creativity methods promote somewhat simplistic structures and techniques which bear little relation to people's intricate ways of thinking. With Mind Mapping, not only can you capture your creative output, you can build more practical meaning from it.[11] It's a way of actually externalising your thinking about a situation so you can explore, elaborate and evaluate that thinking more effectively as the basis for selecting an appropriate course of action.

As highlighted in Chapter 3, Mind Mapping is also a technique that contributes to creative stimulation while you're problem solving. This is because it deliberately signals the need to look for alternatives and extract new ideas through association. In this way it exploits and complements the use of other generative techniques, helping your mind travel further outside the categories and limitations of conventional thinking.

Last but not least, it's an enjoyable process. During typical group problem solving, discussions can become very tiresome and wasteful when each person focuses on getting across their own particular view. With Mind Mapping, the process becomes more stimulating, exploratory and collaborative, making it a fun and pleasurable way to achieve efficient and constructive thinking.

---

11 Jones, Sue and Sims, David (1985), 'Mapping as an Aid to Creativity', *Journal of Management Development*, 4,1, pp. 47-60

A Mind Map externalises your thinking

The Coming Chapters.....

Chapter 9 is devoted entirely to Mind Mapping, teaching you how to use this visual brain-friendly technique for capturing and cultivating your ideas. The remainder of the book is then engaged in guiding you through the Solution Finder process, giving you practical recommendations for each stage and indicating when and how to switch into the most relevant mode of thinking. Several chapters will be spent introducing you to a number of defined tools and techniques for generative thinking. These tools are described in detail and feature easy-to-understand examples to explain the concepts involved. Given the right attention, the Solution Finder will work time and time again in a wide variety of business and personal situations, including both large-scale change initiatives and routine challenges. All it requires is the willingness to cultivate an awareness of your thinking and to look at things in different ways.

Importantly, there's no fixed requirement for using the Solution Finder. The process doesn't have to be followed exhaustively and blindly for every single decision you need to make. For BIG challenges that dictate a major change in direction or use of someone's time, I highly recommend that you try to work through all the stages to attain the highest clarity of thought and objectivity. However, for ordinary, routine decisions, you can be less thorough, picking out the tools that are most useful for the problem you have. A key indication of how methodical you need to be is whether the consequences of getting things wrong are significant, serious or scary!

On the whole, the Solution Finder is intended as a practical working process to help you tackle problems and create ideas and insights where none or few existed before. Over time, practising the stages will become second nature to you, enough so that you can tailor the process to suit your own needs quite easily. All being well, you'll discover that being highly creative and productive becomes part or the course when you use systematic thinking.

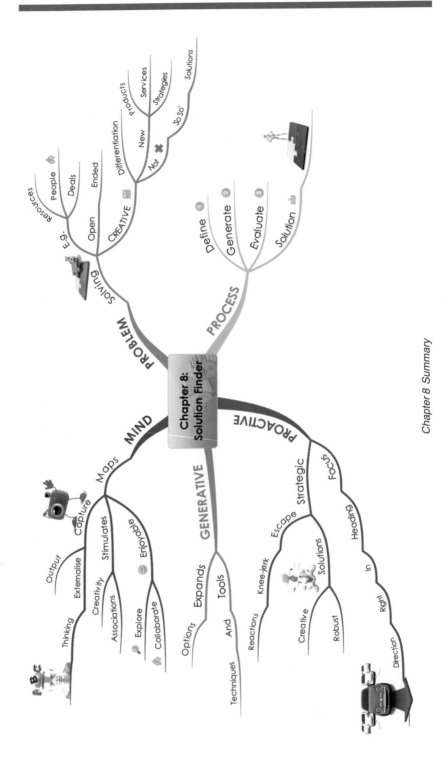

Chapter 8 Summary

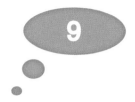

CAPTURING YOUR IDEAS USING MIND MAPS

Creativity is born of new ideas. To achieve stratospheric levels of creativity in the workplace you have to be geared up to generate, assimilate and exploit worthwhile ideas on a consistent basis. But, first things first - how do you capture your ideas to begin with?

Catching ideas as they fly out of your mind is of crucial importance to your innovation efforts. It's a struggle to be fully in command of your creative processes and to realise the value of your ideas if you let them escape! You can lose all sorts of inspirations by failing to note them down. Psychologist Graham Wallas says it best when he tells of a man "who had so brilliant an idea that he went into his garden to thank God for it, and found on rising from his knees that he had forgotten it, and never recalled it."[1] Recording your ideas is what sets off the process that takes them from being mere fancies into tangible and feasible possibilities. Ideally you need a 'hub' for your thoughts and ideas – a place where they can accumulate, interact and grow productively. I propose that place to be the MIND MAP.

No matter what creative systems and strategies you use, a Mind Map allows you to readily capture and consolidate your ideas in physical form. Mind Maps can range from very simple to all-embracing, and are useful at all levels of the creative process from multiple idea generation to rigorous analysis of alternatives. In this chapter, you'll be introduced to the extraordinary potential of Mind Mapping for creative note-taking and you'll be given the know-how to benefit from it directly, both by means of the Solution Finder process contained in this book, and independently.

If you're already familiar with Mind Mapping, please feel free to skip this chapter - though you may find it worthwhile to refresh your memory regarding the key elements that make up a 'true' Mind Map. Often people don't use best practice when it comes to Mind Mapping or they believe

1 Wallas, Graham (1926), *The Art of Thought,* Jonathan Cape

that they're Mind Mapping when, in actual fact, they're doing something else. The term 'Mind Map' is regularly applied to map forms such as spider diagrams, flow charts, concept maps and bubble diagrams. These are NOT Mind Maps and work quite differently. Reading this chapter will help you distinguish between maps that 'follow the rules' and those that don't.

Where Do Ideas Come From?

Your brain is made up of billions of neurons that, during the process of thinking, go firing across your brain in search of new connections. It's effectively an association machine in which every bit of information, every idea, memory or emotion sparks hundreds and even thousands of associations which can be seen to 'radiate' outwards. What's more, each of these associations also has its own unlimited array of neural connections.[2]

Steven Johnson, best-selling author and one of the world's most innovative popular thinkers, explains that a new idea is simply a 'network' of neurons that's never before been formed.[3] It's what comes about when neurons explore the multitude of adjacent possible connections they can make in your mind.

> "To create consists of making new combinations of associative elements which are useful...the most fertile will often be those formed of elements drawn from domains which are far apart."
>
> **Henri Poincare, French mathematician and theoretical physicist**

Contrary to standard thought, good ideas hardly ever occur as 'eureka' moments or 'flash' breakthroughs. In reality, they may take months or even years to culminate and evolve. And Steven Johnson's concept of the 'liquid network'[4] demonstrates that, rather than being something entirely brand new, an idea is the product of a combination of your existing knowledge or ideas, and those of other people, colliding and fusing together in a new way. It's only when the neural connections in your brain reach a state of accessibility or 'liquidity' that the idea can actually materialise.

---

2 Anokhin, P.K. (1973). 'The forming of natural and artificial intelligence', *Impact of Science in Society*, Vol. XXIII
3 Johnson, Steven (2010), *Where Good Ideas Come From: The Natural History of Innovation*, Riverhead Books
4 Johnson, Steven (2010), 'Where ideas come from' (video), TED, Sept 2010, http://www.ted.com/talks/steven_johnson_where_good_ideas_come_from.html

This theory echoes that of the philosopher and physician John Locke[5] who maintained that ideas are derived from 1) sensation - observation of the external world and 2) reflection - our own mental operations and ruminations on our observations. And as Tony Proctor, author of *Creative Problem Solving for Managers* emphasises, ideas are not random, disconnected entities. They can be consciously related to each other through idea processing which "takes individual ideas and manipulates, synthesises and associates them with one another until they form a larger contextual pattern that we can consciously relate to some human concern."[6]

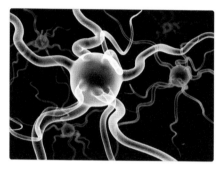

An idea is a 'network' of neurons

"Creativity is just connecting things. When you ask a creative person how they did something, they may feel a little guilty because they didn't really do it, they just saw something. It seemed obvious to them after a while. That's because they were able to connect experiences they've had and synthesize new things... A lot of people in our industry haven't had very diverse experiences. They don't have enough dots to connect, and they end up with very linear solutions, without a broad perspective on the problem."

Steve Jobs, Co-founder and CEO of Apple Inc

With this understanding, it becomes possible to create an external environment that mimics the interactive way in which the brain connects ideas. By bringing together diverse thoughts and people with different backgrounds and interests, snippets of knowledge and assorted ideas can merge to create entirely new configurations. Ideas that are only part ready can connect into something larger and far more exceptional.

5 Locke, John (1964), 'An essay concerning human understanding' in J.V Canfield and F.H Donnell (eds), *Readings in the Theory of Knowledge*, New York: Appleton-Century-Crofts
6 Proctor, Tony (1999), *Creative Problem Solving For Managers,* Routledge

Mind Mapping is essentially a technique that emulates, supports and accelerates this 'dot connecting' process, allowing us to bring new ideas into being in the most liberating and cohesive way. In a Mind Map, information is structured and recorded in a graphic format that mirrors the expansive behaviour of the brain when it creates connections. This allows us to clearly 'see' how our associations can flare into novel and original ideas or solutions. The concept of association is widely believed to be at the heart of any creative act. Popularised by Arthur Koestler[7] under the term 'bisociation', it suggests that linking one area to another gives rise to novel associations and that such associations form the bedrock of creative ideas. On these grounds, it clearly validates the use of many divergent thinking techniques such as Mind Mapping.

Whether we're working on paper or on a computer, alone or in teams, our thoughts and ideas can be captured, co-ordinated and strengthened with great ease and resourcefulness in a Mind Map. Naturally, this makes it an exceptionally powerful tool for solving complex problems, broadening horizons and improving day-to-day decision making.

What Exactly is a Mind Map?

A Mind Map is a visual diagram where thoughts, ideas or facts are laid out on branches around a central theme to form an organic, connected structure which 'radiates' outwards. It uses lines, key words, colour, space and images all according to simple, brain-friendly concepts. The popularity of the Mind Mapping technique has grown spectacularly in the last few decades and it's now used by millions globally as an aid in study, organisation, problem solving and decision making.

> *"Tony didn't invent the brain – he did invent the instructions!"*
>
> **John Husbands, Institute of Management**

The Mind Map was invented and popularised by leading author and 'brain expert' Tony Buzan in the early 1970s. While at university, he learned that conventional linear methods of taking notes and recording ideas such as lists and outlines make inefficient use of the brain's powers and can, in actual fact, be very wasteful to the thinking process.

---

7 Koestler, Arthur (1964), *The Act of Creation*, Hutchinson, London

Drawing on breakthrough scientific insights on the brain and the approaches of the great thinkers, scientists and artists of the past, Tony ultimately devised the Mind Map as a credible alternative to our traditional forms of note-taking. By understanding the operational principles of the brain, Tony was able to purposely formulate a tool to complement these principles, and in doing so, could offer us an incredibly practical and positive way to unleash our thinking capacity.[8]

What's Wrong With Lists?

Creating a linear list or outline forces the brain to work in a way that's not natural for it. Adding new items and sentences to a list in a linear sequence actually funnels out your thinking, so as you get lower and lower down the list, your creativity bottoms out and you stop thinking. As a result your potential to draw out all of the ideas and information available to you is limited – not exactly ideal when you're brainstorming! In effect, this orderly form of note taking is one of the best ways to destroy your creativity as it restricts the flow of your thoughts and dries up your creative juices very early on. That's not to say that it's not useful for analysing and organising your ideas as a SELECTIVE tool, but it's absurd and illogical to try to organise your ideas before you've even generated them.[9]

> "There can be no clearer or more effective mental tool than Tony Buzan's Mind Maps."
>
> **Ray Keene, OBE, correspondent for The Times**

Mind Mapping on the other hand works 'radiantly' and expansively, using associations, connections and triggers to stimulate your brain to respond with more and more ideas. Topics are explored by working from the centre outwards, increasing the depth and breadth of your thoughts. Instead of long, running sentences, you're encouraged to use one key word per branch to open up your thinking and spawn lots of new possibilities. This incites your mind to dig deeper and see greater detail on thoughts that were previously vague, something that isn't easily done when the key word is trapped in a sentence.

For instance, the sentence 'project deadline missed' fuses words together in a way that limits the direction in which the thought process can travel. Switching your focus to the key word 'project' by itself allows you

8 Buzan, Tony and Buzan, Barry (1994), *The Mind Map Book: How to Use Radiant Thinking to Maximize Your Brain's Untapped Potential*, New York: Dutton.
9 Gelb, Michael (2000), *How to Think Like Leonardo da Vinci: Seven Steps to Genius Every day*, Dell

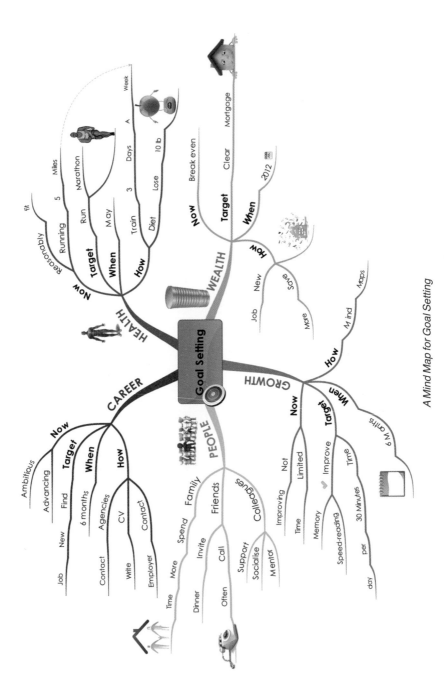

A Mind Map for Goal Setting

to address the subject in a wider context. The 'deadline' then becomes a secondary issue that can also be explored comprehensively as a key word on its own branch e.g. Was the deadline realistic in the first place? What resources were allocated to it? and so on.[10]

A formal list or outline is dull and monotonous – it's monochrome and imposes a restrictive linear and sequential pattern on the user. But the Mind Map encourages the full range of your mental expression by taking on board colour, space, rhythm, image and dimension as well as logic.

What's more, the Mind Mapping process encourages you to keep thinking – it's much easier to 'see' new opportunities between the branches of your map and your thinking will flow naturally to try and fill in the blank spaces. So with Mind Mapping you can think without limitation to explore an infinite number of paths, resulting in it being a GENERATIVE thinking tool.

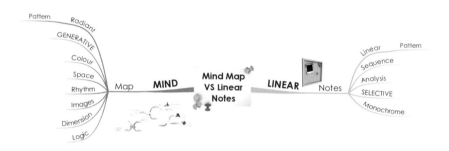

Mind Maps VS Linear notes

Going Beyond Left Brain, Right Brain...

These days, most of us are familiar with the theory of brain lateralisation, i.e. the left and right brain control different thinking functions. This is based on the original research of Dr. Sperry in the 1960s which determined that the Cerebral Cortex, the 'thinking cap' of the brain, is divided into two major hemispheres – a right and left.[11]

---

10 Buzan, Tony and Griffiths, Chris (2010), *Mind Maps for Business*, BBC Active
11 Sperry, R.W. (1968), 'Hemispheric deconnection and unity in conscious awareness'. *Scientific American*, Vol. 23, pp. 723-735

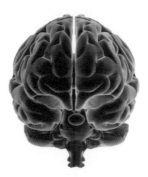

The brain – Divided into left and right hemispheres

The idea that the left and right sides of the brain exhibit different thinking patterns has captured a great deal of public attention over the years and has inspired a multitude of management and educational approaches. These tend to make broad generalisations on how the brain segregates intellectual tasks (cortical skills), for example:

The left brain – The left brain deals primarily with words, numbers, analysis, language, sequence, linearity, lists and logic i.e. analytical processes

The right brain – The right brain is associated with images, colour, rhythm, shape, imagination, seeing the 'whole picture', daydreaming and dimension i.e. creative processes

While it's appealing and helpful to isolate the hemispheres in this way, it's undoubtedly an oversimplification of the facts. Many of the commonly accepted ideas about left and right brain differences have lately come to be regarded as pop-psychology, not hard science, and researchers have heavily criticised such claims. The reality regarding the workings of the hemispheres is a great deal more complex than most of us can envision. Results of neurological scanning (EEG, Isotopic Brain-Scan, Magnetoencephalograpy, Positron Emission Tomography and EMR) show that the brain functions are not as distinct as previously thought. Although the hemispheres operate differently in terms of mental processing, areas of both sides of the brain become active when certain faculties are engaged. Joseph Hellige, a psychologist at the University of California, explains how, under the scanner, language turned out to be represented on both sides of the brain, in matching areas of the cortex. Areas on the left dealt with the core aspects of speech such as grammar and word production, while aspects such as intonation and emphasis lit up the right side.[12]

12 McCrone, John (2000), "Right Brain' or 'Left Brain' – Myth or Reality?', *New Scientist,* RBI Limited 2000

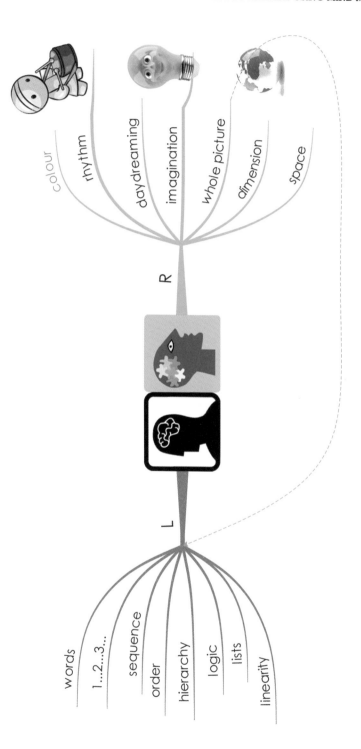

colour
rhythm
daydreaming
imagination
whole picture
dimension
space

R

L

words
1...2...3...
sequence
order
hierarchy
logic
lists
linearity

Left and Right Brain Qualities

This evidence disproves the long-standing perception that the left and right brains are two totally separate entities. They are intricately connected, with every mental faculty shared across the brain and each side contributing in a complementary, not exclusive, fashion. It's less about physical location and more a subtle difference in processing styles that distinguishes the two halves. Dr. Jerre Levy PHD, one of the foremost authorities on the functions of the left and right cerebral hemispheres says:

"To the extent that regions are differentiated in the brain, they must integrate their activities. Indeed, it is precisely that integration that gives rise to behaviour and mental processes greater than and different from each region's contribution."[13]

> *"The more you use your brain, the more brain you will have to use."*
>
> **George A. Dorsey, World War II Veteran**

Despite the existence of the two hemispheres, the brain is designed to be 'whole'. Integrating left and right brain activities forces our brain cells to 'co-operate' to maximise the use of the brain. Jan-Willem van den Brandhof, author of *The Business Brain Book* highlights that using the left and right side of the brain together properly helps us utilise our brains better by a factor of five to ten![14]

When we function within limited preferences, for example, using only a sequential and logical approach (left brain), we reduce our ability to leverage all our available resources during the thinking process. In western society, we predominantly use left brain cortical skills while our right brain abilities are less developed. This is because our schools and workplaces are set up to heavily promote reading, writing, arithmetic and other linear analytical processes. However, each cortical skill works to reinforce and enhance the performance of other areas so the more skills we can learn to integrate, the better. In other words, to perform optimally, we need both sides of our brain working together synergistically – we need whole brain thinking!

Whole brain thinking involves making a conscious and deliberate effort to incorporate our left and right brain cortical skills. When we can think in this way, we strengthen our ability to produce greater associations. This in turn leads to greater creative firepower. Mind Maps work well to enhance creative performance because they're an excellent means for whole brain integration.

---

13 Levy, Jerre (1985), 'Right Brain, Left Brain: Fact and Fiction', *Psychology Today*, May 1985, p.43
14 van den Brandhof, Jan-Willem (2008), *The Business Brain Book*, BrainWare

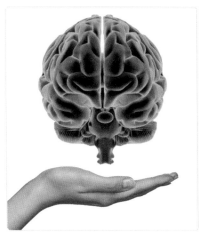

Whole Brain Thinking

When you Mind Map, you're using your entire range of cortical skills and this invokes multiple reference points from which to stimulate your imagination and bring greater clarity to your thinking. Plus, the actual process of Mind Mapping paves the way for new thoughts to surface and new connections to be made. The result is more free-flowing ideas and improved exploration, leading to greater insight and discovery.

> *"Mind Mapping uses the brain in the way it was designed, saves time, improves results and is fun. How can any business person be without this powerful tool?"*
>
> **Stephen C Lundin, Author of the bestseller 'FISH!'**

Consequently, Mind Mapping is an activity that's both logical and creative, engaging your brain in a much richer way for problem solving and decision making. Note-taking using key words and a radiant hierarchical structure draws on the qualities of your logical left cortical skills. Add the use of vibrant colours, striking images and curvilinear lines and you also stir up your creative right cortical skills. Intrinsically therefore, the Mind Map takes all the most significant and compelling qualities of thinking and integrates them dynamically into its own unique structure for better performance all-round!

How to Create a Mind Map

There are two ways of creating a Mind Map: drawing it by hand or on a computer using a bespoke software tool such as iMindMap. If you prefer to work on a computer, the next section introduces you to some of the latest developments in Computer Mind Mapping.

Whichever method you employ, the first and most important step is to clearly identify the topic or issue you want to explore. Be sure to focus on your core question or goal. Creating a Mind Map is a really simple and personal activity, and using the following guidelines will make the process as brain-friendly as possible.

Step 1) Start in the centre with an image

In the centre of a blank sheet of paper or computer screen create a strong, colourful image to represent the main subject or theme of your Mind Map.

Why an image? Well, have you ever heard the phrase - 'a picture is worth a thousand words'? Images are far more suggestive than words and using one in the centre of your map kick-starts your imagination to generate multiple associations, resulting in greater innovative thinking. They make use of a massive range of cortical skills (colour, form, line, dimension, imagination, logic and spatial awareness) so they're a highly potent way to focus your attention. If you're creating a Mind Map on the computer, you have the advantage of being able to use some of the many graphics, photos and other images available in clip art or within your software package.

Step 2) Connect the main topics using organic, curved branches

Next, draw thick, organic, flowing branches radiating out from the central image for your main topics. Curved branches give visual rhythm to the map and their thickness around the centre demonstrates their importance.[15] These first-level branches are your Basic Ordering Ideas (BOIs) and they provide the basic framework and hierarchy that will naturally guide your thinking at lower levels. They help to channel your

---

15 Illumine Training, 'How to Make a Mind Map', http://www.mind-mapping.co.uk/ make-mind-map.htm

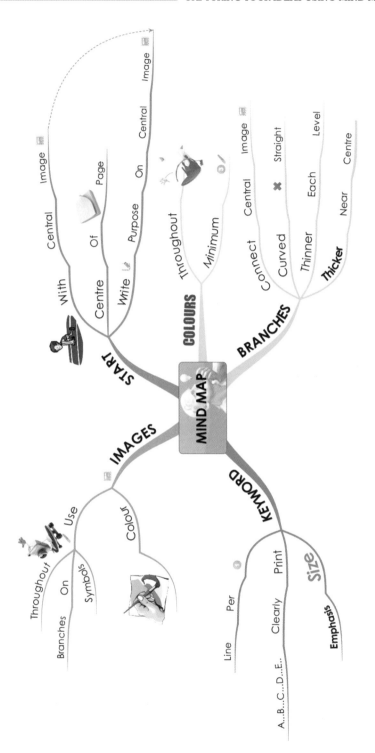

Mind Map Guidelines

creativity in the exact direction you want it to go, maximising the quality of your thinking.[16]

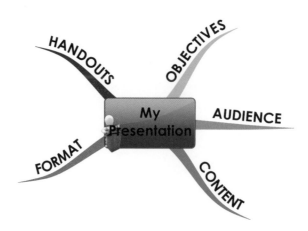

Step 3) Use key words to label branches

Print your main topics onto these central branches. Use single key words or images to label your branches precisely. This stimulates more expansive connections in the brain, boosting creativity and concentration. Using more than one word or a sentence is limiting to the mind and visually cluttering.

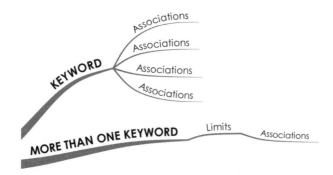

Printing words in upper or lower case letters is also much easier to read than joined up or indistinct writing. Ideally, the word or image should sit on its own branch and the branch should be the same length as the image or word. Leaving too much 'empty' length on the branch after the word or image can disconnect the flow of the thought process.

---

16 Wycoff, J. (1991), *Mindmapping: Your Personal Guide to Exploring Creativity and Problem-solving*, New York: Berkley Books.

Step 4) Apply some colour

Be adventurous and use bold colours in your map to enliven it or as your own special code to differentiate ideas or themes. It's a good idea to use one colour for each major category (BOI) in your map to aid organisation.

Colours stimulate the brain and add impact so that we remember things far better than we would in monochrome.[17] Adding colour is an easy task if you're using a software package with pre-determined colour settings that automatically colour your branches for you.

Step 5) Connect sub-topic branches

Draw thinner lines off the end of the main branches to hold a second level of thought or supporting data (sub-branches). These associations will flow naturally from the main topics. As you delve deeper into the subject, create even more sub-branches to display further levels of information. For example, you can ask questions to explore the Who, What, Where, Why, When and How of the subject or situation.

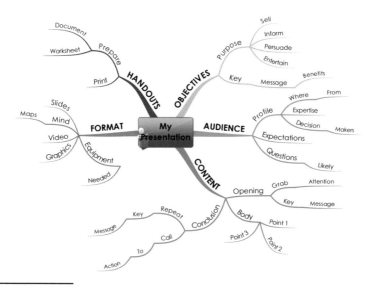

17 White, J. V. (1997), *Color for Impact,* Berkeley: Strathmoor Press.

All the connected branches will cause the Mind Map to take on a recognisable shape and structure. Using progressively thinner branches illustrates the different levels of importance in topics.

Step 6) Use images and symbols where possible

Try to use images throughout your Mind Map, not just for the central theme. Where possible, use them instead of key words on branches or to add visual impact to specific topics. Images convey more information than any amount of words that you could legibly fit into a single Mind Map so your notes can be as brief and compact as possible. They also prompt your imagination and stimulate your memory – what you see, you remember![18]

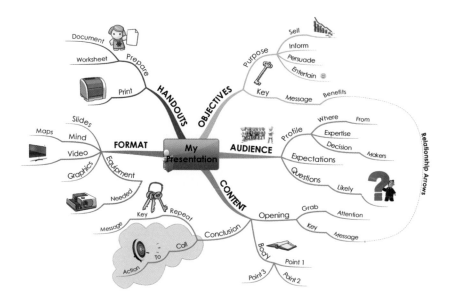

18 Haber, R.N. (1970), 'How we remember what we see', *Scientific American,* Vol. 222, pp. 104-112

Step 7) Show relationships within your map

Information in one part of the map may relate to another part. Use relationship arrows or lines to visually connect concepts across different areas of the map. By encouraging you to link apparently different ideas and concepts in this way, this activity actually promotes divergent and highly creative thinking.[19]

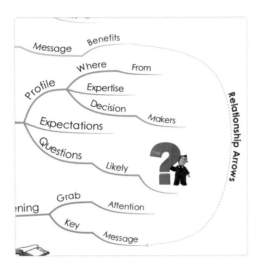

Step 8) Emphasise important topics or areas

If you like, you can go even further to draw attention to key parts of your map. Adding highlights in the form of clouds or other outlines can make specific topics or ideas 'stand out' so that they're easier to remember and/or communicate to others. Simply surround a topic branch and/or its sub-branches with an enclosed shape, preferably containing a background colour.

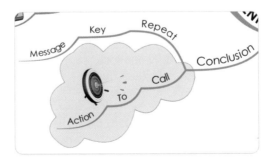

19 White, R. and Gunstone, R. (1992), *Probing Understanding*, New York: Falmer Press.

Mind Mapping is a highly personal and idiosyncratic activity where your thoughts can reach out in any direction. Once you know how to Mind Map, you can develop your own distinctive style to make your maps more meaningful.

Mind Maps, Concept Maps, Spider Diagrams – What's the Difference?

It's important to be able to differentiate between a 'true' Mind Map and a 'proto' Mind Map such as a concept map, flow chart or spider diagram. There are considerable differences among the map styles that can impact negatively on the creative output of your note-taking. The following examples represent proto-Mind Maps that, while having a similar appearance, don't contain the essential properties of a Mind Map.

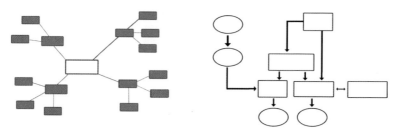

Examples of non Mind Maps

At first glance these diagrams may seem acceptable, but unfortunately, they overlook principles that are vital for effective idea capture and organisation. For instance, they may contain more than one main concept; many words can be used per idea; lines are not hierarchical or differentiated; and colours and images are merely optional.

All of this can hinder the dynamic connection between ideas and disengage the flow of thought. There's little to inspire your brain to spark with new ideas and using phrases instead of key words also limits associations. Compare this with a Mind Map that closely follows all the important principles – there's only one focused theme; only one word per line; lines are related in terms of hierarchy; lines go from thick to thin; and colours and images are VERY important.

When you're first learning to Mind Map, it's a good idea to stick to the Buzan Mind Mapping principles as much as possible as they provide a reliable and consistent framework for your thinking. Once you're comfortable with the principles, feel free to experiment a bit more and do what works best for you.

Computer Mind Maps – an Essential Modern-Day Tool

While you can use pencil and paper to draw Mind Maps the traditional way, you now have access to computer software that can help you produce top quality Mind Maps that are not only visual representations of your ideas, but incredible facilitators for your varying business needs and requirements. For instance, software tools bring a whole host of features for rapidly generating, reorganising, structuring, presenting and sharing ideas and information. There are many stand-alone software programs available as well as web-based applications, most of which allow you to:[20]

- Automatically generate neat and professional Mind Maps quickly and with little effort;
- Edit and enhance your Mind Maps as much as you like;
- Analyse and manage your data at intricate levels using a range of tools;
- Share and present your Mind Maps through a variety of modes;
- Convert your Mind Maps into different communication and reporting formats such as reports, presentations, project plans and spreadsheets;
- Leverage group ideas and comments through collaboration;
- Organise, implement and track projects from start to finish;
- Improve knowledge management through links to external information sources.

Of course, being able to create Mind Maps on screen and having access to a wide range of additional features and functions makes life considerably easier. But it's important not to lose sight of why you're using Mind Maps in the first place – to activate the different areas of your brain through a multi-sensory approach and spark more immediate creativity and innovation. To this end, your Mind Map software should be 'fit for purpose' and allow you to express yourself in harmony with your brain's thought processes. Any software labelled to be a Mind Mapping tool must be able to follow the guiding principles of Mind Mapping to spur your creativity in a truly limitless way.

This is the exact thinking behind the creation of iMindMap software. In 2005, Tony Buzan and I teamed up to produce a tool that could accurately reflect the imagination and association processes of his successful organic Mind Mapping formula. Our focus was not so much on the technology as it was on the process. iMindMap is a tool for thinking first and foremost – you can capture your ideas within a comfortable software environment that's purposely designed to stimulate and draw out as

20 Buzan, Tony and Griffiths, Chris (2010), *Mind Maps For Business*, BBC Active

many of your brain's resources as possible. And now, with the launch of iMindMap 5, it also contains most of the exciting features and capabilities that you could possibly want in today's modern, technological world. (For more information, visit www.ThinkBuzan.com).

Case Study: Mind Maps for Strategic Change

The Children in Distress Network (CINDI) has been in existence for around 12 years, located in the KwaZulu-Natal province of South Africa. KwaZulu-Natal has the highest prevalence of HIV and AIDS, and is rife with unemployment and poverty. CINDI works with about 300 non-profit organisations in the area; from emerging grassroots, community-based organisations, to larger NGOs. All have the common goal of wanting to help children, who are infected by, or affected by HIV and AIDS.

CINDI provides coordination and collaboration between these different organisations. It helps them to share information, work together, avoid duplication and improve their organisational capabilities.

We at ThinkBuzan have been in regular contact with Neill Stevenson, a programme manager at CINDI, since we donated iMindMap licenses to the organisation in 2009. He has reported on how they've been using iMindMap to facilitate an entire strategic planning process in the network.

The project that Neill works on is funded by a large international donor. It includes a consortium of 4 fairly large non-profit organisations who are working together in a partnership and providing a comprehensive package of services to 13,000 orphans and vulnerable children in the area. It's a big project, with lots of funding, a big staff and a lot of collaboration and coordination that needs to take place. Neill has been using iMindMap to facilitate a process of strategic planning and change on the project.

"We review and revise our strategic plan every couple of years and this was the first time we tried using Mind Mapping. We had to do a very thorough process of consulting various internal and external stakeholders, capturing their information and putting it all together into different components of the strategic plan."

1. Brainstorming

"I was able to use the iMindMap software to capture the different thinking of people in the various consultations as we gathered information and brainstormed ideas. We worked with a laptop and a projector, so that as people were sharing their ideas, I was able to get it all into a Mind Map and project it onto the screen. Everyone could see the thinking evolving as I drew links between branches, and shifted priorities by moving branches around."

"Previously, we have just used flipcharts, which is fine as far as it goes – but it's not dynamic. But with iMindMap, whilst we were talking, we were immediately able to cluster ideas together, prioritise them, and create new themes. It was a much more engaging and fruitful process. Then at the end of it we had a document that everybody has consensus on. Rather than going away and creating minutes using the various sheets from the flipchart, and circulating them to everybody to get their feedback, this was all done in one step. "

2. Analysing

The information then needed to be pulled together and analysed. Different strategic themes had to be identified and the priorities going forward determined.

With the help of iMindMap software, CINDI were able to decide that there were two main themes, or areas. The networking and advocacy that had always been the core of what they did, and another area that had emerged as being of new importance.

Far more new members were small, emerging organisations – small groups of people who have come together in the community in order to respond to a particular need, with minimum resources and minimum skills, and very little organisational capacity and structure.

"They register as a non-profit organisation, which is fairly easy to do, but they will have very little chance of actually mobilising further resources, because they don't have the skills and the structure."

"We realised we needed to place more emphasis on capacity building and resource mobilisation. We decided we would need to develop a whole new division of the organisation which is devoted to that area."

3. Strategising

"We were able to very clearly show how the various components fit together. We developed a modular system where small organisations can receive a small amount of money that could be used to implement their projects and also receive both training and mentoring. The larger organisations would mentor the smaller organisations and we would outsource training on the key areas that organisational sustainability is founded on – things like project management, monitoring and evaluation, basic financial management and human resources. "

By the time an organisation has gone through the whole programme, not only have they been able to offer services to their beneficiaries, the children, but they have been able to demonstrate that they have the training and capacity necessary and so are able to attract funding in their own right.

To find out more about CINDI and the work they do, visit their website: www.cindi.org.za. For information on iMindMap or to download it for **FREE**, visit www.ThinkBuzan.com.

So many people are doing their creative thinking and problem solving using tools that aren't designed for these tasks. By learning to Mind Map, on paper or on a computer, you can support good thinking practices and reach greater heights in your creative performance. As a note-taking platform, it can multiply dramatically the advantages you get from using your brain, and integrated within the Solution Finder process, it becomes even more highly targeted. Don't be reticent; Mind Mapping is fun and easy to do – precisely because it's a natural reflection of your internal thinking processes.

And it's a skill you can use for the rest of your life!

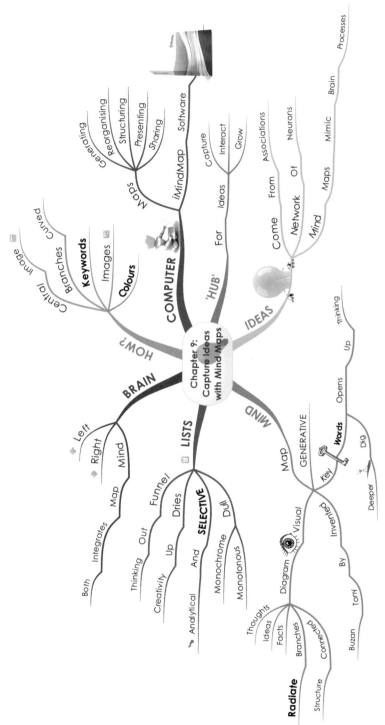

Chapter 9 Summary

STEP 1: DEFINE THE PROBLEM

Einstein once said that if he had one hour to save the world he would "spend 55 minutes defining the problem and only five minutes finding the solution."

What Einstein clearly understood is that the starting point of any creative problem solving process is to invest time in **defining your problem correctly**. Problems and challenges can take on a vast number of shapes and sizes - they may represent shortcomings ('repeat sales are falling', 'our budget has been reduced') or goals ('design an up-to-date product', 'regain market share'). They can be broad or specific, internal or external, and can vary from a relatively minor hiccup to a major switch in operational focus.

How you define your problem sets the principal direction for all your solution finding efforts and so it's your job to make sure that you're addressing the right problem from the outset. This might appear to be a simple task, but it's often where people struggle. In many organisations, people will spend hours finding solutions to issues that are trivial, or in some cases non-existent.[1] Why? Because they're **reacting** to what they think the problem or opportunity is; and wasting valuable time, energy and resources doing it!

> *"From my personal experience, most organizations spend 60 minutes finding solutions to problems that don't matter. Doing this wastes your money and the energy of your people."*
>
> **Stephen Shapiro, Author of '24/7 Innovation'**

---

1 Shapiro, Stephen (2009), 'Innovating in Tough Times', *Stephen Shapiro's 24/7 Innovation*, 29th April 2009, http://www.steveshapiro.com/blog/page/22/

When you were at school, do you remember being told to make sure that you read the question in the exam properly before answering? The same advice applies to problem solving. Instead of rushing into finding solutions, we must devote our early attention to formulating a sharp and thorough understanding of our problem, even if we're under time constraints or pressure. It could be that we're mistaken about the real problem or challenge and that there is a more influential, worthwhile or fundamental issue at hand. Naturally, we have to be able to distinguish whether the area we're focusing on is the actual problem or merely a symptom.

Step 1 of the Solution Finder: Define The Problem

The way we define our problem influences the line of thought that we follow and has a powerful effect on the solution strategies we consider. In other words, it's what drives our generative, analytical and selective processes, which is why it's so important to get it right. Problems that are badly defined inevitably lead to bad solutions and vice versa. Individuals and businesses that I work with seem to have incredible realisations when they go through this stage – but this is the stage of the creative process that most of us tend to skip! If it's ignored entirely, many problem solving activities can fail before they even start because we haven't got to the heart of the challenge itself.[2] While enthusiastic action and energy can be a huge help in overcoming challenges, this effort is a complete waste if it's misguided!

> *"A problem well stated is a problem half solved."*
>
> **Charles F. Kettering, American electrical engineer & inventor**

Developing a focused and well-honed description of the problem demands a proactive orientation to investigate the facts and clarify your

---

2 Byron, Kevin (2005), *Creative Problem-Solving*, ETC (Education and Training in Creativity)

thoughts around it. Some probing and exploration is necessary to help you shape and refine the problem in terms of the most relevant issues. In a sense, you're preparing the problem in readiness to prompt a good range of choices and solve it at the right creative level. For group problem solving this is a vital activity so that the energies of everyone involved are focused in the same direction. The upcoming method is really handy for breaking down your problem in a way that improves and verifies your understanding of it.

Five Wives, One Husband and a Map

Rather than creating a plain statement, it's helpful to define and describe the problem in a much wider sense. Once we've identified the overall challenge that we want to work with, we need to use divergent thought processes to find facts and locate the most relevant elements of the situation. These are the things that will help us better understand the current reality of our task, as opposed to those that will distract us from our real goal.[3]

Within the Solution Finder, this stage is structured around a simple technique based on the maxim of **Five W's and One H**. This involves mapping out the problem using the question prompts: **What? Why? Where? Who? When? and How?**

Five W's and One H

Questions are a key device through which you challenge yourself to generate the explicit answers you need – answers that are necessary to illuminate the problem. These, in turn, assist you to consider different problem perspectives for stimulating ideas when you move on to the next stage of the Solution Finder process. Some of the information you need

3 Treffinger, Donald J., Isaksen, Scott G. and Dorval, Brian D. (2003), 'Creative Problem Solving (CPS Version 6.1™): A Contemporary Framework for Managing Change', *Center for Creative Learning Inc and Creative Problem Solving Group Inc,* www.creativelearning.com and www.cpsb.com.

might be starkly apparent, but other data might be missing which is why going through the process is so critical. Note the distinction between 'relevant' information and 'available' information.[4] A classic mistake problem solvers make is to look at the information at their disposal and attempt to mould it towards their problem. Make a point of asking yourself if the information you have is actually relevant. If not, then you'll need to set about obtaining the 'right' information using appropriate research methods.

Undertaking this stage of the Solution Finder process within a **Mind Map** helps to spark off the divergent thought pattern that assists you in gathering everything you need. When the problem or challenge is crystallised within the central theme, you can explore it clearly, carefully and comprehensively by mapping out your thoughts and data under each question category - **What? Why? Where? Who? When?** and **How?** The Mind Map format is particularly helpful for highlighting any misconceptions about the problem. If the same word or concept appears on several branches, the chances are it's more fundamental to your problem than the one you've placed in the centre!

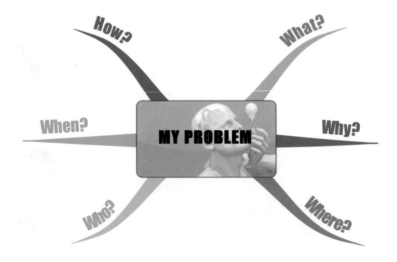

Define your problem using Five W's and One H

1) WHAT

What are the **facts**? Investigate the circumstances of the problem and probe details about it. Your aim at this point is to outline the facts clearly and accurately without any assumptions. Breaking the problem down into strict components and features allows each chunk to be addressed

---

4 Adair, John (2007), *Decision Making and Problem Solving Strategies*, The Sunday Times, Kogan Page

separately and clarifies anything about the problem that's ambiguous or fuzzy. This process is even more important if your problem is vague. For instance 'productivity is declining' is an uncertain assignment because it doesn't specify the area where the decline is occurring or by how much. This makes it difficult to determine how to make improvements. The added benefit of breaking down what seems to be a BIG problem into smaller pieces is that it also becomes more manageable and far less intimidating!

Ask questions that help you delve into the specifics of the problem: What is or is not happening? Where is it happening, when is it happening, who is it happening to, and how is it happening? For instance, what aspects of productivity in particular are declining? Where is the decline in productivity occurring most? When is the productivity declining? How much decline in productivity is involved and how serious is it?[5]

Look at both **hard data** such as statistics, history and time factors and **soft data** such as opinions, human factors, attitudes and behaviours. Including both elements provides a balanced perspective and helps you elicit the most significant symptoms, constraints and impacts. It might be helpful at this point to gather information using a mixture of research methods such as interviews, statistics, questionnaires, technical experiments, checklists or focus groups. Each bit of information contributes to you gaining a fuller understanding of the nature of the problem and will stimulate better ideas later on. In fact, the more focused you are at this stage, the fewer resources and energy you'll need for generating original and worthwhile solutions in the next stage.

What are the facts?

This is also the perfect point to state **what** you're trying to achieve. Are you clear about what you want to happen and where you want to get to? Without a sense of purpose, the whole process of problem solving can be obscured in a haze – aimless creativity is usually just that. As outlined

5 Proctor, Tony (1999), *Creative Problem Solving For Managers*, Routledge

by Stephen Covey, author of *The 7 Habits of Highly Effective People,* you must "begin with the end in mind".[6] Setting out your goal need only be a case of identifying a key word or phrase such as 'understand our customers better' or 'win a government contract'. You've diverged your thoughts to work out your problem, now you're converging them towards your vision.

When you have a target in sight, all your thinking can be done in context of the whole and your actions can contribute meaningfully and beneficially to your objective. In other words, you can proactively manage the problem solving process to line up positively with what you want to accomplish, increasing your odds of coming up with the best ideas.

2) WHY

If your challenge relates to an actual 'problem' or difficulty, ask yourself, "why has the problem occurred?" Like a good doctor who wants to be sure he prescribes the right treatment, you need to identify and investigate not only the presenting symptoms of the problem, but the underlying conditions. It's astounding how little you probably know about why the problem is happening. Your overall goal at this point should be to uncover the root cause i.e. the condition or event that, if corrected or eliminated, would prevent the problem or challenge from occurring. A useful approach to use here is the 'Five Whys'. Ask the question "why?" repeatedly until you get to the bottom of things. Note that the term Five Whys is figurative and you might need more or less whys for the base cause of the problem to become apparent.

Here's an example. Your problem is that the employee turnover rate has been increasing. Why? Employees are leaving for other jobs. Why? Employees are not satisfied. Why? Other employers are paying higher salaries. Why? Demand for such employees has increased in the market.[7] As you can see, this little tip is useful for sorting through the cause and effect relationships or patterns at work within the problem.

Use 'Five Whys' to determine the root cause of the problem

6 Covey, Stephen R. (1989), *The 7 Habits of Highly Effective People*, Simon & Schuster UK Ltd
7 A Course on Analytical Thinking, www.exinfm.com/...files/Analytical%20Thinking% 20Training.ppt

Alternatively, for a challenge which represents a new opportunity or goal such as 'improve my creativity', it's nice to outline **why** you want to achieve that particular goal, or why that decision is important. For example - "because I want to offer my workshop audiences a unique experience." Again, we reach the underlying reason for the challenge, giving us a more complete outlook of what we're working towards and further helping to frame our decision making.

3) WHERE

Where can you **resolve** the problem? At this point, you want to determine the best place or environment for working things out or implementing the solution. Where will you need to be located or positioned? This will be indicated by the types of facilities and people you need to help you. For instance, the problem may be something that can be resolved quite easily at the office or in a specific department, for example, production or customer services. Or it may relate to specific branches, shop locations or even a client's office.

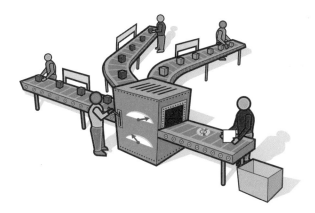

Where can you resolve the problem? e.g. production line

4) WHO

Who can **help** to solve the problem? Here you will identify the person or people who can be involved in the solution, both directly and indirectly. For example, if the problem relates to poor customer service in a supermarket chain, the responsibility for enacting the solution lies most obviously with the shop service counter staff as they're in direct contact with the customer. And it will also involve the supervisors who oversee their interactions. Indirectly, it could involve lots of others, for instance, key members of the head office who can help research and develop better customer service initiatives to roll out across the company, and perhaps human resources personnel to provide support for dealing with low staff morale. A problem such as 'increased incidents of machinery failure' has a bearing on the operations manager who is responsible for maintaining productivity output and on the maintenance team who are called out to repair the machinery. It's likely that both parties will need to be involved in terms of 1) investigating the root cause of the problem e.g. is the equipment being misused or is it not being adequately maintained? and 2) determining appropriate solutions.

Huge, complex problems may call for external help in the form of consultants, technical experts, agencies or freelancers. For example, developing new products almost always involves relationships with outside suppliers. Recognising this early on means that you can look into potential ways of sharing the investment risks. In some instances, you might also need to seek approval for a project from more senior staff or stakeholders.

If you're stuck at this point, you can turn to a useful method devised by Reg Revans, best known for his work on Action Learning. In this approach you ask:[8]

Who knows? – about the situation/opportunity, or who has the information we need to solve it/realise it.

Who cares? – that something is done about it.

Who can? – do something about the solution.

For significant challenges, try and spend some time at the affected department or doing a certain task so that you become immersed personally in the problem. This will help you to see everything from a more concrete perspective so you can pinpoint more accurately the people who can assist. Identifying these people now is far more effective than waiting until you're ready to implement a solution as it offers the opportunity to come up with solutions and strategies that are more workable later on.

5) WHEN

When do you need to have a solution ready? Strictly speaking, what is your deadline? This is a key question as it helps you establish a time frame for the rest of your problem solving. If your challenge is to develop a new marketing campaign, when do you plan on launching? Your

---

8 'The Seven Step Problem Solving Technique', *The Happy Manager,* http://www.the-happy-manager. com/seven-step-problem-solving.html

decision here will feed into your implementation planning, helping you build in time for earlier tasks and keep on track. Quite a lot of business problems require an urgent response. This could indicate that you need to put in place a temporary or interim solution before you can fully explore possibilities and conduct more analysis. You might only have a chance to fleetingly visit each step of the Solution Finder, or may even skip stages. Of course, this means that you should recognise that there are likely to be limitations inherent in that interim solution.[9]

When is your deadline?

6) HOW

How does the problem or challenge influence people or activities? This line of questioning explains the impact of the problem in terms of specific tasks, departments, resources, products or tools. A problem concerning the 'poor record of recruitment and retention of sales staff' could have a bearing on the activities of human resources and the sales manager in a number of ways such as:

• The way in which job descriptions are modified and updated.
• The way advertisements are placed in the media when a vacancy arises.
• The quality of information given to prospective applicants.
• The policy of how many candidates are shortlisted for interview.
• The manner in which face to face interviews are conducted.

> *"The mere formulation of a problem is far more often essential than its solution, which may be merely a matter of mathematical or experimental skill. To raise new questions, new possibilities, to regard old problems from a new angle requires creative imagination and marks real advances in science."*
>
> **Albert Einstein, Nobel Prize winning theoretical physicist**

9 Heiser, Daniel R. 'Problem Solving', *Encyclopedia for Business*, 2nd Ed, 18th January 2011, http://www.referenceforbusiness.com/management/Or-Pr/Problem-Solving.html

Outlining all of these factors at this early stage contributes to more meaningful idea generation. They act as key stimulators for ideas, resulting in suggestions that have brilliant potential in terms of their application to the problem.

In any creative process, the quality of your output always depends on the quality of your input. The Solution Finder is no different. Each problem or challenge requires its own special treatment in terms of the people involved and the information brought to bear on it. How well you define the problem makes a massive difference to your outcome as it's the precept for how you apply your resources and energy while problem solving. What you'll find as you map through Step 1 of the Solution Finder is that each question forces you to look at the problem from different angles so that you develop a total view of what you're dealing with. It's such a simple yet powerful way to isolate the key elements and salient facts that form your final problem definition. Once this step is complete, you've set the scene to invite ideas for solutions using generative thinking strategies.

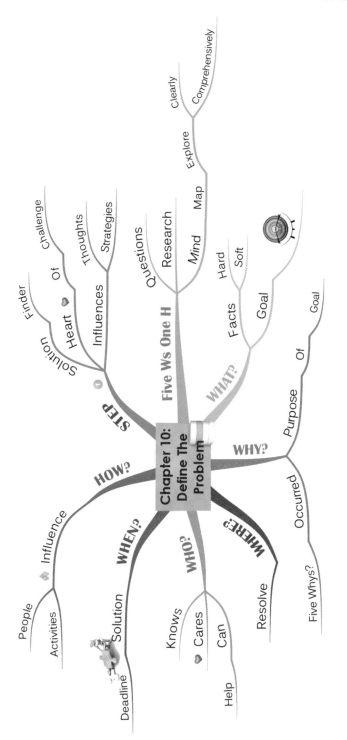

Chapter 10 Summary

STEP 2: GENERATE IDEAS
Correct Brainstorming Strategy

Step 2 is the idea generation phase of the Solution Finder process. Here you map out plenty of creative solutions to the problem you articulated in Step 1. In other words, it's the brainstorming step – the part when your 'ideas machine', **generative thinking**, comes fully into gear.

In the first step of the Solution Finder, you put lots of effort into understanding and defining your problem and outlining what you want to achieve. During that time, you probably built up a hoard of ideas and thoughts that are itching to get out. The brainstorming stage helps you release the energy you stored up in the first stage to bring forth these ideas... and many more. Used correctly with a team, it helps you draw on the diverse experience and perspectives of a range of people to increase the richness and originality of the solutions you could potentially bring to bear on your problem.

> *"Three humble shoemakers brainstorming will make a great statesman."*
>
> **Chinese Proverb**

The Traditional Brainstorming Process

In recent decades, brainstorming has become part and parcel of problem solving and decision making. When new ideas are needed to deliver a better outcome, people will gather together to brainstorm. The original approach to brainstorming was developed by Alex Osborn in the 1950s who found that the creative productivity of groups was often held back due to the largely evaluative nature of conventional business meetings.[1]

1 Osborn, Alex F. (1953), *Applied Imagination: Principles and Procedures of Creative Problem Solving*, New York: Charles Scribner's Sons

He designed the brainstorming session as a creative conference for the sole purpose of generating lots of ideas and finding fresh approaches to problems. These would be evaluated and processed at a later stage. A basic assumption of brainstorming is that 'two heads are better than one' and that, in groups, we can gain insights into problems we might otherwise overlook and generate a much wider range of possible ideas.

While brainstorming is universally viewed as 'free' thinking, it isn't a random activity. A brainstorming session needs to be carefully planned and structured if you're to break away from the norm and elicit novel solutions, particularly if you're applying it in a group context for large, complex challenges. A well organised brainstorming process keeps your thoughts flowing and provides a good 'breeding ground' for unexpected solutions to emerge.

> *"Did you ever observe to whom the accidents happen? Chance favors only the prepared mind."*
>
> **Louis Pasteur, French chemist and microbiologist**

Alex Osborn believed that the ideal size for a brainstorming group was between five and ten people, however, that's not to say that with the right kind of strategy and facilitation larger numbers couldn't successfully participate. A brainstorming session requires a facilitator, a meeting space and something on which to record ideas such as a flip chart, whiteboard or software tool. The facilitator is there to guide the session, encourage participation and write ideas down for everyone to see. In classic brainstorming, the following process is typically used:[2]

1) Assemble your team. This should ideally be a healthy mix of people with varying tasks and responsibilities and a blend of experts in the subject matter and non-experts. Why is this important? People from diverse disciplines and backgrounds will tend to approach a subject from different perspectives and viewpoints, so the chance for 'different' ideas to filter through is increased. As Jerry Hirshberg points out in his book, *The Creative Priority*, it's the differences in the way people think that often stimulates new and interesting ideas.[3]

2) Ensure the team understands the problem and clarify the aim of the brainstorming session.

---

2 Adapted from Slocum, Michael S., 'The Simple Steps of Classic Brainstorming', http://www. realinnovation.com/content/c070604a.asp
3 Hirshberg, Jerry (1998), *The Creative Priority: Driving Innovative Business in the New World,* HarperCollins

3) Explain the principles for effective brainstorming/generative thinking - a) strive for quantity, b) encourage wild and unusual ideas, c) postpone judgement and d) build and combine ideas (see Chapter 3). These principles are designed to jolt people out of their normal modes of thinking and stimulate creativity. They must be understood by all group members for the brainstorming effort to be successful.

4) Initiate brainstorming as a group, recording each idea as it comes up. At this point you can engage in a variety of creativity techniques to fire up people's imaginations, all the while adhering to the principles of brainstorming.

5) Clarify and conclude the session. Ideas that are identical or similar can be combined and clustered, while other ideas can be refined ready for evalution.

Traditional Group Brainstorming

Though brainstorming has become a popular group technique, several studies point to its ineffectiveness in delivering both quantity and quality of ideas when used in a traditional group setting. The next section examines some of the research which has lately enhanced our understanding of how to productively apply brainstorming.

Individual vs Group Brainstorming

Here's something interesting. Despite the widespread notion of a 'brainstorming group', research evidence strongly suggests that individuals working alone come up with more and better quality ideas than people working together in a group. This area was originally explored by Taylor, Berry and Block in 1958[4] and there have since been at least 25 tests of groups versus individual idea production. Diehl and Stroebe have reviewed these tests as well as contributing their own series of experiments.[5]

By and large the findings indicate that, for initial idea generation when dealing with real world, complex problems, individuals working alone have an immense advantage over those working in a brainstorming group. For instance, Diehl and Stroebe[6] found that, with a time limit of only 15 minutes for idea production, the average number of ideas for individuals was a staggering 84, with those of high quality numbering 13. In stark contrast, brainstorming groups produced an average of only 32 ideas, with only three being high quality. Thus, compared with groups, individuals produced four times as many high quality ideas.

What are the reasons for this creative idea production loss in brainstorming groups?

Diehl and Stroebe propose three explanations:

1) **Evaluation Apprehension** – This is when the presence of other group members inhibits people from expressing their wilder, oddball ideas due to fear of them being shot down or critically picked to pieces. Additional research supports this explanation in that productivity loss is greater when an authority figure is present[7] and when some or all of the group members, typically the quieter ones, are anxious about social interaction. This factor also relates to people's desire to go along with the dominant or established pattern of idea generation, also known as uniformity pressure.[8] As researchers from A&M University in Texas found:

"Fixation to other people's ideas can occur unconsciously and lead you to suggesting ideas that mimic your brainstorming partners. Thus, you potentially become less creative."[9]

2) **Social Loafing and Free Riding** – A less significant factor, social loafing occurs when individuals don't feel as accountable for producing

4 Taylor, D.W., Berry, P.C. and Block, C.H. (1958), 'Does group participation when using brainstorming facilitate or inhibit creative thinking?', *Administrative Science Quarterly*, 6, pp. 22-47.
5 Rossiter, John R. and Lilien, Gary L. (1994), 'New "Brainstorming" Principles', *Australian Journal of Management*, June 1994, 19, 1
6 Diehl, M. and Stroebe, W. (1987), 'Productivity Loss in Brainstorming Groups: Toward the Solution of a Riddle', *Journal of Personality and Social Psychology*, 53 (3), pp. 497-509.
7 Mullen, Brian, Johnson, Craig and Salas, Eduardo (1991), 'Productivity loss in brainstorming groups: A meta-analytic integration', *Basic and Applied Psychology*, 12: 2-23
8 Camacho, L.M. and Paulus, P.B. (1995), 'The role of social anxiousness in group brainstorming', *Journal of Personality and Social Psychology*, 68, 1071-1080.
9 Kohn, Nicholas W. and Smith, Steven M (2010), 'Collaborative fixation: Effects of others' ideas on brainstorming', *Applied Cognitive Psychology*, 29th March 2010

ideas when working in a group project and will slack off, putting in less effort than they would when working alone. They 'free ride' on other's ideas because they perceive their own contributions to be relatively anonymous or superfluous.[10]

3) Production Blocking – This was found to be the most significant explanation of creative idea production loss in groups by far. Production blocking occurs when individuals, after thinking of some initial ideas, are 'blocked' from verbalising all of these initial ideas and from generating further ones by having to wait for other people to report *their* ideas. Most commonly, people will forget their ideas while waiting their turn to speak or will be distracted while listening to others. This explanation is supported by the general finding that the larger the brainstorming group, the fewer the ideas produced compared with the same number of brainstormers working individually, mainly due to the context that only allows one person to speak at a time.[11]

Production blocking - Waiting for others to voice their ideas

"The ideas that come out of most brainstorming sessions are usually superficial, trivial, and not very original. They are rarely useful. The process, however, seems to make uncreative people feel that they are making innovative contributions."

A. Harvey Block, Author

---

10 Lattane, B., Williams K. and Harkins, S. (1979), 'Many hands make light work: the causes and consequences of social loafing', *Journal of Personality and Social Psychology*, 37, 822-832
11 Myers, D. (2005), *Social Psychology*, McGraw-Hill Higher Education: New York

Given these findings, Diehl and Stroebe concluded that group brainstorming should not be used to generate creative ideas - at least not initially. Still, we mustn't completely abandon it! Despite the superiority of individuals for generating preliminary ideas, group conditions are actually better for amalgamating and refining ideas after the initial idea output. Group brainstorming can develop ideas more deeply and effectively, as whenever someone gets stuck on an idea, they can draw on other people's creativity and experience to build on the idea and take it to the next stage.

This is supported by additional research which suggests that groups are better at convergent thinking while individuals are better at divergent thinking. When a problem has a single 'best' possible answer, a group is more effective at reaching it than individuals working alone. But when lots of diverse options and possibilities are needed, a group will come up with more conventional, 'run-of-the-mill' ideas in comparison to the more unique suggestions put forward by individuals.[12]

Contrary to the opinion of most researchers, Andrew Hargadon and Robert Sutton from Stanford University believe that building on ideas is a more important measure of effective brainstorming than the quantity of ideas generated.[13] They found that the best innovators systematically use existing ideas as the raw materials for one new idea after another and, in highly creative companies, people will typically switch between both solitary and group modes. Andrew Hargadon emphasises that the power of group brainstorming comes from creating a safe place where people with different ideas can share, blend and extend their diverse knowledge. If your goal is just to 'collect the creative ideas that are out there', running a group session is of very little worth.[14]

While the explicit goal of a group brainstorm is to generate ideas, the secondary benefits of gathering groups of people from around a company to talk about ideas might ultimately be more important for stimulating creativity. Group brainstorming actually fosters a supportive company culture where the true value of ideas can be understood and appreciated. As Nick Souter, author of *Breakthrough Thinking* says, "Creative people cannot survive in an environment that does not nurture and support them."[15]

12 Thompson, Leigh (2003), 'Improving the Creativity of Organisational Work Groups', *Academy of Management Executive,* Vol. 17, No.1
13 Sutton, Robert I. and Hargadon, Andrew (1996), 'Brainstorming Groups in Context: Effectiveness in a Product Design Firm', *Administrative Science Quarterly,* 41, 685-718
14 Hargadon, Andrew (2003), *How Breakthroughs Happen: The Suprising Truth about How Companies Innovate,* Harvard Business School Press, Boston
15 Souter, Nick (2007), *Breakthrough Thinking: Using Creativity to Solve Problems*, ILEX Press

> "The good ideas are all hammered out in agony by individuals, not spewed out by groups."

Charles Brower, American advertising executive and author

The distinctive yet complementary strengths of individual and group brainstorming indicates that it needn't be a case of 'either or'. We can set up the right conditions and procedures to get the best out of both worlds. Indeed, when group brainstorming was first born Alex Osborn had suggested it as a supplement to individual 'ideation', not a replacement!

In the next section, I put forward a strategy for combining solitary and group brainstorming effectively to raise your output of top quality creative ideas.

The Correct Brainstorming Strategy

Poor brainstorming occurs when it's done too loosely and the principles aren't followed. To be successful, brainstorming has to be a proactive and purposeful activity. The best results come when you embrace both individual and group brainstorming in a carefully managed process. The process is what allows you to steer the mode of thinking of the group so that creativity isn't stifled due to premature analysis or selectivity. There are dozens of generative thinking tools that can support the brainstorming activity by acting as triggers to reveal fresh and original solutions to your problem. A selection of what I believe to be the most user-friendly, well-attested and idea-boosting techniques are outlined in subsequent chapters.

Instead of listing ideas, I recommend you use Mind Maps to record, develop and arrange ideas. With a Mind Map, the brainstorming process is always guided by your highest intentions as the central theme maintains your focus on your key problem or goal. What's more, the informal nature of a Mind Map helps to encourage playfulness, humour and innovation. This means that people are less restricted by formal and stuffy thoughts or ways of approaching problems and can produce more original and diverse ideas.[16]

After forming your team, define the problem you want solved clearly and concisely and lay down the four principles for optimal brainstorming and

---

16 Buzan, Tony and Griffiths, Chris (2010), *Mind Maps for Business,* BBC Active

generative thinking - a) strive for quantity, b) encourage wild and unusual ideas, c) postpone judgement and d) build and combine ideas. Then use the following three-stage process to run your session effectively:

1) Individual Idea Generation

Ask each person to prepare for a group session by brainstorming and working individually with their own Mind Maps first. The idea is that all team members should clean out the corners of their mind to map as many potential solutions as they can before any discussions take place. If you wait until everyone is huddled together in a group to begin brainstorming, you'll find that the meeting becomes governed by reactive thinking, potentially resulting in harmful evaluation apprehension, social loafing or production blocking.

Every individual has their own creative ideas but it becomes easy to be influenced by the thoughts of others. More forceful personalities can dominate the group in communicating their ideas, meaning that true brainstorming is inhibited and fewer innovative ideas are unleashed. In contrast, when individuals work alone they aren't under any social pressures and are free to explore their thoughts without any fear of criticism, and so even the quietest members of the group are able to contribute ideas. Rather than relying on stimuli provided by other members of the group, individuals are spurred by their own originality. And importantly, they aren't held back from thinking by having to wait for others to voice their ideas.

2) Small Group Brainstorming

The next stage is to divide everyone into small groups of approximately three to five people to exchange ideas and produce a single Mind Map which pools together the ideas from the individual maps. What's the benefit of this? In a small group, people feel more likely to contribute. It presents a safe space for them to share as the dynamics are more controlled and the strongest communicator can't dominate. Plus, people aren't automatically led into reactive thinking as they've already stated their position and sketched out their ideas in their individual Mind Maps. There is much greater objectivity and focus to the whole process and participants can work collectively to review their output, eliminate duplicates and select the ideas that they want to take forward to the next stage.

3) Entire Group Brainstorming

The final stage is to draw everyone together for a large group meeting to discuss the ideas generated and construct a conclusive Mind Map. This is best carried out by the facilitator taking one idea serially from each participant, putting all the ideas on a common Mind Map, either on paper or on screen, and then allowing equal time for discussion of each idea.[17] Colour and codes for the Mind Map should be agreed in advance to ensure clarity of thought and focus.

Working collectively, the group should clarify, combine and refine ideas or springboard off existing ideas to create new ones. If connections aren't clear between ideas, then the group should make some! The unique perspectives and associations of each individual contribute to the whole in a highly visible and dynamic way. It's important that all ideas are supported and taken on board by all the other members, even the ideas that seem weak, ridiculous or irrelevant. Bad ideas can very easily be stepping stones to good ideas - the Mind Map helps you explore the chains of associations that can turn a seemingly useless idea into something inspirational and ground-breaking. The purpose of this phase is not to evaluate or judge ideas but to make constructive suggestions to improve ideas without passing a final vote on the best ones.

The final Mind Map becomes the external reflection, the 'hard copy' record of the brainstorming session. At the end of the process, all members of the group are united with a shared vision as it's understood that the Mind Map has been created together without anyone exerting excessive influence on other people's thinking.

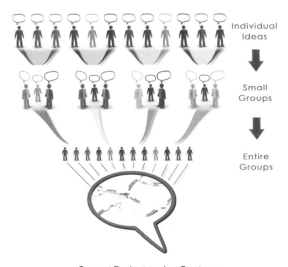

Correct Brainstorming Strategy

---

17 Delbecq, A.L, Van de Ven, A.H and Gustafson, D.H (1986), *Group Techniques for Program Planning: A Guide to Nominal Group and Delphi Processes*, Green Briar Press

As we've seen, conventional group brainstorming can be hugely detrimental to initial idea generation, mainly because conditions allow for undesirable factors such as 'production blocking' and 'evaluation apprehension' to arise. This points us towards an important fact - you could have the best people and brainstorming techniques at your disposal, but if you haven't set up the environment and process correctly for generative thinking, you're not going to get optimum results from your brainstorming sessions.

The strategy I introduced in this chapter takes on board the research findings which show individuals to be consistently superior to groups in generating more initial high quality ideas, yet also incorporates the benefits of group interaction for combining and 'building up' ideas. The use of Mind Mapping for note-taking endorses a steady, proactive focus throughout the brainstorming session and combines the energy of everyone involved in a way that produces more profound insights and fresh perspectives.

The next six chapters explore a set of fun, field-tested tools that you can apply during brainstorming to support your generative thinking efforts. Many business problems, opportunities and situations require new perspectives to be successfully tackled. These tools are therefore designed to encourage you to look at things differently, lighting up your thinking from a variety of angles. If your brain is the computer, then these tools are the software applications that help your brain find different ways of processing and interpreting the information related to your challenge. They're all simple and immediately usable so I invite you to choose those that you're drawn to and integrate them into your brainstorming.

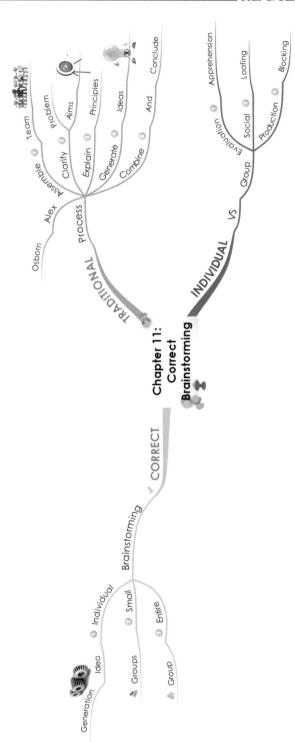

Chapter 11 Summary

Chapter 11: Correct Brainstorming

TRADITIONAL

- Osborn
- Alex
- Process
  - Assemble — Team
  - Clarify — Problem — Aims
  - Explain — Principles
  - Generate — Ideas
  - Combine — And — Conclude

INDIVIDUAL VS Group
- Evaluation
  - Apprehension
- Social
  - Loafing
- Production
  - Blocking

CORRECT Brainstorming
- Individual — Idea — Generation
- Small — Groups
- Entire — Group

REFRAME THE PROBLEM

A great place to begin idea generation is with the problem itself. In Step 1 of the Solution Finder you went through the process of defining your problem; you dismantled it, searched it and verified that it was the correct one. So, the good news is that you know exactly what the problem is. The not so good news is that a single definition of the problem places limits on your generative thinking as you'll be inclined to connect only with that definition when considering potential solutions. For this reason, one of the most beneficial techniques for generating lots of novel ideas is to *reframe the problem*.

Reframing is simply "changing the way you understand a statement, situation or behaviour to give it new meaning."[1] In the context of idea generation, reframing the problem allows you to examine it in a new light to reveal solutions that might otherwise remain hidden.

Reframing the problem

---

1 O'Connor, Joseph and Seymour, John (2000), *Training with NLP: Skills for Trainers, Managers and Communicators*, Thorsons

The Power of Words

Words have a powerful effect on the direction of our thoughts. To quote Nick Souter, author of *Breakthrough Thinking*, words act as "on-ramps, stop lights and intersections on the neural pathways in our minds."[2] Different words can therefore impact on the mental route we take while thinking up ideas.

Fundamentally, words are associations and they can mean different things to different people. For instance, ask anyone to form associations with the word 'Love' and you'll get a multitude of varying responses. The word itself opens up an infinite number of pathways.

> *"Handle them carefully, for words have more power than atom bombs."*
>
> **Pearl Strachan Hurd, British politician**

The wording of a problem plays a massive role in how we come to perceive it. When we're handed a specific definition of a problem, we'll contemplate solutions from the angle set by that definition. As an example, if you were a line manager and approached your employee with the statement "we're going to look at ways to increase your productivity", the employee's response will be affected by the implicit wording of this statement. For most employees, this would undoubtedly have negative connotations, suggesting that their productivity is pretty poor at the moment. This would stifle their ability to come up with diverse suggestions as the overall solution seems to be pre-determined i.e. they need to 'work harder'.

However, if you rephrased the statement to "we're going to look at how we can make your job easier", the employee would be motivated to produce lots of ideas as it comes across as being for their own benefit as well as the company's. You've changed the angle of the problem from negative to positive. In the end, the problem is still the same, but the feelings and viewpoints associated with it are different. The actual problem itself is not nearly as important as how we think about it. If we think about the problem another way, we gain an alternative perspective on it and can respond to it more creatively.

---

2 Souter, Nick (2007), *Breakthrough Thinking: Using Creativity to Solve Problems*, ILEX Press

Examine how you word a problem

Step 1 of the Solution Finder is hugely important in getting us to a point where we have a sound understanding of our problem. The reframing technique stretches our understanding further. If we can get into the habit of restating a problem multiple times before generating solutions, we can get past some of the ambiguities related to language and tap into its core essence. This helps us to build a new momentum for seeking out more varied and meaningful solutions.

The Technique

Reframing is a technique that jars our normal idea generation patterns, shifting us to a new starting point. By looking harder at the problem and searching for diverse ways to present it, we enrich our perception of it so we aren't limited to the obvious, ready-formed solutions (i.e. the boring ones!). Sometimes a simple rephrasing of the problem makes solutions that weren't so clear before, blindingly apparent.

To get the best out of this technique, I recommend you take the current expression of the problem or challenge and try to reframe it at least 5 times. Play freely with it, change verbs and nouns and examine it from all kinds of angles. Here are a handful of approaches you can use to help you:

1) Use Questions

Try converting your problem into a question to provoke a search for answers. As Tim Hurson, author of *Think Better*, points out, "Problem statements are usually inert. Problem questions, on the other hand, invite answers."[3] For instance, the statement 'we don't have enough budget' has no drive or energy. It doesn't build any motivation or enthusiasm for discovering creative ideas because it's little more than an opinion about a condition. On the other hand, the question 'how might we increase our

---

3 Hurson, Tim (2008), *Think Better: An Innovator's Guide to Productive Thinking*, McGraw-Hill Professional

budget?' opens the door wide for new answers to come in.

Experiment with different questions for rephrasing the problem. It's said that Henry Ford invented the assembly line simply by changing the question from 'how do we get the people to the work?' to 'how do we get the work to the people?' Pointedly, one of the underlying reasons that new products or initiatives fail is that so many of us ask the wrong question in the first place. The questions we ask shape the answers we get, so it's worth taking time to pose the right ones. It gives us a much better chance of coming up with good solutions.

Convert your problem into questions to invite answers

If you've been asking 'why aren't people buying my product?' try asking the following questions instead:[4]

• Why are people buying my product?
• Why aren't people who do buy my product buying it more often?
• Why aren't people who do buy my product buying more of it?
• Why are people buying my competitor's product?
• How else can my product help people?

...Different questions lead to different solutions for the same problem.

> *"It is not the answer that enlightens, but the question."*
>
> **Eugene Ionesco, French playwright**

---

4 Foster, Jack (1998), 'Re-Define the Problem: You May Get the Answer', *Innovative Leader*, #317, Vol 7, No.1

2) Switch Words and Meanings

A more precise approach is to take single words from your problem definition and substitute variations. For instance, if your challenge is 'increase sales', try replacing 'increase' with words like 'attract', 'develop', 'extend' or 'repeat' and see how your interpretation of the problem changes.[5] You might want to use a thesaurus to broaden your vocabulary. This type of reframing can help you go as far as to change the entire meaning of a situation – the situation will still be the same but what it denotes will change. A famous army general once reframed a distressful situation for his troops by telling them "We're not retreating, we're just advancing in another direction."[6] Exchanging the word 'retreating' with 'advancing' sets off a more positive series of beliefs and thoughts about the situation, which builds motivation and enthusiasm for coming up with more productive and creative ideas.

3) How To...

Using the term 'how to...' is a nifty approach for improving how you frame your underlying goal. Too often we phrase problems in a definitive way which makes them seem overwhelming or insurmountable. For instance, 'staff morale is low' is a conclusive statement – it feels final and ends up creating our reality unless we change it. By rephrasing it to 'how to improve staff morale' we invite brainstorming on the issue by indicating that we can do something about it.

To use another example, if you're looking for your next great product, the problem might be variously defined as:

• How to introduce winning new products
• How to satisfy customer's wants and needs
• How to identify successful new products

After coming up with several new frames for your problem, select one or more to focus on for idea generation. These should be the statements or questions that best capture the 'real' problem. Use a Mind Map to generate ideas for each one of the selected problem definitions in turn. You'll find that each definition releases a dam of previously untapped choices. Problems that seemed unsolvable or arduous at best become

---

5 Passuelo, Luciano (2010), 'Einstein's Secret to Amazing Problem Solving (and 10 specific ways you can use it)', *Litemind*, http://litemind.com/problem-definition/
6 Gardner, James F. and Nudler, Sylvia (1999), *Quality Performance in Human Services*, Brookes Publishing

solvable simply because you've changed what people pay attention to.[7]

The bottom line is that reframing takes the same problem and expresses it differently. This alternate expression allows us to see the situation in a new way and uncovers greater possibilities for the actions we can take to solve it.

7 Kurke, Lance and Ball, Dave (2011), 'Solving the Unsolvable Problem: Achieving Results Through Enactment', Growth and Leadership, *Business Know-How*, http://www.businessknowhow.com/growth/unsolvable.htm

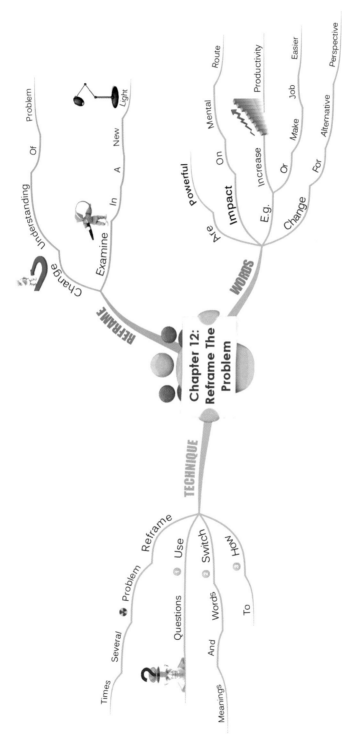

Chapter 12 Summary

METAPHORIC STIMULATION

The Greek philosopher, Aristotle, is quoted as saying, "The greatest thing by far is to be a master of metaphor." Metaphors change our way of looking at the world and so there's a certain skill, even a kind of genius, in being able to use them to express situations in an original way.

A metaphor is the concept of understanding one thing in terms of another. A word or phrase is applied to something it doesn't literally denote in order to suggest a similarity. For instance, Shakespeare's expression 'all the world's a stage' and the popular idiom 'time is money' are metaphors.

> *"The metaphor is perhaps one of man's most fruitful potentialities. Its efficacy verges on magic, and it seems a tool for creation which God forgot inside one of His creatures when He made Him."*
>
> **Jose Ortega y Gasset, Author of 'The Dehumanisation of Art and Ideas About the Novel'**

If we want to originate breakthrough solutions to our challenges, we have to be able to think differently than we usually do. In the words of a universal metaphor, we've got to 'think outside of the box'. The power of using metaphors as a creative thinking technique lies in the way they spark the imagination and allow us to go beyond the boundaries of conventional thinking. Creating a metaphor is like creating a verbal image... and we all know how powerful images can be in freeing the mind to make greater associations. Metaphors inspire new ideas and connections by allowing us to picture how our problem is similar or dissimilar to something that might at first seem totally unrelated.[1]

---

[1] Steward, D. and Simmons, M. (2010), *The Business Playground: Where Creativity and Commerce Collide*, Financial Times / Prentice Hall

They change the subject of our thinking,[2] taking us away from the familiar characteristics, demands and assumptions we impose on our problem to allow new and original insights to bubble to the surface. From these we can draw relevant connections and ideas back to our particular challenge or task.

Metaphors can be used for creative thinking

Metaphors in Action

As we saw in Chapter 9, it's natural for the human mind to want to look for associations, connections and relationships and this is why the metaphor is such a fantastic tool for encouraging creative thinking. Poets and writers have relied on the power of metaphors for years, using them to open readers' minds to new worlds of perception, understanding and experience. Even scientists are no strangers to their usage. For example, Friedrick Kekule, the renowned German chemist, described his breakthrough understanding of the benzene molecule as a 'snake biting its own tail.'[3]

Using a metaphor or analogy from nature is a popular and effective way to identify new ideas and models for all sorts of business challenges, even those that are very technical. For instance, Velcro was inspired by an analogy with plant burrs.[4] The story of Pringles (curvy crisps) is another case in point.

William J. Gordon,[5] the creator of the 'Synectics' problem solving approach,

2 Treffinger, Donald J, Isaksen, Scott G. and Dorval, Brian (2000), *Creative Problem Solving: An Introduction*, Prufrock Press
3 Ditkoff, Michael (2005), 'Unlock the power of metaphorical thinking', *Innovation Tools*, 17th June 2005, http://www.innovationtools.com/Articles/ArticleDetails.asp? a=188
4 Mital, Anil, Desai, Anoop and Subramanian, Anand (2007), *Product Development: a structured approach to consumer product development, design and manufacture*, Butterworth-Heinemann
5 Gordon, William J. (1961), *Synectics*, Harper & Row, New York

was called in to help Proctor & Gamble resolve a problem with its potato crisps manufacturing. Customers were expressing their disappointment at opening a seemingly full bag of crisps only to find a relatively small amount of broken crisps at the bottom! While raking leaves in his yard, William noticed that on sunny days when the leaves were dry, they would crumble as he shoved them into a bag. But on rainy days the wet leaves would cling together, their shapes conforming to each other without breaking, making it easy to bag them. This sparked the brilliant idea of wetting and freeze-drying potato flour to create Pringles – crisps that can be packaged with very little breakage.[6]

Nature is a source for many metaphors

William Gordon linked the creative process with certain psychological states, believing that if these could be induced, then the number of creative breakthroughs would increase. He emphasised the need to make the strange familiar, and vice versa, to improve the likelihood of gaining new insights into problems. Metaphors offer a valuable way of doing this:

1) Make the Strange Familiar

"Everything has been thought of before, but the problem is to think of it again."

Johann Wolfgang von Goethe, German playwright, poet and novelist

---

6 Inge (2010), 'Find metaphors in dogs and potato chips', *Focus & Flow*, 10th July 2010, http://www.creativeexpeditions.com/blog/2010/07/find-metaphors-in-dogs¬and-potato-chips/

Use a metaphor to reframe the problem so that everyone understands it.

When you're faced with a complex challenge that's difficult to get your head around, you can use metaphors to make the strange familiar i.e. to convert the problem into something from your known experience that exhibits similar patterns. This helps to conceptualise and deepen your understanding of the problem, making it easier to explore possibilities and suggestions for solving it.

For instance, when primitive natives in New Guinea saw an aircraft for the first time they called it 'the big bird'. Their first step towards comprehending something totally strange and unfamiliar to them was to assume it was an unusual example of something already known to them – birds! This was a handy way for them to begin to understand a new phenomenon.[7]

To use another example, an engineer looking for a way to hold together a multi-part machine in a high-vibration environment was able to take the metaphor of shivering with cold and come up with ideas for encasing the system in a flexible jacket.[8]

2) Make the Familiar Strange

> "Discovery consists of seeing what everyone has seen and thinking what nobody has thought."
>
> **Anon**

Use metaphor to view familiar situations in a new light.

The more you're used to a situation, the less stimulating it is for your brain. Familiarity breeds conformity. When a familiar problem anchors you into a routine pattern of thoughts, you can use a metaphor to reform the situation into something different, something that's strange to you.

This causes friction which restarts the engine of your mind to think in new ways to comprehend and explore an unknown world. To quote the authors of *Metaphor: Implications and Associations*, Jeffery Mio and Albert Katz, "Only when the familiar is made strange... and the resulting strangeness is used to alter or recast ordinary perceptions are we in a revolutionary

---

7 Adair, John (2009), *The Art of Creative Thinking: How to be Innovative and Develop Great Ideas*, Kogan Page
8 ChangingMinds.Org, 'Creativity and Metaphor', http://changingminds.org/techniques/languagemetaph or/creativity_metaphor.htm

setting."[9]

For an example, consider the product designer who applies the metaphor of a tiny Napoleon Bonaparte marching around inside the printer, issuing orders, capturing territory and forcing the paper to go in any direction.[10]

> "The essence of the creative act is to see the familiar as strange."
>
> **Anon**

Using Metaphors to Solve Problems

How exactly can you use metaphors for idea generation? The following is a simple process that you can apply for any business challenge:[11]

1) Identify the Challenge

Take the problem definition that you came up with in Step 1 of the Solution Finder as your starting point. For the purpose of illustration, we'll use the problem 'I want more customers'.

2) Reframe the Problem with a Metaphor

Now rephrase the original problem into a similar or unrelated problem by means of a metaphor. An easy way to do this is by replacing the verb (which represents the process) and noun (the content of the challenge).

Start by breaking down the verb and noun as follows:

I **want** more **customers**

VERB   **NOUN**

---

9 Mio, Jeffery Scott and Katz, Albert N. (1996), *Metaphor: Implications and Applications*, Routledge
10 ChangingMinds.Org, 'Creativity and Metaphor', http://changingminds.org/
11 Adapted from 'Metaphor and Problem Solving', http://www.angelfire.com/nd/ wraith/meta.html

Think of how you could change the verb and noun to create a new statement. There are no limitations. For instance, you could substitute 'want' for 'how' and 'customers' could be changed to 'fish' to give you the new challenge of 'how to catch a fish'. Now you have a new angle from which to look at the issue!

Metaphor – 'how to catch a fish'

To give you another example, the challenge 'dealing with a difficult person' could become 'training a stubborn dog'.

It's better if there's a vague similarity between the old verb and new one (since verbs represent process), otherwise you could struggle to relate the concept back to your problem. As human beings we're essentially curious and readily stimulated by obscure tasks. However, if a task is too vague we tend to ignore it rather than attempt to get to grips with the difficulties it presents. It becomes a block rather than a stimulus for creative thinking.

On the other hand, we must also be wary of working with metaphors which are too close to the problem at hand as we won't be making the familiar strange enough to gain any useful insights or ideas.[12]

---

12 Proctor, R.A. (1989) 'The Use of Metaphors to Aid the Process of Creative Problem Solving', *Personnel Review*, 18, 4

If you're struggling to come up with a metaphor, ask yourself if your challenge might be similar to a distant parallel activity. This could come from nature or any other realm that's quite different from that of your problem. Here are some random examples:

• Riding a bike
• Planning a holiday
• Cooking a meal
• Going on a diet
• Raising a child
• Running for political office

3) Solve the Metaphor

Next, focus your attention on solving the problem presented by the metaphor. Completely erase all thoughts of the original problem from your mind. Create a new Mind Map for the metaphor subject of 'how to catch a fish' and generate ideas and associations to solve it as if it were the real issue. What solutions work in that particular scenario? Some possible solutions for our example of 'how to catch a fish' could be:

• Use correct bait
• Ask a fisherman
• Buy a good rod
• Use a net
• Go spear-fishing
• Read a book on it
• Use a lure
• Learn the habits of fish

> *"An idea is a feat of association, and the height of it is a good metaphor."*
>
> **Robert Frost, American poet**

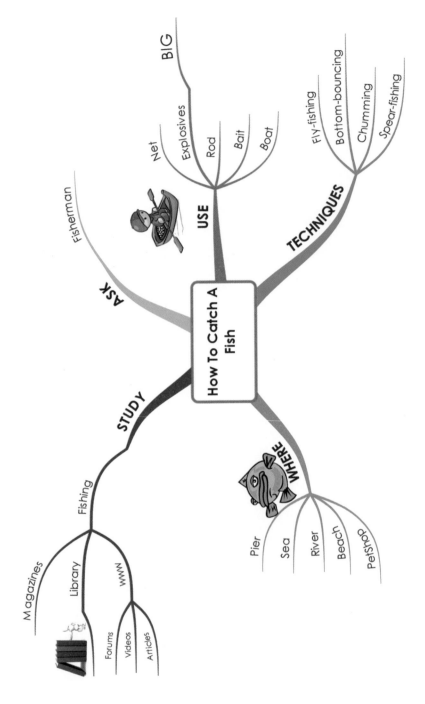

How To Catch A Fish

- **USE**
  - Net
  - Explosives
  - Rod
  - Bait
  - Boat
  - BIG
- **ASK**
  - Fisherman
- **TECHNIQUES**
  - Fly-fishing
  - Bottom-bouncing
  - Chumming
  - Spear-fishing
- **STUDY**
  - Fishing
    - Magazines
    - Library
    - WWW
      - Forums
      - Videos
      - Articles
- **WHERE**
  - Pier
  - Sea
  - River
  - Beach
  - PetShoP

Solve the Metaphor

4) *Map it Back to the Original Challenge*

In this final step, map each idea that you generated to solve the metaphor back to the original problem. Using a Mind Map helps you make use of the natural drive of the human brain to look for and create connections between two items, regardless of how dissimilar or unrelated they may be. Ask yourself how you might relate the same actions or responses that work well for the metaphor back to the original problem. For example, some of the ideas from step 3 could be converted as follows:

- Use correct bait – use appropriate advertising, make products more appealing
- Ask a fisherman – ask a sales expert/consultant, find a mentor
- Use a net – make sure the message appeals to as wide an audience as possible
- Go spear-fishing – target individual customers, focus on repeat sales
- Read a book on it – study new sales techniques

The solution 'ask a fisherman' becomes 'ask a sales expert'

This process is often very enlightening, revealing some new and promising ideas that you might not have picked up using more direct techniques.

"Metaphors have a way of holding the most truth in the least space."

Orson Scott Card, American author and public speaker

In conclusion, you can see how generating solutions based on a metaphor opens up new perspectives with respect to your challenge. These alternate perspectives can expose creative ideas to solve your challenge that aren't likely to have surfaced otherwise. All in all, the metaphor is a valuable prompt that lets you move beyond the conventional and predictable to come up with something truly unprecedented.

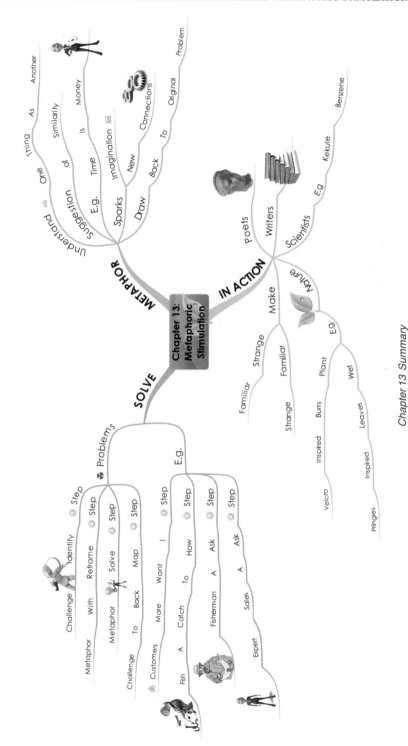

Chapter 13 Summary

THOUGHT EXPERIMENTS

When we want to come up with creative solutions, it's sometimes more productive to take a step back from the problem and let our minds wander rather than trying to aggressively force new ideas. In other words, it's good to allow ourselves to daydream once in a while.

Daydreaming has for years been attributed to a lazy, undisciplined mind but, in reality, it holds tremendous power and can be highly constructive in lots of contexts. Going into a daydreaming state can be an excellent means of encouraging creative visualisation and insights which can go a long way towards helping us solve our problems.

"The intellect has little to do on the road to discovery. There comes a leap in consciousness, call it intuition or what you will, and the solution comes to you and you don't know how or why."

Albert Einstein, Nobel Prize winning theoretical physicist

A great many of the world's most acclaimed inventors and scientists have credited daydreaming for their moments of brilliance. For instance, Sir Isaac Newton was in a tranquil and relaxed frame of mind sitting under a tree when, with the falling of the apple, he envisioned the phenomenon of gravity. He would often deliberately engage in daydreaming to free his imagination. Albert Einstein also relied heavily on his ability to visualise during his daydreaming episodes, referring to them as 'thought experiments'. It's said that he came up with the theory of relativity by picturing himself sitting on a beam of light and imagining the journey he was going to take. There are also numerous examples of people in creative or artistic careers, such as composers, novelists and filmmakers, developing new ideas through daydreaming. Hollywood filmmaker Tim Burton would spend hours holed up in his bedroom as a child daydreaming about an imaginary horror film series.

Think about it - how many times have you had a great idea in the shower, when taking a walk or while driving? It's common to be at our most creative when we aren't actually 'working' - often it's just a question of letting go and allowing our minds to do the work for us.[1] We've all experienced those occasions when we struggle for hours to solve a problem without any success, and then just as we give up and start to relax, the answer arrives seemingly out of nowhere.

When we're relaxed, we're more creative because we have more brain capacity available.[2] We can tap into this capacity through daydreaming. Daydreams are uncensored and free associating, helping us discover solutions that the rational, focused mind, locked in its tunnel vision, can't access.[3] However, as with anything in the creative process, the key to successful daydreaming is that it should be purposeful and deliberate. We still need to put in the groundwork and preparation for our mind to 'incubate ideas', and be mindfully alert to these ideas when they come. As Dr Jonathan Schooler, psychologist at the University of California says, "For creativity you need your mind to wander but you also need to be able to notice that you're mind wandering and catch the idea when you have it. If Archimedes had come up with a solution in the bathtub but didn't notice he'd had the idea, what good would it have done him?"[4]

Is it Allowed?

For most of us, daydreaming and idly musing over things isn't perceived to be the best way of getting ahead in life. If you were to go into a meeting with the Board of Directors and suggest that employees should put their feet up on their desks and spend time daydreaming, how would they react?...

...It would probably not be a popular idea!

While setting time aside for conscious and rational thinking is acceptable in business, the same courtesy isn't extended to daydreaming. For most of us it's simply out of bounds. Society has been ingrained to think that daydreaming is a time-squandering, self-indulgent and frivolous activity. This creates a conflict in business. People need and want to be creative, yet they're uncomfortable with the concept of daydreaming, failing to see it as the incredibly useful tool it is. As Amy Fries, author of *Daydreams At Work* humorously points out, "We worship at the altar of focus while

1 Hurson, Tim (2008), *Think Better: An Innovator's Guide to Productive Thinking*, McGraw-Hill Professional
2 van den Brandhof, Jan-Willem (2008), *The Business Brain Book*, BrainWare
3 Fries, Amy (2009), *Daydreams at Work: Wake Up Your Creative Powers*, Capital Books
4 Tierney, John (2010), 'Discovering the Virtues of a Wandering Mind', *The New York Times*, 28th June 2010

making daydreaming the crazy uncle in the attic." But what else can help us visualise, imagine, model and create with our minds as much as daydreaming?

Daydreaming at Work

The fact that the unconscious mind plays a part in decision making, problem solving and creative thinking has been known for some time. This dimension is what John Adair, author of *The Art of Creative Thinking* has named the Depth Mind, professing it to be one of the most important elements in creative thinking.[5] He uses the metaphor of the submarine at sea to illustrate that thinking can sometimes leave the surface and proceed into the depths of the sea on its unique voyage. Later on, it can surface again into the conscious mind. Many of us are apt to believe that the unconscious mind is chaotic and disorderly. In fact, it's perfectly capable of good hard 'purposeful' work. It can synthesise and connect information, releasing it back into our conscious mind in the form of intuitions, inklings and insights.

> *"Without leaps of imagination, or dreaming, we lose the excitement of possibilities. Dreaming, after all, is a form of planning."*
>
> **Gloria Steinem, American political activist and author**

Our mind is an endless reservoir of possibility, harbouring a vast store of knowledge and experience. The unconscious, daydreaming aspect of our mind simply links this knowledge and experience together in ways that

5 Adair, John (2009), *The Art of Creative Thinking: How to be Innovative and Develop Great Ideas*, Kogan Page

the focused, conscious mind can't envision or even attempt. This leads to those magical 'A-ha' moments when the answer to our problem seems to suddenly arrive.

So, while the process of daydreaming might not be valued by our bosses, it remains that being able to tap into the unconscious mind can bring up remarkably brilliant, quirky and original ideas, especially when a more direct and rational approach doesn't seem to be generating any answers. With a degree of simple awareness, understanding and skill we can easily work with this wonderful innate capacity that we all possess.

The Great Geniuses Loved to Daydream

Most of the geniuses of the past used some form of directed daydreaming to help them solve problems, generate ideas and achieve their grand goals. Einstein, in particular, was very outspoken about his love of daydreaming. It's reported that he attributed his greatest work to ideas that would come while he engaged in his 'thought experiments'.

> *"Creative scientists are the ones with access to their dreams."*
>
> **Albert Einstein, Nobel Prize winning theoretical physicist**

Such 'thought experiments' were also used by other innovators and scientists to shed light on our world and how things work. We all know the story of Sir Isaac Newton's discovery of gravity while sitting beneath an apple tree. Less well known is how he came up with the theory of Orbit. While contemplating the law of gravity, he imagined shooting a cannonball parallel to the Earth's surface from the top of a very high mountain. He understood that the cannonball would fall to the earth under the influence of gravity. If the initial speed and force of the cannonball was low, gravity would pull it down and the ball would fall to earth at some distance from the mountain. However, at a certain speed the cannonball would fall towards the earth at the same rate as the earth's surface curved away – i.e. it would orbit the earth.[6]

While a thought experiment won't serve to prove anything in the same way a real experiment could, it still has incredible value. Newton couldn't test or verify his theory in a practical sense but he was still right! Through imagination and visualisation, his thinking was stimulated to uncover the creative insights and understandings he needed to develop his concept.

6 Newton's Cannon, http://www.smaphysics.ca/phys40s/field40s/newtmtn.html

Newton's Orbital Cannon

Thomas Edison, inventor of the electric light bulb (among many other things!), had his own unique way of harnessing the power of daydreaming. It's reported that he would hold ball bearings in each hand, sit down in a comfortable chair and doze off to sleep. Just as he was relaxing into sleep, his hands would loosen their grip and the ball bearings would fall to the floor, waking him up. Immediately after waking, Edison would note down any ideas that had come to him.[7]

Thomas Edison used daydreaming for his creative work

What Edison instinctively knew is that, if he could get into that 'twilight state' between wakefulness and sleep, he could access the pure creative genius of his unconscious mind. His mind would take over the challenge for him and offer its solutions in due course.

Interestingly, Thomas Edison gave a much-quoted definition of genius as

7 Innovation-Creativity.com, 'Thomas Alva Edison', http://www.innovation¬creativity.com/thomas-alva-edison.html

"1% inspiration and 99% perspiration". This statement is often used to argue against the value of spending time thinking creatively. It implies that taking action is difficult and that thinking is the easy, straightforward part of the innovative process. I beg to differ - thinking is incredibly hard work. When you're not getting the results you want, you have to continue thinking until you do. Inspiration doesn't occur by complete chance. To quote John Adair, "Creative thinking, paradoxically, is for 99 hours out of every 100 not very creative: it is endlessly varied combinations of analysing, synthesising, imagining and valuing. The raw materials are sifted, judged, adapted, altered and glued together in different ways."[8]

Newton arrived at the law of gravity by repeatedly thinking about it. Einstein tried for years to clarify the relation of mechanical movement to electromagnetic phenomena.[9] Thus, thinking effort is vital to lay the foundations for creative work, you can't just wait for the right mood or you might just wait forever. The key is recognising when to stand back and let all that research and hard work simmer and stew in your mind until it's ready to release its results. You need to submerge yourself in the problem, while at the same time stay sufficiently detached so you can still look at it in fresh ways - something known as 'detached devotion'.

The incubation period suggested by Graham Wallas[10] in his model of the creative process is possibly one way to achieve the right balance of devotion and detachment. During incubation, we allow our minds to mull over the problem while getting on with something else. This works best if the unconscious mind already has lots of information to incubate i.e. if you've already done a lot of work on the problem.

> "You expend effort and energy thinking hard. Then, after you have given up, they (thoughts) come sauntering in with their hands in their pockets. If the effort had not been made to open the door, however, who knows if they would have come?"
>
> **Johann Wolfgang von Goethe, German playwright, poet and novelist**

What the Science Proves

In the past, the act of daydreaming was broadly considered by science to be counter-productive; a failure of mental discipline and functioning.

8 Adair, John (2009), *The Art of Creative Thinking: How to be Innovative and Develop Great Ideas*, Kogan Page
9 Wertheimer, Max (1982), *Productive Thinking*, University of Chicago PR
10 Wallas, Graham (1926), *The Art of Thought*, Jonathan Cape, London

In recent years, however, scientists have begun to see it very differently. They've demonstrated that daydreaming is a fundamental feature of the human mind – so fundamental that it's actually referred to as our 'default' mode of thought.[11]

"Daydreaming may sound like a mental luxury but its purpose is deadly serious."

Douglas Fox, 'Private Life of the Brain', New Scientist.

While attempting to discover what the brain gets up to when we're idle, Marcus Raichle and Gordon Shulman, neuroscientists at Washington University, made a fantastic discovery. They found that, rather than shutting down when a person was resting, more of the brain would start firing up. The same areas of the brain would then quieten down as soon as a person started a mental exercise. This research led to the recognition of a new functional system within the brain, which Raichle and Shulman called the 'default network'.[12]

The default network consists of the areas of the brain that become active whenever we're unoccupied and the brain is at wakeful rest. Its subsystems include part of the medial temporal lobe for memory, part of the medial prefrontal cortex for theory of mind and the posterior cingulate cortex for integration. The default network is largely held to be responsible for producing the spontaneous thoughts we have during daydreaming episodes. It's a system involved in the acts of mulling over past experiences and speculating about the future, acts that are so essential that the brain engages in them whenever possible.[13]

Building on this research, a later study by Psychology Professor Kalina Christoff at the University of British Columbia reveals that daydreaming activates even more of the brain than previously thought.[14] As well as the 'default network', she found evidence through fMRI scanning that the brain's 'executive network' is simultaneously engaged. This is the network involved in activities such as high-level problem solving, reasoning and 'goal-directed deliberate thinking'. Prior to this study, scientists had supposed that the two networks operated on an either-or basis – when one was activated the other was thought to be dormant.

11 Lehrer, Jonah (2009), 'Daydreams', *ScienceBlogs*, 15th May 2009, http://scienceblogs.com/cortex/2009/05/daydreams_1.php
12 Raichle, M. E., MacLeod, A. M., Snyder, A. Z., Powers, W. J., Gusnard D. A. and Shulman, G. L. (2001), 'A default mode of brain function'. *Proc National Academic Science* U S A 98:676–682
13 Fox, Douglas (2008), 'Private life of the brain', *New Scientist*, 8th November 2008
14 Christoff, Kalina, Gordon, Alan M., Smallwood, Jonathan, Smith, Rachelle and Schooler, Jonathan W. (2009), 'Experience sampling during fMRI reveals default network and executive system contributions to mind wandering', *Proceedings of the National Academy of Sciences*, DOI: 10.1073/pnas.0900234106

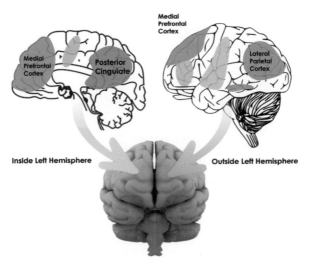

The Default Network

Christoff believes this research provides vital scientific justification for the value of daydreaming as an important cognitive stage for complex problem solving. More areas of the brain fire up when we daydream than when we're using conscious thought. As Christoff says, "You have this unique brain state where instead of having one or the other shut down, both networks are available to be used. It's a mental state that's really not lazy, from the point of view of the brain."[15]

In an as yet unpublished study, Dr Jonathan Schooler and his colleague, Jonathan Smallwood asked 122 undergraduates at the University of British Columbia to read a children's story and press a button each time they caught themselves tuning out. They found that those who regularly caught themselves daydreaming seemed to be the most creative, scoring higher in the standard creativity test.[16]

All this evidence supports the idea that when we're daydreaming, we're literally in our most creative state of mind, tapping into and connecting the most complex regions of the brain. The quantity and quality of brain

15 Dooley, Roger (2009), 'Daydreaming Key to Creativity', *NeuroMarketing*, 1st June 2009, http://www.neurosciencemarketing.com/blog/articles/daydreaming-creativity.htm
16 Glausiusz, Josie (2011), 'Living in A Dream World', *Scientific American Mind*, Vol 22, No 1, March/April 2011

activity suggests that, when we're struggling to solve a complicated problem, we can benefit by switching to a simpler task and letting our mind wander. If we really want to encourage the creative process Dr. Schooler advises that we go jogging, take a walk, do some knitting or just sit around doodling. These relatively undemanding tasks will free our mind to roam productively and engage in abstract thought. To quote Christoff a second time:

"After all that mind-wandering, eventually you start seeing connections that you wouldn't have seen before, because you would never have logically allowed your mind to make those connections."

When we give our mind space to go about its business, it will do the imaginative work for us!

How to Daydream Productively

While scientific research supports the benefits of daydreaming for integrating knowledge and producing new insights and intuitions about our future, we have to be mindful of how we use it as a creativity technique.

Daydreaming and thought experiments require more than just relaxing and being passive. Inspiration is a system – it has to be goal-orientated and purposeful. The problem with unconscious creativity is that it tends to remain unconscious, so we never become aware of it or use it.[17]

Daydreaming only works productively if the unconscious mind already has lots of information to ponder and ruminate on, so you have to do your preparation and homework first. And as with any other system, you need to put yourself in the right environment and apply appropriate skills to get the best out of it.

"It is no good trying to shine if you don't take time to fill your lamp."

Robert Frost, American poet

For many of us, it can feel frustrating when we first start to use daydreaming as a creativity technique in business. It's different from how we normally go about thinking creatively. We're used to a reactive climate filled with time-pressures, so getting away from the problem to mull it over feels uncomfortable because we can't rush and we're not sure of the outcome.

17 Dean, Jeremy (2010), 'Get Creative: 7 More Psychological Techniques', *PsyBlog*, http://www.spring. org.uk/2010/06/get-creative-7-more-psychological-techniques.php

We have to get over this. Daydreaming is probably one of most powerful tools we could have at our disposal, especially when we're dealing with complicated issues where attempting to solve the problem directly gets us nowhere.[18]

Focused daydreaming is a simple two-step approach:

1) Preparation

If you're thinking along certain lines with respect to your problem and nothing is happening – stop! The longer you struggle against a problem, the less likely you are to solve it. Although creative thinking requires sustained attention, it doesn't always have to be conscious attention. The best solutions almost always occur after we take a mental break from the problem. Before we do this, however, we must put in the groundwork.

Collect and sort all relevant information in relation to your problem and explore possible solutions using a variety of other avenues and creativity tools. You can see how important Step 1 of the Solution Finder is here for organising all relevant data on your problem. And there's a compendium of creative techniques in this book that you can use to generate ideas in an active way. It's useful to view this process of preparation as a means of briefing and programming the deeper parts of your mind.

2) Let your Mind Wander

Next switch off your attention and let the problem and all the information germinate in your mind for a while i.e. let it incubate. The unconscious mind has ways of connecting unrelated information. These may involve other elements or bits and bobs stored away in your memory.

Our creative thinking is often influenced by what we're used to in real life. The beauty of daydreaming is that it gives us permission to let go of the reality we're used to so that the ideas we generate are likely to be more unusual and engaging.

Allowing our unconscious to work on the problem doesn't require any specific tools or techniques; we simply need to get ourselves into the right frame of mind. When we plant a tree in the correct conditions and keep watering it every now and then, we know that it will grow. Similarly, we must plant our problem or question in our mind and trust that creative ideas will emerge without any pressure or force. The whole point is to let go of our need to control the entire thought process. Instead we must cultivate a detached interest. Saying that, it really helps if you maintain an

---

18 Mind Gym (2005), *The Mind Gym: Wake Your Mind Up*, Sphere

attitude of faith and expectancy in the process.

Conducive states for daydreaming can be reached through lots of different ways:

- Having a bath or shower
- Walking in the park or other, preferably natural, setting
- Sitting on a train or plane
- Lying awake in the morning or night

Taking a walk - One way to encourage daydreaming

For instance, it was while walking his dog in a field that George de Mestral noticed burrs sticking to his trousers and thought of the idea for Velcro.

And the great Austrian composer, Mozart, would be at his most creative when lying awake in the still of the night, warm and relaxed in bed. In a letter to his father he wrote, "When I am completely myself, entirely alone or during the night when I cannot sleep, it is on these occasions that my ideas flow best and most abundantly. Whence and how these come I know not and nor can I force them."

A heightened awareness plays a huge part in creating the right mental climate for ideas to arise. This comes through Mindfulness. Mindfulness is the art of paying careful attention to the details of the present moment, without judgement. By observing and recognising your thoughts as they come to pass, you can begin to see things from a shifted perspective and play with new concepts in your mind.

"The past is history. The future is a mystery, but today is a gift. That's why it's called 'the present'."

Bill Keane, American artist

How Do You Practice Mindfulness?

Forget any preconceptions that you have to sit in an awkward position and do funny breathing exercises in the middle of the office to ground yourself to the present. For a simple mindfulness technique, take a leaf out of Leonardo da Vinci's book and cultivate your senses. Set aside 5 minutes and try to see through the eyes of an artist, to hear through the ears of a musician, to feel with the sense of a lover, to smell with the nose of a perfumist and taste with the palate of a chef. This exercise heightens your awareness within just 20 seconds and brings you into focus to look at your situation with greater clarity. It helps to clear your head and harmonise you so you can produce ideas in the right frame of mind.

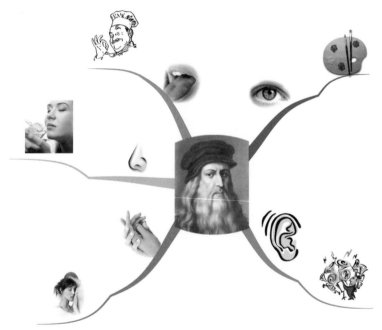

Leonardo da Vinci – Mindfulness

If you're at home or in the office and getting stressed trying to come up with ideas, take a short excursion, preferably somewhere in nature to help you tune out. Think mindfulness – take a notebook and list the things you notice. Use all your senses to make the experience richer and more engaging. Note the different things you see, hear, taste, smell or feel. What ideas do these things stimulate as you relate them to your problem?

After attempting this exercise, you'll be surprised at just how creative you can be. Mindfulness helps you develop your inner sensitivity and awareness so that you're open to the slightest suggestion of an idea. Pay attention to what arises and make sure you record it on a Mind Map or in your notebook. As Dr. Schooler explains, "You need to have the mind-wandering process, but you always need to have meta-awareness to say, 'That's a creative idea that popped into my mind."[19]

Our education and work life trains us to perform conscious logical thinking really well, while the more relaxed and playful methods of creative problem solving such as daydreaming are usually ignored or disparaged.[20] This is incongruent with what's now being revealed to us through science. Our brains are, in reality, more active when we daydream than when we're engaged in vigorous, conscious thought.

Daydreaming is a fantastic process for generating huge creative leaps, particularly if we're stuck on a complex problem. It helps us make sense of concepts, connect different thoughts and see new possibilities to spark truly original ideas. We must always remember, however, that the key to productive daydreaming is that it should be goal-orientated and purposeful.

19 Glausiusz, Josie (2011), 'Living in a Dream World', *Scientific American Mind*, Vol. 22, No.1, March/April 2011
20 Mind Gym (2005), *The Mind Gym: Wake Your Mind Up*, Sphere

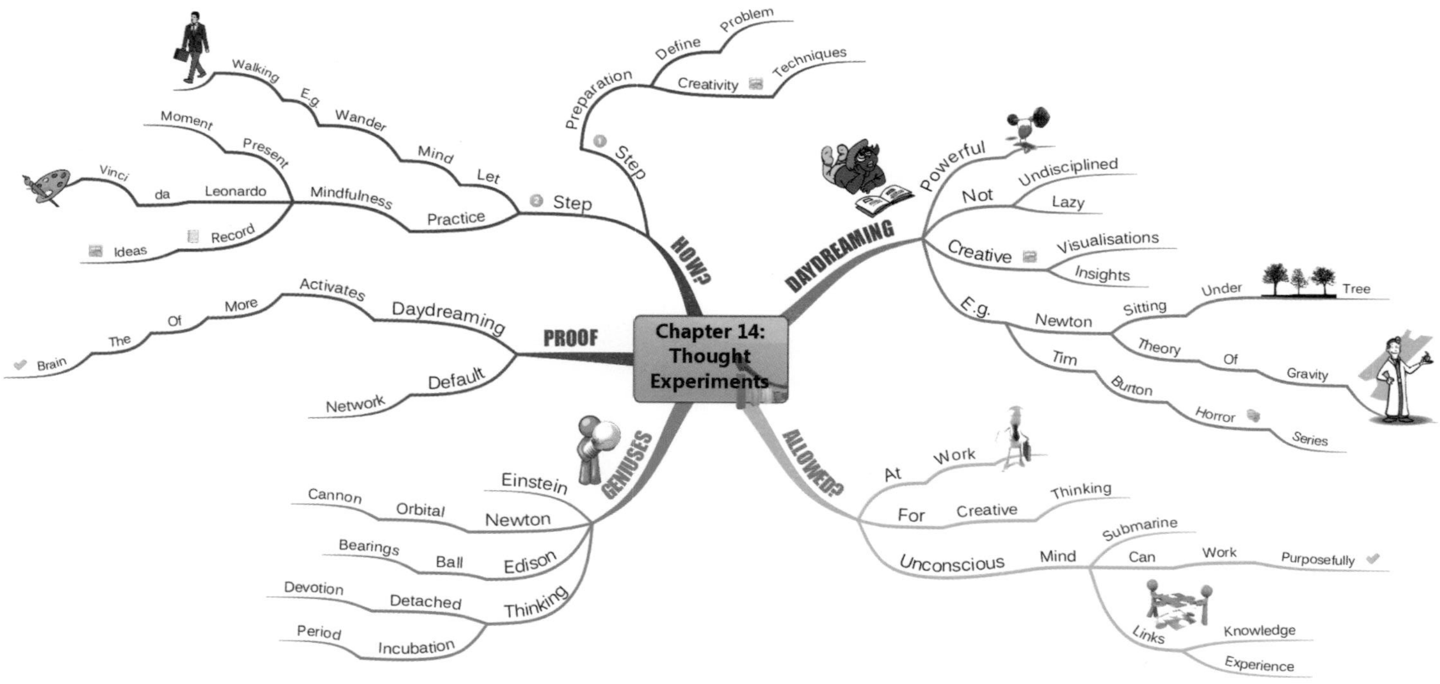

Chapter 14: Thought Experiments

DAYDREAMING
- Powerful
  - Not
    - Undisciplined
    - Lazy
  - Creative
    - Visualisations
    - Insights
  - E.g.
    - Newton
      - Sitting
      - Under
      - Tree
    - Theory
      - Of
      - Gravity
    - Tim
    - Burton
      - Horror
      - Series

ALLOWED?
- At Work
  - Thinking
  - For Creative
  - Unconscious Mind
    - Submarine
    - Can Work
    - Purposefully
    - Links
      - Knowledge
      - Experience

HOW?
- Creativity
  - Techniques
  - Define Problem
- Step
  - Preparation
- Step
  - Let Mind Wander
    - E.g.
    - Walking
  - Practice
    - Mindfulness
      - Present Moment
      - Leonardo da Vinci
    - Record
      - Ideas
  - Activates
    - More
    - Daydreaming
      - Of The Brain
    - Default
      - Network

PROOF

GENIUSES
- Einstein
- Newton
  - Cannon
  - Orbital
  - Bearings
  - Ball
- Edison
  - Devotion
  - Detached
  - Period
  - Incubation
- Thinking

Chapter 14 Summary

204

CHALLENGE ASSUMPTIONS

We make assumptions all the time and in almost every situation. Whenever we approach a business problem, whether simple or complex, we attach assumptions to it before we try to solve it. What's an assumption? It's a belief or idea that we hold to be true – often with little or no evidence. Our assumptions help shape our point of view in relation to our problem or challenge.[1] Some typical assumptions in business might be 'product cost is the main base for determining selling price' or 'our largest clients are our most important clients'.

Sometimes our assumptions are accurate and help us find the right solutions quickly. But most of the time, they limit our perception of the problem and misdirect our creative efforts. There's a great saying that goes, "Assume makes an 'ass' out of 'u' and 'me'". Assumptions are dangerous because they lead us to think we know more than we do. Remember, the aim in Step 2 of the Solution Finder is to be generative in our thinking and many of the assumptions we take for granted can actually stifle this process. They encourage us to focus on ideas that maintain the status quo instead of letting our thinking branch off into new terrain. Before we unleash our creative energy on finding solutions, we need to question the assumptions we're making about a business problem and get rid of the ones that don't hold true.

> *"Begin challenging your own assumptions. Your assumptions are your windows on the world. Scrub them off every once in a while or the light won't come in."*
>
> **Alan Alda, American actor, director and author**

Challenging assumptions is a powerful creative technique and it's particularly beneficial for livening up an unproductive brainstorming session or when people are stuck in their existing thinking paradigms.

---

1 Paul, Richard W. and Elder, Linda (2002), *Critical Thinking: Tools for Taking Charge of Your Professional and Personal Life*, Financial Times / Prentice Hall

Challenging Assumptions is an effective creative technique

What Do We Take For Granted?

The mind works as a self-organising information system.[2] Our incoming experiences, knowledge and education form the programs i.e. concepts and assumptions, that we conform to as we go about our daily lives. These programs, known as 'heuristics', come from our parents, teachers and society in general and are immensely useful for helping us navigate the many choices confronting us each day.

When we come face to face with a challenge, it's tempting to do what we've always done - what's been programmed in us by our past and by the opinions and customary ways of society. But while our programs are valuable for helping us make sense of the world and operate efficiently within it, they can act as mental straight jackets at times when we need to be highly **generative**; constraining our thinking and reducing the range of possible answers we can produce. In the words of Albert Einstein, "Few people are capable of expressing with equanimity opinions which differ from the prejudices of their social environment. Most people are even incapable of forming such opinions." We tend to accept what society tells us as true, without questioning its validity. These assumptions become so entrenched that they're below our level of conscious awareness and it never really crosses our minds to challenge or debate them. But if we do, we can reach genius levels of innovation. It's no coincidence that the greatest and most innovative thinkers would usually take great pains to distance themselves psychologically from the powerful influences of societal opinion.[3]

2 de Bono, Edward (1982), *Thinking Course*, BBC
3 Adair, John (2009), *The Art of Creative Thinking: How to be Innovative and Develop Great Ideas*, Kogan Page

> *"The best assumption to have is that any commonly held belief is wrong."*
>
> **Ken Olsen, Founder and CEO of DEC**

You'll be surprised how many aspects of life are tainted by false assumptions that prevent us from seeing something new and different. In the Middle Ages, the definition of astronomy was the 'study of how the heavenly bodies move around the Earth', i.e. the Earth was considered to be the centre of the universe. This assumption resulted in a series of poor explanations regarding various phenomena. In 1510, the Polish astronomer Nicolaus Copernicus challenged this belief by hypothesising that the sun was the centre of the solar system and that the Earth (and indeed all planets) revolved around the sun. His theory flew totally in the face of convention but made complete sense in explaining the motions of the planets.[4]

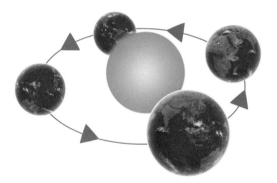

Challenging Assumptions – The earth revolves around the sun

Sometimes our assumptions can go as far as to seriously distort our thinking and could even have deadly results. Ian McGammon, a researcher at the University of Utah, examined the patterns behind experienced backcountry skiers who had died in avalanches to find out what caused them to take the risky decisions that led to their deaths. His results revealed that the poor choices made by the skiers occurred because of heuristic traps – lapses resulting from the skiers assumptions. For the skiers the terrain was familiar to them and therefore safe, causing them to make decisions that should not be made by experienced skiers.[5] This demonstrates how imperfect our assumptions can be. They can be serious traps when we rely heavily on them to make decisions.

4 Sloane, Paul (2009), 'Challenge Your Assumptions', *Blogging Innovation*, 3rd Dec 2009, http://www.business-strategy-innovation.com/2009/12/challenge-your-assumptions.html
5 Herbert, Wray (2010), *On Second Thought: Outsmarting Your Mind's Hard-Wired Habits,* Crown / Random House

In tackling challenging business situations, we really must learn to question the ingrained beliefs we take for granted. If we don't they can get in the way of our creativity and result in more or less the same set of tried and tested solutions. Many tremendous industry breakthroughs were the brainwaves of unconventional thinkers or newcomers who were able to challenge false assumptions and bring new insights to their field. For instance:

• Henry Ford challenged the assumption that automobiles were expensive, hand-built carriages for the wealthy.[6]

• Apple challenged the assumption that a personal computer needed to be just functional and that aesthetics weren't important.

• Jorma Ollila of Nokia questioned the assumption that the company needed to have lots of diverse and unrelated businesses to survive and it transformed its fortunes by specialising in mobile phone manufacturing.[7]

• McDonald's challenged the assumption that assembly lines are for cars, not food. The company re-engineered its kitchen for mass production and speed with an assembly line procedure.[8]

• The low-cost airline easyJet challenged the assumption that all air travellers are prepared to pay for a meal and drinks during their flights.[9]

> *"Creativity requires the courage to let go of certainties."*
>
> **Erich Fromm, German-American psychologist and philosopher**

But I'm an Expert...

We're all experts to a degree in that we have specialised knowledge in some area or another. The more knowledgeable and practiced we are in something, the more likely we are to make assumptions by inferring from known facts and experiences. Often this can get in the way of our ability

6 Sloane, Paul (2009), 'Challenge Your Assumptions', *Blogging Innovation*, 3rd Dec 2009, http://www.business-strategy-innovation.com/2009/12/challenge-your-assumptions.html
7 Steward, D. and Simmons, M. (2010), *The Business Playground: Where Creativity and Commerce Collide*, Financial Times / Prentice Hall
8 Mork, David (2009), 'Reversing assumptions can often lead to innovation', *Examinercom*, 6th September 2009, http://www.examiner.com/economy-in-national/reversing-assumptions-can-often-lead-to-innovation
9 McDonald, Malcolm and De Chermetony, Leslie (2001) 'Corporate Marketing and Service brands: Moving beyond the fast moving consumer goods model', European Journal of Marketing, Vol. 35,pp.335-53

to see new and different solutions to a problem as our expertise makes our vision narrow and selective. It's as if we're looking at the problem through a microscope - we're convinced we're seeing it clearly, but we're missing everything that's around it.[10]

This is demonstrated in an experiment where a group of expert magicians were asked to watch one of their fellow conjurors perform a trick. The trick involved the magician pulling an ace from a shuffled pack of cards every single time. A group of novices also observed the same trick and, afterwards, both groups were asked to explain how they believed it was done.

Drawing on their expertise, the magicians gave long convoluted explanations of how a well-practiced sleight of hand could allow the magician to access the exact position of the ace and pull it from the pack. The novices simply suggested that that the pack contained only aces so the magician could turn any one of them over... and they were correct. In this experiment, the expertise of the magicians obstructed them from thinking clearly to identify the solution that was staring them in the face the whole time! The one that ultimately made the most sense.

> "Preconceived ideas are like searchlights which illumine the path of an experimenter and serve him as a guide to interrogate nature. They become a danger only if he transforms them into fixed ideas – that is why I should like to see these profound words inscribed on the threshold of all temples of science: 'The greatest derangement of the mind is to believe in something because one wishes it to be so.'"
>
> **Louis Pasteur, French chemist and biologist**

As we age, our creativity diminishes because of our fixed beliefs and assumptions which blind us from seeing the world objectively. Children don't have the same mental restrictions as adults and can therefore be more creative. Pablo Picasso, the Spanish artist and painter, illustrated this point perfectly when he said, "It took me four years to paint like Raphael but a lifetime to paint like a child."

When it comes to creativity, being too literal is a major hindrance. It prevents us from seeing what 'could be'. Children have this ability naturally as they aren't bound by assumptions about 'what is'.[11] This is evident when they play. For instance, in the next picture, the box the child is playing with isn't a box – to her it's a bus, train, building, mountain

10 Souter, Nick (2007), *Breakthrough Thinking: Using Creativity to Solve Problems*, ILEX Press
11 Mind Gym (2005), *The Mind Gym: Wake Your Mind Up*, Sphere

or anything else her imagination wants it to be. By the same token, a simple twig can become an aeroplane or a sword. Children can be free with their imagination as there aren't any assumptions holding them back. By eradicating our assumptions, we can rediscover this ability and experience the magic of creativity that we all knew as children.

The box is a 'bus' – Children are uninhibited by assumptions

How to Challenge Assumptions

First we must recognise that we and others are bound to have unquestioned assumptions about the problem we're dealing with. It helps to use a process to deliberately seek out and challenge these assumptions. Using a Mind Map, we can apply the following three-step method. The Mind Map supports us in being generative to expose as many assumptions as possible. It also brings more clarity in testing assumptions for validity.

1) State your Problem or Challenge

The problem you defined in Step 1 of the Solution Finder becomes the central theme of your Mind Map. For illustration purposes, let's take the following challenge as an example: 'Set up a restaurant business'.

2) Map out Assumptions

Map out all the assumptions, boundaries and ground rules you're holding with respect to the situation. Doing this makes them explicit. Examine different elements of your problem closely. What seems so obvious or impervious that you wouldn't normally think about challenging it?

Typical assumptions can include:[12]

• That it's impossible to do something given constraints such as time and cost.
• That something works because of certain rules and conditions that are in place.
• That people believe, think or need certain things.

In our restaurant scenario, some of our assumptions in setting up a successful restaurant could be that it has to have:

• A menu
• Food
• Staff

Restaurant = Menu = Food = Staff

If you get stuck looking for assumptions, a helpful tip is to highlight important words and phrases in the problem statement that could be examined for hidden assumptions. For instance, if your problem is 'how to generate more sales', you can pick out the word 'sales' as a major basis for assumption. Can your goals only be achieved by more sales or could targeting more 'income' or 'profits' provide a better approach for generating solutions. Perhaps there are avenues other than sales through which you can generate income. Also, more sales do not always equate to greater profits. Are you better off looking at how to increase profits instead?

> *"Don't let assumptions stifle your capacity. Throw away every one of them."*
>
> **William N. Yeomans, Author of '1000 Things You Never Learned in Business School'**

3) Challenge Each Assumption

Now challenge the validity of each individual assumption. Your aim here is to determine whether any of your assumptions are actually correct. Ask questions to get to the bottom of things and trigger new lines of thought. For instance:

---

12 CreatingMinds.org, 'Assumption-busting', http://creatingminds.org/tools/assumption_busting.htm

- What would happen if we deliberately broke this rule?
- Why do we do it this way?
- How might this assumption be false?

The results of this process may surprise you. At first glance, your assumptions might seem blindingly true, but you'll soon find that a lot of them don't stand their ground and can be easily dropped. Many of them are likely to be self-imposed boundaries and limits. Once all your unwarranted assumptions are out of the way, lots of new solutions can be brought to light. You might even happen upon an interesting new business model or pioneering industrial breakthrough!

Referring to our restaurant example, how could we challenge each assumption and uncover new options?

Do we need to have a menu?

Perhaps not. There are several alternatives we could consider:

- Customers could bring dish ideas for the chef to cook
- The waiter could inform customers of the dishes available
- It could be a buffet restaurant or a restaurant that only offers a set meal

Do we need to offer food?

While this may appear to be a pointless question at first, when you think about it more deeply it can throw up lots of ideas. For instance, people could bring their own food and pay a service charge for the location. Or we could offer another type of product such as:

- Wine
- Food for thought
- …Even software

Do we need to have staff?

Again, not necessarily:

- The restaurant could operate via vending machines or a self-service counter
- Customers could serve other customers

Through re-examining our assumptions, we've gained a series of new perspectives on our challenge and are able to create more original ideas to explore. It doesn't matter if the new ideas are odd or silly. Remember we're aiming to be as generative as possible so we have to be able to push past our usual boundaries.

Not only can you drop assumptions, you can also **reverse** them. Turn the assumption on its head by looking at its exact opposite. This is a great thing to try when your problem is a logical paradox, for instance, when you need to do more with less; but it can also be applied to varied business challenges.[13] Essentially you're aiming to find out if the reverse of the assumption could be true. It involves:

• Mapping out all the assumptions associated with your problem
• Reversing each assumption in any way you want
• Using the assumption reversals to stimulate new ideas regarding the situation

Try reversing your assumptions to stimulate new ideas

This is a powerful approach as it gets you looking beyond the normal and obvious solutions i.e. you can think 'out of the box'. For example, in setting up your restaurant you might hold the assumption that all 'restaurants charge money for food'. This could be reversed to 'restaurants do not charge money for food'. All sorts of ideas for solutions can be triggered by this reversed assumption. Instead of charging for food, you could charge customers for the time they spend in the restaurant. Or perhaps selected low cost food and beverages could be provided for free.

Not accepting the way things are now is a great starting point for thinking more innovatively. Challenging assumptions is a valuable tool which

13 Proctor, Tony (1999), *Creative Problem Solving For Managers*, Routledge

forces us to look beyond what's already accepted in our industry and identify the less recognisable solutions for the issues we face. If we don't challenge assumptions we risk overlooking those new possibilities that don't necessarily fit in with our patterns, and might well set ourselves down the well-trodden path of conformity. By eradicating our assumptions, we can reach the kinds of perceptual breakthroughs that encourage us to stretch our creativity and construct our own paths.

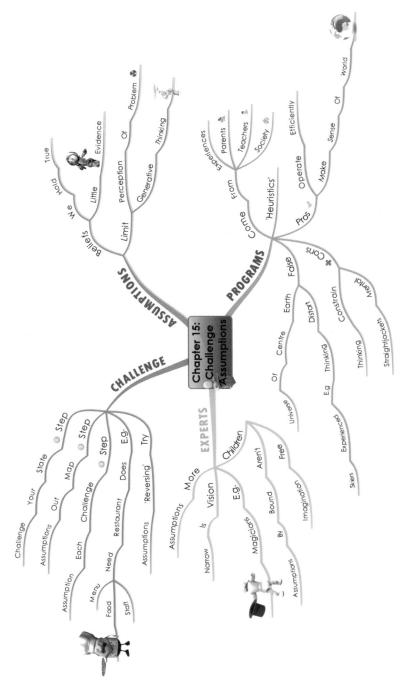

Chapter 15 Summary

CHANGE YOUR POINT OF REFERENCE

There's an old proverb that says, "What you see depends on where you stand." When it comes to solving problems and making decisions, this couldn't be more correct! Where we stand - our point of reference or perspective - has a tremendous influence on how we perceive and respond to the issues and challenges in our life. Indeed all our thinking takes place from a particular standpoint - it's such a core element of how we think that we can't think without it.[1]

> *"The real magic of discovery lies not in seeking new landscapes but in having new eyes."*

Marcel Proust, French novelist and author

When faced with an issue or challenge we need to solve, most of us look at it only from our own individual perspective - the ingrained mental view formed by our history, opinions and expertise. But the simple act of adopting another point of reference can make a huge difference in how creatively we approach the problem. Different people with varied backgrounds, experiences, professions and interests all look at things in different ways. In an organisation, a product manager will view a marketing problem differently to someone in customer service. And a finance person might have another totally new way to address a customer service issue.[2]

By stepping out of our own little world to examine the problem from multiple perspectives, we can greatly expand the insights and resources we bring to bear on it. We can look at the problem with fresh eyes and

---

1 Paul, Richard W. and Elder, Linda (2002), *Critical Thinking: Tools for Taking Charge of Your Professional and Personal Life,* Financial Times Prentice Hall
2 Carpenter, Hutch (2010), 'The Benefits of Letting Others Recast Your Problem', *CloudAve*, 11th October 2010, http://www.cloudave.com/6325/the-benefits-of-letting-others-recast-your-problem/

might uncover terrific solutions that were invisible to us before.

In this chapter, I outline a technique that encourages you to put yourself into the minds of different people and imagine how they would view the problem. For instance, how would a politician see it? A nurse? A child? A bus driver? Mentally taking on their perspectives can help you make new connections and creative leaps to spark original solutions to the problem, rather than variations on the same old ideas.

This is a particularly powerful technique when you've exhausted all other options for producing novel ideas and have fallen into a rut. You can escape your narrow perspective and discover new and meaningful ways to look at things. It's also a highly playful and imaginative approach, livening up any lacklustre brainstorming session.

Changing perspective helps you look at a problem with fresh eyes

Our Point of Reference

Our unique point of reference is created from the moment we're born and continually evolves as we learn new information and gain experiences. It's fashioned by innumerable factors such as our IQ, age, race, genes, gender, culture, education, upbringing, personality, experiences, spiritual beliefs, work experience, social conditions and much more. Every one of these factors creates a filter through which we view the world. These filters in their entirety help to create the distinct perspective which governs how we solve problems and make decisions as we go about our lives.[3]

The problem with this is that our point of reference is singular – it's just one mental model or perceptual position that could be used to tackle problems, challenges and decisions. In the words of Professor Scott Page of the University of Michigan, "A perspective is a map from reality

3 Problem-Solving-Techniques.com (2009), 'Frame of Reference', http://www.problem-solvingtechniques.com/Frame-of-Reference.html

to an internal language such that each distinct object, situation, problem, or event gets mapped to a unique world."[4] We all have different maps of reality and any single perspective is far from being completely objective in making sense of the whole problem and recognising how to deal with it.

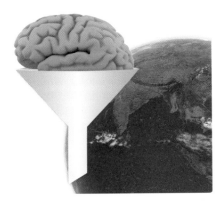

Our filters affect our perspective of the world

"You have your way. I have my way. As for the right way, the correct way, and the only way, it does not exist."

Friedrich Nietzsche, German classical scholar and philosopher

When we rely too much on our own perspective we limit the awareness of how we might do something differently or better. We get stuck on our problems and run through the same ideas over and over again, ending up with the same predictable solutions.

Sometimes our perception causes 'functional fixedness'.[5] This is the tendency to view objects in terms of their traditional uses. In problem solving, this can box us in by limiting our ability to find more inspired and unconventional uses for products or services. For instance, the computer had been in use for a long time as a calculator before its potential as a general symbol manipulator was seen.[6] An object like a hammer isn't just useful for driving or removing nails, it can also be an effective paperweight, nutcracker, pendulum weight or even a murder weapon!

4 Page, Scott (2007), *The Difference: How the Power of Diversity Creates Better Groups, Firms, Schools and Societies,* Princeton University Press

5 Duncker, K. (1945), 'On problem solving', trans L.S. Lees, *Psychological Monographs*, 58, 5 (Whole No. 270)

6 Weizenbaum, J. (1984), *Computer Power and Human Reason,* Penguin: Harmondsworth

What this means is that we have to be able to detach ourselves from our own world view to open up more creative possibilities. Creative thinkers understand that considering a challenge from another standpoint brings a new dimension to how effectively you can generate ideas. For example, when Dr. Jonas Salk was asked how he discovered the vaccine that cured Polio, he replied, "I learned to think as Mother Nature thinks."[7] His answer illustrates just how important it is to let go of your own 'map of reality' and adopt a new angle to make new discoveries and breakthroughs.

Sometimes we're far too close to a situation to see it neutrally and objectively. We assume that the way we see the problem is the right way to see it but this isn't always the case. An outsider's take on the problem might be radically different from ours - triggering solutions we might never have come across while stuck in our own perspective. The scientific research paper 'The Value of Openness in Scientific Problem Solving' is intriguing in that it reveals that the probability of solving a problem actually *triples* when the problem is out of the individual's realm of expertise:

"We reason that the significance of this effect may be due to the ability of 'outsiders' from relatively distant fields to see problems with fresh eyes and apply solutions that are novel to the problem domain but well known and understood by them."[8]

More recent research by Evan Polman of New York University and Kyle J. Ernich of Cornell University supports this.[9] Across four studies involving hundreds of undergraduates, they found that when people solved problems on behalf of others, they produced faster and more creative solutions than they did when they solved the same problems for themselves. This is because we think in more abstract terms about problems belonging to distant people, and thinking at a more abstract level generates more creative ideas – a principle known as 'construal-level theory'.

The conclusion from all this is that new ideas come from distance and differences, not closeness and similarities in thinking. By staying alert to other perspectives, we can move out of instinctual, reactive thinking into a more constructive, abstract and creative state of awareness. We basically create more psychological distance from the problem so we can solve it better.

---

7 Caroselli, Marlene (1997), *That's No Problem! A Problem-Free Approach to Problem-Solving*, Coastal Training Technologies Corp
8 Lakhani, Karim, R et al (2007), 'The Value of Openness in Scientific Problem Solving', http://www.hbs.edu/research/pdf/07-050.pdf
9 Polman, Evan and Ernich, Kyle J. (2011), 'Decisions for others are more creative than decisions for the self', *Personality and Social Psychology Bulletin*, April 2011

Generating Ideas Using Multiple Perspectives

How can we look at and address our problem from different perspectives? The following is a simple technique that encourages you to take a mixed variety of distinct viewpoints into account for responding to your challenge.

1) Identify Different Points of Reference

Create a Mind Map with the main branches representing different people whose viewpoint you'd like to explore. Use a random selection of people in different roles, circumstances or professions to encourage diverse thinking. You can include people affected by the problem such as staff, customers or partners, but it's far better to use people unrelated to the problem - Bill Gates, your sister or a librarian for example. You can even use archetypes such as the Hero, Lover, Sage or Magician or characters like Snow White.[10] The more assorted the choice, the broader your base for generating solutions. Here's a sample of perspectives you could explore:

Mother/Father; Superman; Flight Attendant; Clown; Librarian; Child; Doctor; Minister; Politician; Accountant; Musician, Leonardo da Vinci; Stand-up comedian; Retired person; Sales Manager; A dog; Doctor; Bill Gates; An inventor; A football player; Homer Simpson; Teacher; The Dalai Lama; Hitler; Cinderella.[11]

Find multiple perspectives from which to view your problem

---

10 Souter, Nick (2007), *Breakthrough Thinking: Using Creativity to Solve Problems,* ILEX Press
11 *NHS Institute for Innovation and Improvement* (2008), 'Fresh Eyes – Seek Out and Use the Wisdom of Others', *NHS Institute for Innovation and Improvement,* Quality and Service Improvement Tools, http://www.institute.nhs.uk/quality_and_service_improvement_tools/quality_and_service_improvement_tools/creativity_tools_-_seek_out_and_use_the_wisdom_of_others_(fresh_eyes).html

While some perspectives will work better than others, all will stretch your thinking to offer valid alternatives. It's recommended that you come up with at least four different points of reference. Try to keep them unrelated to each other for more divergence.

2) Expore Each Viewpoint

Next, consider how each of these people would view your particular challenge. Put yourself in their shoes - their mindset or environment - and imagine how they would think about it or describe it. Try asking the following questions:

• What would be the important factors?
• What aspect of the issue might they focus on?
• How would they describe the problem?
• How would their description differ from mine?
• Would they even see a problem at all?

You'll find that it's quite easy to get into other people's heads and see the world through their eyes. Map out the thoughts from each perspective. For instance, what do you think your father would say about your problem? What would a clown say? Entirely different, perhaps even absurd explanations might come up.

If possible, talk directly to some of these people and record what they say in your Mind Map. Notice the similarities and differences in how each person would approach the problem.

This is a brilliant technique for opening your mind. At a recent seminar in which I demonstrated this technique, one attendee was particularly amazed at how well it worked for him. As a representative of the United Nations, he was in the process of helping to resolve some issues concerning the political system of an Eastern European state. After applying this technique, he was taken aback by how easily he was able to imagine the situation from the perspective of different factions and stakeholders such as the Israelis, Arabs etc. Thus, no matter how serious or seemingly complex our problem may appear to be, we can all benefit by leveraging the different perceptual models that others hold to view the situation afresh.

Examine the problem from each perspective

"I see and write things first as an artist, second as a woman, and third as a New Yorker. All three have built-in perspectives that aren't neutral."

Laurie Anderson, American performance artist and musician

3) Generate New Ideas

Reflecting on these perspectives, map out the new ideas that come to mind for solving your challenge. How would these people address the challenge? What ideas or approaches might they have? What actions would they take? Can these ideas work for your situation? This activity is likely to draw out lots of inventive approaches to your challenge. Sometimes the perspectives that seem to be completely unrelated to your problem can give you exactly the inspiration you're looking for.

For example, if your problem is to 'increase sales', and you're viewing it from the perspective of a child, this might give rise to ideas such as adding more playful and entertaining features to your product that customers would be willing to pay more for.

We all have our own unique way of seeing the world – our own point of reference. When we get stuck on a problem and are having difficulty generating options and possibilities it's usually because we're relying too much on this single perspective. It's important, therefore, for us to learn to shift perspectives to examine the issue in new and varied ways. In using the technique outlined in this chapter, we're essentially adopting different filters through which to look at the problem. When the flow of ideas has dried up, this can be incredibly powerful in restarting it and helping us ready ourselves to forge new and unlikely directions.

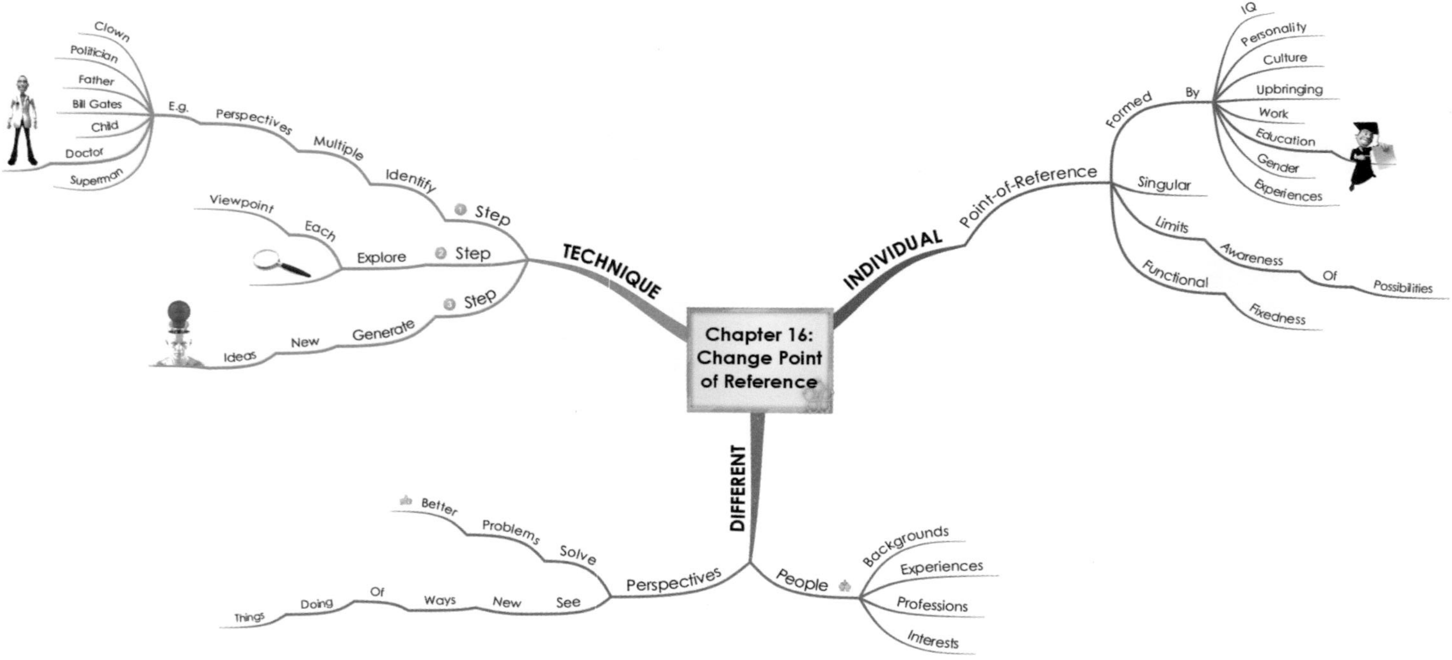

Chapter 16: Change Point of Reference

INDIVIDUAL

Point-of-Reference

- Formed By
  - IQ
  - Personality
  - Culture
  - Upbringing
  - Work
  - Education
  - Gender
  - Experiences
- Singular
  - Limits
    - Awareness Of Possibilities
  - Functional
    - Fixedness

DIFFERENT

- People
  - Backgrounds
  - Experiences
  - Professions
  - Interests
- Perspectives
  - Solve Problems Better
  - See New Ways Of Doing Things

TECHNIQUE

- Step 1: Identify Multiple Perspectives
  - E.g.
    - Clown
    - Politician
    - Father
    - Bill Gates
    - Child
    - Doctor
    - Superman
- Step 2: Explore Each Viewpoint
- Step 3: Generate New Ideas

Chapter 16 Summary

REVERSE THE CHALLENGE

The world is defined by opposites. The classic Chinese philosophical text, the *Tao Te Ching* ('way of virtue') teaches us that any attribute or concept is meaningless without its opposite.[1] Beauty is beauty because ugliness is perceived and good is good because we observe there to be bad.

By recognising the opposites all around us, we can bring a huge amount of creative strength and power to our goals, problems, challenges and tasks. Take leadership for example – in order to lead successfully, a leader must be able to follow. And in order to prosper, a leader must first learn to live simply.[2] Learning to see things in reverse – 180 degrees from the usual or common view – allows us to instigate greater movement and expansion in our thoughts. When we switch to an opposite perspective, we have a new base from which to approach things far more creatively than we would when locked into our normal patterns of thinking.

> *"Our mind is capable of passing beyond the dividing line we have drawn for it. Beyond the pairs of opposites of which the world consists, other, new insights begin."*
>
> **Hermann Hesse, German-born Swiss novelist and poet**

The premise of the 'Reverse the Challenge' technique is really very simple. It takes your original problem statement and uses the opposite as a springboard to create new and different solutions. It's a provocative technique that forces you to think in opposite directions to go beyond boundaries and conventions. Rather than thinking about 'what to do', you think of 'what not to do'. If you're struggling to find ways to get more customers, find ways to lose them instead. If you want to reduce the number of faulty goods you produce, find ways to create *more* faulty goods. While this might appear paradoxical and absurd, recognising the actions you want to avoid actually gives you

---

1 Tzu, Lao (1990), *Tao Te Ching*, Shambhala Publications Inc
2 Thompson, Charles (1992), *What a Great Idea! Key Steps Creative People Take*, HarperPerennial

better scope to identify lots more interesting alternatives to reach your desired results.

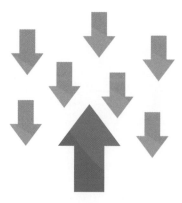

Reverse the challenge - View your problem from the opposite direction

Brainstorming In Reverse

When we brainstorm normally, we state our problem then try to generate a multitude of possible solutions to solve it. While this can be a highly productive process most of the time, sometimes it's tough to identify solutions to the problem when we're looking at it face-on. The Reverse The Challenge technique works in a similar fashion to conventional brainstorming but instead of coming up with solutions, you brainstorm ways to **make the problem worse.** You work against the flow of your natural thought process to look for 'anti -solutions' to the problem.[3] Once you've done this, you can draw parallel positive solutions to your original problem by simply reversing your ideas.

Reverse The Challenge is useful as both an individual and group technique for brainstorming. In a group, it offers a playful and humorous approach leading to lively (and sometimes feisty!) exchanges over the possibilities presented by the reversals. When people get stuck, it can be used to jump-start creativity as it throws everyone off balance to start thinking afresh. And the unique angle it provides makes it great to use when people are finding it difficult to break off from analytical and judgemental tendencies and preferences.[4] In situations where you really need to generate a huge volume of ideas, this is definitely one of the most valuable techniques to have at your disposal. The results are usually very surprising, ranging from the 'obvious' answers to fairly radical solutions that wouldn't normally come to mind.

3 Dayne (2009), '5 Powerful Creative Thinking Techniques', *TheHappySelf.com*, 3rd December 2009, http://www.thehappyself.com/5-powerful-creative-thinking¬techniques
4 TRACTORS Project, Training Material in Creativity and innovation For European R&D Organisations SMES, http://www.train4creativity.eu/dat/C0C4F57E/file.pdf? 634349294081200786

Brainstorming in reverse helps you generate a broad range of solutions

Edward de Bono describes a similar technique which he calls the 'Intermediate Impossible'. This is built upon the concept that wrong and/or impossible ideas can be used as gateways or stepping stones to good ideas. Basically, you allow your thinking to work in a seemingly wrong direction so you can explore unfamiliar landscape.[5] For instance, when working on a challenge to prevent factories that are built on rivers polluting the towns that are downstream from them, de Bono used the statement 'the factories should be downstream of themselves'. This statement appears incongruous and illogical on first sight. Normally a factory's input is upstream of its output. However, reversing this approach led to the idea of legislating that factory inlet pipes must be downstream of their outlet pipes. So if the factories polluted the water, they would be the first to suffer!

> *"Reverse every natural instinct and do the opposite of what you are inclined to do, and you will probably come very close to having a perfect golf swing."*
>
> **Ben Hogan, American golfer**

Reverse the Challenge Step-by-Step

The following is a simple process you can use for reversing your challenge and stimulating new ideas:

---

5 de Bono, Edward (1982), *Thinking Course*, BBC

1) State Your Problem

Start by stating the problem you defined in Step 1 of the Solution Finder. We'll use the example of 'how to get more customers'.

2) Reverse Your Problem

Change the wording of the problem to the exact reverse or opposite. Instead of asking 'how do I solve or prevent this problem?' try asking 'how could I cause the problem?' And instead of asking 'how do I achieve these results?', ask 'how could I achieve the opposite effect?'[6]

For instance, we can easily reverse 'how to get more customers' to 'how to lose more customers'. This alters our immediate focus from how to solve the problem to how to cause it.

3) Brainstorm Ideas for the Reversed Problem

When you brainstorm directly on your original problem, you can end up following a certain, predictable path in terms of the solutions you come up with. For instance, for 'how to get more customers', you might come up with the following ideas through traditional brainstorming:

- New advertising strategy
- Offer discounts
- Find new markets
- Door-to-door sales
- Change or improve packaging

Once you reverse the problem, however, your perspective on the situation changes completely! Start Mind Mapping ideas for addressing your reversed problem. You might well be surprised at the insights this new angle gives you into the fundamental nature of the problem. For instance, when the ThinkBuzan team performed this exercise, we found that our priorities altered dramatically as we shifted our focus from getting more customers to losing more customers. 'Offer bad customer service' was identified as the most significant way to lose customers in our organisation. This expanded our outlook on the importance of good customer service and support profoundly.

---

6 MindTools (2010), 'Reverse Brainstorming: A Different Approach to Brainstorming', *MindTools Career Excellence Club*, http://mindtools.com/community/pages/article/ newCT_96.php

Reverse your solutions to identify those that 'fit' the problem

4) Reverse Your Solutions

Finally, reverse the 'anti-solutions' you generated to identify ways of solving the original problem or challenge. See if any of the solutions provide a good 'fit' to your problem or can be adjusted to work. As you look over your answers, you'll find that there are many more ways to solve the original problem than you could initially envisage. In our example, we can reverse the solution 'offer bad customer service' to 'offer excellent customer service'. At ThinkBuzan, we increased our level of customer support considerably after using this technique!

> *"The solution of every problem is another problem."*
>
> **Johann Wolfgang von Goethe, German playwright, poet and novelist**

To demonstrate this technique further, we can adopt the previous solution as an entirely new challenge - 'offer excellent customer service'. Instead of mapping out ways to improve customer service, we reverse the problem and look at ways to offer bad customer service, for instance:

• Not answering telephones
• Opening late and closing early
• Staff have very little product knowledge
• Answering customer queries incorrectly
• Not providing a warranty
• Staff are rude to customers

Afterwards, we can reverse the answers to see if any relate back to the initial problem. Perhaps we could provide additional training for our customer service operatives to improve product knowledge and their handling of customers, or we could begin working in shifts to open earlier and close later.

The benefits of using this technique in business situations are clearly apparent, yet it can also be tremendously effective for dealing with issues in your personal life. To really understand how powerful it is, try it out with the statement 'how to keep your partner'. Reverse the statement to 'how to lose your partner' and map out all the things you could do to lose your partner. Then highlight all those that you currently do. You'll find it's a real eye opener in showing you exactly what you need to change in your relationship!

In any situation, identifying ways to make the problem worse helps develop a deeper understanding of the things you're actually doing wrong at the moment. This then places you in an effective position to generate better solutions for positive change.

Reverse The Challenge is a fantastic technique for encouraging you to 'think outside the box' by approaching your problem from a completely different angle. The process of reversing your problem, issue or goal offers an easy way to view it differently, bringing a new dimension to your brainstorming and allowing you to break free of established mindsets. All things considered, it provides an effective trigger for discovering novel ideas that you wouldn't be able to detect when looking at your problem head-on.

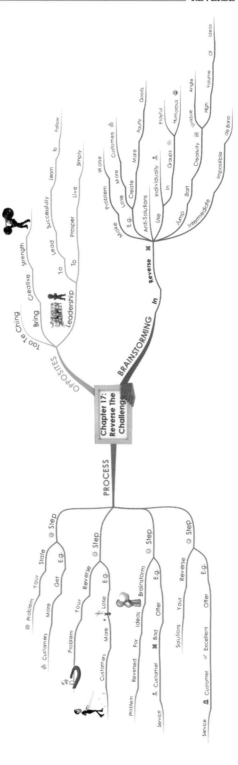

STEP 3: EVALUATE

In Step 2 of the Solution Finder, we unleashed our generative thinking skills during brainstorming to create lots of new and different ideas. We allowed our thoughts to **diverge** substantially to improve our chances of finding solutions that would help us positively address the problem or challenge we defined in Step 1. At the end of this process, we're likely to be sitting on an output of dozens, hundreds or even thousands of ideas. This presents us with a formidable yet exciting challenge. We must now 'mine' our huge pit of ideas to locate the precious diamond that's hidden in there somewhere - the brilliant solution that will solve our problem in the best way possible.

Step 3 of the Solution Finder is the evaluation stage – the stage when you **1) sort, 2) screen** and **3) select** the idea or ideas that you'll implement to successfully deal with your challenge. It's important to note that the hardest part of problem solving and decision making is not producing ideas, but making creative use of them. The usefulness of all your creative efforts relies heavily on your ability to analyse all of the ideas you've generated and make well-reasoned choices amongst them.

> *"The object of analysis is clarity of thought. For clear thinking should precede and accompany creative thinking."*
>
> **John Adair, Author of 'The Art of Creative Thinking'**

A good evaluative system helps you to effectively manage the volume and complexity of the ideas you came up with during brainstorming to **converge** to the right answer. It brings analytical thinking to the fore so you can subject your ideas to critical tests, kill off the weak ones and figure out which are worth keeping. As with the previous steps of the Solution Finder, tools and techniques have a valuable role to play. After all, the better able you are to 'mine', the greater your chances of finding a diamond or two.

The right methods and tools help you stay in tune with your goal and maintain objectivity as you analyse. Without them, it's tempting to fall into long-standing habits and patterns and gravitate towards the same old 'tried and true' ideas.

The evaluative approach I outline in this chapter - **the 3S Analysis System (Sort, Screen and Select)** encompasses simple, yet incredibly powerful tools for analysing ideas using 'whole brain' thinking. Unlike more complex and sophisticated analytical approaches, it doesn't overwhelm you with lots of complicated weights and calibrations. And instead of relying solely on convergent thinking practices, it also employs divergent thinking to blend imagination and discovery into the exploration of your options.

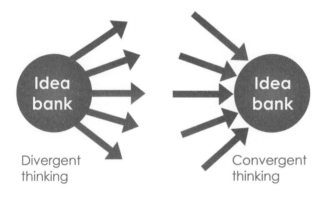

Analysing ideas using both convergent and divergent thinking

As we saw in Chapter 5, divergent and convergent thinking don't have to be distinct strategies.[1] In fact, when carried out simultaneously they better engage the left and right brain thought processes required to help you build practical meaning from the pile of ideas you've now got.

By and large, the 3S Analysis System gives you proactive control over your analytical thinking and assists in maintaining objectivity. This helps you be confident that your analytical endeavours will result in a positive outcome. As with the previous steps of the Solution Finder, Mind Mapping remains the note-taking method of choice for keeping you organised and focused as you work out the correct solution. It's particularly valuable as a device through which you can make your analytical thought process explicit, regardless of whether you're working alone or in a team.[2]

1 Guilford, J.P. (1975), 'Creativity: a quarter century of progress', in I. A. Taylor and J. W. Getzels (ed), *Perspectives in Creativity*, Chicago, Ill: Aldine
2 Jones, Sue and Sims, David (1985), 'Mapping as an Aid to Creativity', *Journal of Management Development*, 4, 1, pp. 47-60

Why Use a System to Evaluate Ideas?

Making good use of the right ideas requires that you take all the different options spawned by generative thinking and subject them to the bright glare of 'positive judgement'. To do this successfully, you must be able to draw fully upon the wide range of personal experience, logic, imagination and gut feeling which you and others can bring to the situation. Without a carefully balanced and structured system, you're limited in how well you can do this.

Too many people brush over the evaluation stage of the problem solving process. They stop brainstorming and just pick the solution they believe to be correct – "That's the best solution. We should go for it." Why? Often that's just what their reactive instinct is telling them. They haven't stopped to examine the true potential of the solution. In some cases, particularly those involving 'soft' decisions, people don't believe that an analytical system or method will help them reach the right answer. Instead of being guided by a well-rounded process, they allow themselves to be blindly led by tradition, beliefs or emotional impulses. Their prejudices make the decision on how they should feel about an idea pretty much straightaway. In other words, they become *selective* far too early in the process.

> *"One should never impose one's views on a problem; one should rather study it, and in time a solution will reveal itself."*
>
> **Albert Einstein, Nobel Prize winning theoretical physicist**

Applying a careful and considered analytical system helps you overcome obstacles caused by selective preferences, prejudices and assumptions. With the aid of appropriate tools, you can suspend selective thinking to prevent the power struggles and difficulties that can occur when people endorse the wrong views and illogical conclusions.

As we saw in Chapter 6, being over-confident in your preferred or known solutions can be extremely harmful to creative problem solving. Remember, just because something worked in the past, it doesn't mean it will work again. What's more, initial impressions aren't always correct.[3] So many people 'shoot from the hip' when evaluating ideas i.e. they let their immediate reaction determine their choice. This is easy to do when there's no clear picture of what you're looking at. Making the effort to work through a system or process first helps you take better aim at your target. Instead of

---

3 Hammond, John, Keeney, Ralph and Raiffa, Howard (1998), *Smart Choices: A Practical Guide to Making Better Decisions*, Harvard Business School Press

your intelligence being used to support a particular prejudice or belief, it's used for further screening and exploration. In this way you can line up your insights and those of others to determine a positive direction which you can all be fully committed to.

Applying 'Whole Brain' Skills

The purpose of the 3S Analysis System is to arrange our thinking and make sure both our rationality and creativity are guided towards a successful decision. We need to employ analytical thinking to choose from all the ideas that we have, but instead of evaluating ideas in a conventional manner using 'checklists' or weighted measurements, we can increase the productivity of our analysis by using a *generative* and *whole brain* approach.

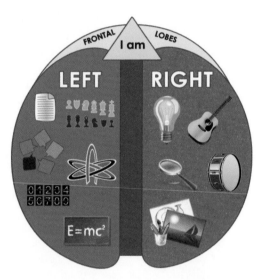

Productive analysis requires balanced use of our cortical skills

When we focus heavily on logic, judgement and criticism, our left brain cortical skills become excessively dominant and skew our thinking. It's important to engage other right brain cortical skills to balance things out and bring our mental strength fully into gear for more constructive analysis. Contrary to standard thought, this also encompasses the use of emotion, intuition and gut feeling to fuel our interpretation of the situation and assist in judging options (see Chapter 5). The danger in using emotion only comes about if we place it above everything else and use it as a substitute for careful and considered thinking. As a contributory element it's positively instrumental for whole brain thinking.

"The intuitive mind is a sacred gift and the rational mind is a faithful servant. We have created a society that honours the servant and has forgotten the gift."

Albert Einstein, Nobel Prize winning theoretical physicist

During the evaluation stage, your ability to imagine, feel and see the whole picture must be equally as strong as your faculty of valuing and judging. Without this balance, you potentially lose more than half of your effectiveness. To understand this, imagine that you're running a marathon as you would normally with two arms and legs working freely. Then visualise that you're running with your left hand tied to your left foot. This affects the distribution of your body weight massively, increasing the chance of you falling over and causing damage to yourself! While you're still using half of your running resources i.e. one arm and leg, the reduction in your power and efficiency is far greater than 50 per cent. It's closer to a deterioration of 99 per cent.[4] This analogy is parallel to your thinking. You need to engage the gears of your brain fully (i.e. your individual cognitive skills) when conducting analysis otherwise you're potentially not even half as effective as you could be. If you use only your left brain cognitive skills to manage and evaluate ideas, you're wasting the majority of your resource capability. Needless to say, this can be disastrous when it comes to making important decisions!

Using only left brain skills to evaluate is like running with your left hand tied to your left foot

When used together each side of your brain reinforces the other in a way that strengthens your ability for greater intellectual and intuitive reasoning. So rather than separating your analysis and rationality from

4 Buzan, Tony and Griffiths, Chris (2010), *Mind Maps For Business*, BBC Active

your creative abilities and emotional responses, you should aim to apply them simultaneously to get the best results.

The process of creating a Mind Map brings your entire range of cognitive skills into play at the same time, so in popular terms it can be seen as a 'whole brain' thinking tool. When you evaluate using a Mind Map, you open up multiple synaptic connections so you can be generative in your thinking while converging towards your solution. This helps you to explore and engage with each idea much more fully and explicitly than you could with other note-taking methods.

The '3S Analysis System' for Evaluating Ideas

How can we apply whole brain skills, integrate emotion as well as logic and take advantage of the generative nature of Mind Mapping during the analytical stage of problem solving, yet still keep things very simple? The following is the three-step system we devised for this very purpose. It walks you through the evaluation process and directs your attention positively for constructive analysis.

1) SORT

Before jumping into detailed analysis of your ideas you need to look at editing them down to a manageable quantity. Broadly, your aim is to come out of this phase with a shortlist of between three and six promising options to explore. This initial step is crucial to prevent you from drowning in a sea of possibilities.

If you have a huge volume of ideas to work through, say 50 to a 100, it helps to first categorise them into clusters or groups based on important themes. For instance, if you've come up with lots of ideas for designing a new product, you could create clusters for the ideas that relate to 'practicality', 'differentiation' etc. Or you can group ideas in terms of time and financial requirements such as 'simple', 'hard' and 'difficult'. Simple ideas are those that can be put into action with a minimum of expenditure of time and money. Hard ideas require more expenditure, while difficult ideas require the most expenditure.[5]

Yet another approach could be to distinguish groups of ideas according to the type of innovation they promote, for instance, product innovation, technical/technological innovation, organisational innovation, managerial

---

5 Moore, L.B. (1962), 'Creative action – the evaluation, development and use of ideas', in S. J. Parnes and H.F. Harding (eds), *A Sourcebook For Creative Thinking*, Scribner's: New York

innovation or methodological innovation.[6]

This activity is easily performed in a Mind Map. The structure of a Mind Map lets you synthesise large amounts of data meaningfully by forming relationships between ideas. You can move back and forth and arrange and rearrange ideas in line with the flow of thoughts during the thinking session or group discussion. Once your ideas are in clusters, it becomes easier to identify which ones you can kill off. It could be that they don't fall into any obvious grouping for helping you solve the problem. Perhaps even whole clusters can be eliminated if they don't fit in with your ultimate goal.

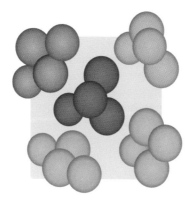

Sort ideas into clusters/groups to aid initial evaluation and elimination

If there are any particularly crazy ideas that you're inclined to instantly dismiss as impractical, you can use an excellent method suggested by Tim Hurson, author of *Think Better*, to test their validity. The method, called 'What's UP?', is very simple.[7]

The UP stands for the 'underlying principle'. For each of your wild ideas, simply ask yourself "what is the underlying principle behind this idea?" This gets you thinking of how the idea could be practically applied, helping you better work out if it could actually be feasible in reality. Remember, the whole point of going through the Solution Finder process is to look for imaginative ideas and you can jeopardise your creativity by limiting yourself only to 'safe' or tested ideas.

Use the principle of **positive judgement** to maintain an open mind. It's

6 Rebernik, Miroslav and Bradac, Barbara, 'Idea Evaluation Methods and Techniques', Module 4, *Creative Trainer*, http://www.creative-trainer.eu/fileadmin/template/ download/module_idea_evaluation_final.pdf

7 Hurson, Tim (2008), *Think Better: An Innovator's Guide to Productive Thinking*, McGraw-Hill Professional

tempting to charge in and start discarding ideas immediately. However, if you do this while focusing on negative characteristics of ideas as the basis for elimination, you risk rejecting alternatives that have real potential. Rather than paying attention to the negatives, concentrate on the positive and novel aspects to help you decide which ideas to keep. At the same time, keep your eyes on your objective so that your shortlisted ideas are all highly relevant to your goal. By the end of this stage, heaps of your original ideas will have been discounted, while the few most promising and attractive alternatives remain to be explored further. These ideas form your input into the screening process.

2) SCREEN

It's my personal belief that 'ticking off' ideas against a long list of predetermined criteria isn't a beneficial or constructive way to evaluate. For the most part, it doesn't make full use of the rich and complex workings of all of our cortical skills. Very little positive judgement or intuition is engaged in such a fixed procedure which means people can easily lose their creativity. We need to employ generative and 'whole brain' aids and tools if we're to effectively tap into all our resources and connect with both the quantitative and qualitative sides of our thinking.

As a result of your efforts in the sorting stage of the 3S Analysis System, you now have approximately three to six ideas that you feel are worth exploring further. Ideally, at least some of them will be paradigm breaking ideas – ones that you wouldn't normally have thought of, ones that may even be a little crazy! The screening process for these ideas has been kept very simple and is based on relatively relaxed criteria and standards – you don't want to be overwhelmed with the task. In Mind Map form, evaluate each of your ideas in turn using the following measurement factors:

a) Heart Rating and Head Rating

Take one of your ideas and begin your evaluation by examining it from the perspectives of both your heart (emotions) and head (logic).

Heart - Under the 'Heart' sub-branch of your Mind Map, consider how you 'feel' about the idea i.e. think with your heart. What is your gut feeling on it? Does it excite you? Add a further sub-branch entitled 'Rate' and score the idea in terms of how positive you are about it emotionally. Use a 10-point scale where 10 indicates that you feel 'very positive' and 1 'very negative'.

Head - You then follow the same process using intellectual reasoning i.e.

think with your head. Does the idea make sense to you logically? Is it robust? Can you rationalise and justify it? Score it on this basis under the 'Rate' sub-branch.

The results of this activity are usually fascinating. You could find that for some ideas your heart says yes but your head says no, and for others both your heart and head concur. Rating scales such as this are quantitative forms of evaluation that provide a clear-cut and definite way to determine your best ideas. A strongly positive score indicates an attractive option and a strongly negative score suggests the idea is poor. While figures and scores are helpful for evaluating alternatives, we also need to use generative thinking to broaden and deepen our analysis. In other words, we need to use **'generative analysis'**. On your Mind Map, branch out to examine the idea from the following angles:

b) Greens and Reds

Conduct a pros and cons analysis. Use divergent thinking to stretch your mind to explore all the positive and negative features of the potential solution. Consider financial, marketing and organisational aspects and implications. You may need to get hold of additional data and research to increase your chances of making an informed and intelligent decision. The good news is that all your data can be collected in an integrated form all on one map, making it easier to 'see' it clearly and holistically.

Greens - What are the positive aspects about this solution? Its strengths? What do you like about it? Why might it succeed? What might others like about it? Be as generative as you can here. For example, if your idea relates to a new kind of product offering, some of its greens may include: it's a good differentiator; it's difficult for competitors to replicate; and there is high consumer demand for it. The Mind Map format will help you conduct a detailed examination of all the positive attributes and their inter-relationships. Consider whether you can build on these attributes to make the idea bigger and better.

Reds - What are the negative aspects of the solution? Its weaknesses? What do you dislike about it? Why might it fail? Why will others reject it? Be its worst critic. Again the Mind Map assists you to be generative in exploring the flaws and downsides of the idea. This could spark ideas on how to erase a red point or even transform it into a plus! For instance, you can use the Mind Map to change your perspective. If one of your negatives is that the solution would cost too much, switch your thinking to 'how could I afford to pay for this?' If you're able to map out answers to the question, the barrier is no longer a real negative.

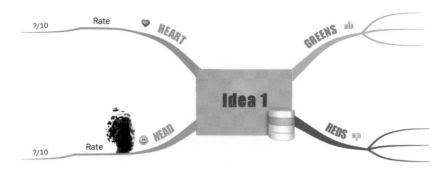

Evaluating your ideas using a Mind Map

Follow this activity for all your shortlisted ideas and you'll end up with a complete and robust description of each one. Through this process, every idea is transformed from something vague into something solid and real. It's great for identifying the 'deal makers' and 'deal breakers' of each idea, boosting your chances of picking the best possible option to run with.

The problem with a lot of traditional evaluation systems is that they can trick us into thinking we're being highly analytical with their use of numbers, probabilities and detailed calibrations. However, these are solely left brain dominant elements. When you appraise the value of a home you don't only look at the square footage to figure out the value. You take lots of balancing factors into account. Is it in good shape or does it need repairs? How many finishing details does it have? Is there a garage? etc. The procedure outlined here is comparable to conducting a full appraisal on a house as it encourages you to combine both quantitative and qualitative factors so you end up with a 'whole' picture of each idea. It balances rational and logical elements against your intuition and stimulates you to be generative to explore each idea as fully as possible.

For some people this system might appear too rough, simplistic or 'soft'- i.e. not 'analytical enough'. But lots of more complex analytical systems are unsuccessful precisely because they are 'too analytical'. While being highly logical is valuable for decision making, it can be detrimental when we overdo it. As human beings, we find it difficult and awkward to judge options using multivariate analysis. Having to apply intricate measurements and weights to different attributes can jumble our choices and leave us confused. We end up suffering from 'analysis paralysis'.

Complex analytical measures can lead to 'analysis paralysis'

There are several cognitive studies, such as that conducted by researchers Daniel Kahneman, Paul Slovick, and Amos Tversky, which have established that intense analysis can actually hinder decision making.[8] In many situations, the quick emotional or 'gut' choice can prove to be far superior to the 'reasoned' choice. This tells us that it's usually not worth the time and effort going into in-depth numerical detail to compare one alternative to another. When you overanalyse it makes it difficult for your intuition to communicate with you so your evaluation process ends up missing a vital ingredient.

Even if an idea has the highest score of those available it might still not be the best one to adopt as there are always other factors to take into account that are difficult to quantify. In Chapter 5, I explained how we at ThinkBuzan would have discounted what turned out to be an excellent solution for improving the audio notes feature in the iMindMap software if we had focused purely on the numerical aspects of our analysis. We believe it's much more useful and accurate to get a broad sense of how your options fare against both your logical and intuitive thought processes, as we suggest in the 3S Analysis System.

This system overcomes the limitations associated with using weights and scores by bringing generative thinking into the evaluative process and by factoring in the value of emotion. And Mind Mapping your way through the system helps you go further in uncovering new connections and associations to furnish the analysis.[9] Using a Mind Map you can easily move backwards and forwards from one arena of discussion to another without losing focus, as the central theme draws you back to task every time.

8 Kahneman, Daniel, Slovic, Paul and Tversky Amos (1982), *Judgment under Certainty: Heuristics and Biases,* Cambridge University Press
9 Ones, Sue and Sims, David (1985), 'Mapping as an Aid to Creativity', *Journal of Management Development,* 4,1 pp. 47-60

3) SELECT

Now it's time for the final step, selecting the solution. If you've followed the 3S Analysis System correctly so far, it's likely that one or two particular alternatives will stand out more than others. Yes, this evaluation process involves some effort, but in the long run it saves time and money by helping to make sure that your resources aren't wasted on poor choices. If you're dealing with major issues such as strategic initiatives and changes, this effort is more than warranted.[10]

> "Two roads diverged in a wood, and I – I took the one less travelled by, and that has made all the difference."
>
> **Robert Frost, American Poet**

Pick the idea that you believe is the 'best' – the one that will be most valuable in *creatively* meeting the challenge you defined in Step 1 of the Solution Finder. If you've been working in a group, then a simple voting system should be enough for selecting the final solution.

Before you make a decision to implement that solution, however, verify that it's the correct one by asking yourself the following:

a) Will the solution achieve what you want?
In the end, the solution you choose has to 'pay off'. It has to have huge merit and originality in addressing the problem - it can't just be 'satisfactory'. This comes back to the crucial importance of the work you did in Step 1 of the Solution Finder to define the problem as a precursor to effective problem solving. In understanding your exact challenge, you're better able to determine whether the solution you pick will help you to successfully meet it head-on.

b) Is the solution in line with your ultimate goals and objectives (individual or organisational)?
Your final selection should be made in the context of your overall goals and objectives. For instance, will the solution contribute to a company objective of increased competitiveness and create a sufficient level of profit? It's important to bear in mind that the solution isn't going to exist in isolation - it will be part of a broader picture that includes goal setting and action planning at a more comprehensive level.

---

10 Caroselli, Marlene (1997), *That's No Problem! A Problem-Free Approach to Problem-Solving*, Coastal Training Technologies Corp

c) What are the possibilities it will fail and in what way?

Assess what could go wrong with the solution after it is implemented. What are the impacts of any changes that might result from the idea being put into action? Could it create more problems in the long run? Many times the solutions with the greatest potential can also bring the greatest risk. Try and work out the dangers of the solution failing and think seriously about whether you're willing to take on that amount of risk.

Your answers to these questions present a brief case for and against the solution which will help to validate why it was chosen above the others. If you've worked in a team to get to this point, you'll find that everyone involved in the process will feel a sense of ownership over the solution, having all contributed a good amount of mental energy to finding it!

———

To succeed in meeting your challenges creatively, you not only have to produce new ideas, you have to exploit them. This means being able to choose the best ones to bring to reality. In this chapter, I outlined an effective and straightforward method for idea evaluation which can be applied to broad areas of business life – the **3S Analysis System**. This method puts you in the right mental context to think constructively and harmonises your use of both logical and creative skills during analysis. It lets you see everything clearly from both a holistic and detailed perspective – the woods, the trees, even the birds. From this vantage point, you can easily kill off worthless ideas and leave the way clear for the best ideas to move forward.

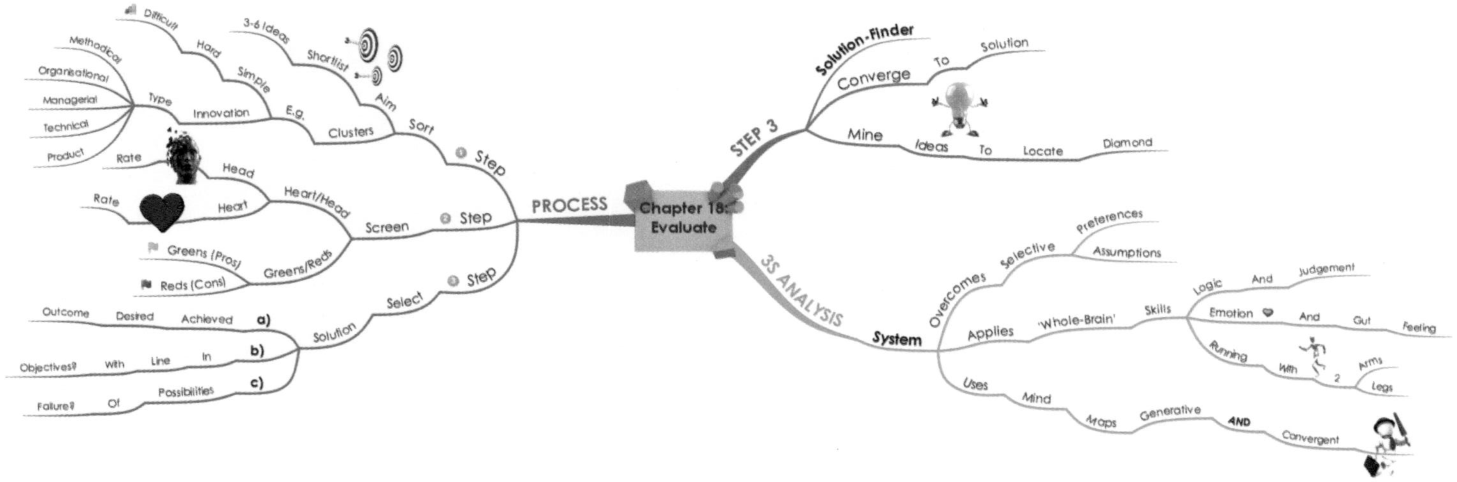

Chapter 18: Evaluate

STEP 3 — Solution-Finder
- Converge To Solution
- Mine Ideas To Locate Diamond

3S ANALYSIS — System
- Overcomes Selective preferences / Assumptions
- Applies Whole-Brain Skills
- Uses Mind Maps
- Generative AND Convergent
- Logic And Judgement
- Emotion And Gut Feeling
- Running With 2 — Arms / Legs

PROCESS

Step — Sort — Aim
- 3-6 Ideas
- Shortlist
- Hard
- Difficult
- Simple
- E.g. Innovation
- Type: Methodical / Organisational / Managerial / Technical / Product
- Clusters
- Rate

Step — Screen — Heart/Head
- Head
- Heart
- Rate
- Greens/Reds
- Greens (Proj)
- Reds (Cont)

Step — Select — Solution
- a) Outcome Desired Achieved
- b) Live In With Objectives?
- c) Possibilities Of Failure?

Chapter 18 Summary

STEP 4: THE SOLUTION

We've selected our solution, so what's next?

Now it's time to move into the action phase of the Solution Finder process and bring our chosen solution to life! In lots of businesses, the innovative process comes to a halt once the solution has been decided, and soon enough it's forgotten or fades away from neglect. It's important to avoid falling into this trap as it's a complete waste of your creative energy and leaves a bitter aftertaste of disappointment and disillusionment. Up to now, you've adopted a proactive focus with your thinking and this must end in proactive action if you're going to achieve the innovative results you want.

This final step of the Solution Finder is the real challenge of creative problem solving - converting your solution into reality. As the saying goes, "good ideas are a dime a dozen" but success or failure is in the execution. You have your 'good' idea, now it's time to take the results of the earlier analysis, strengthen the idea and drive it forward through goal setting and action planning. You have to make sure that the solution you worked so hard to come up with actually pays off for you and your company.

> *"You don't make progress by standing on the sidelines, whimpering and complaining. You make progress by implementing ideas."*
>
> **Shirley Hufstedler, American lawyer and former US Secretary of Education**

It's at this point that positive selective thinking comes into play to help you create the best possible chance for success – you imbue your solution with the belief, intention and commitment that will make it happen.

There are a number of activities involved in the implementation stage:

Developing the Solution - Looking at ways to strengthen, develop and refine the solution, transforming it from a 'good' idea into a powerful and workable solution.

Preparing for Action - Setting goals and planning effective ways to implement your chosen solution. This includes considering ways to build support and/or decrease or overcome resistance to the solution.

Taking Action - Launching your solution according to your plan.

Follow-up - Post-implementation evaluation of results and effectiveness. Have you achieved your target outcome?

For many people, the creative process of solving the problem is usually easier than the process of putting the solution to work. Although the first part requires several steps (define the problem, generate ideas, evaluate and select a solution) and the latter involves only one (implement the solution), the latter can be a lot tougher because it demands a heavy amount of change, motivation and commitment of time and energy.[1]

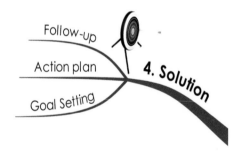

Step 4 of the Solution Finder

The launch stage is the culmination of all your earlier thinking, but it doesn't necessarily signal the end of thinking. Indeed, this entire step is about the thought processes involved in bringing your new idea into existence. Even post-launch, you need effective thinking to evaluate your decision. Did you get it right? Could you have gone about things differently, more quickly, perhaps at less cost to others?

Believe In Your Solution

Some people are hugely successful in accomplishing their goals while others fail to even get started. What is it that makes successful people so successful?

---

1 Caroselli, Marlene (1997), *That's No Problem! A Problem-Free Approach to Problem-Solving*, Coastal Training Technologies Corp

In chapter 6, we discussed how people who have achieved great things in life and business tend to display a common ingredient that contributes massively to their success – BELIEF. They believe they will succeed and they do. Belief is what gives high achievers such as Donald Trump and James Dyson the confidence to go out with their heads held high and strive for success. They are positive, focused and driven in how they approach their goals, tasks and challenges.

> *"As long as the mind can envision the fact that you can do something, you can do it – as long as you really believe 100 per cent."*

Arnold Schwarzenegger, Austrian born American actor and former governor of California

Belief is self-fulfilling. The pioneering psychologist, Albert Bandura, who developed the theory of self-efficacy,[2] observed that one of the reasons why effective and decisive people succeed in being that way is because they *believe* they are effective and decisive.[3] By the same token, if people think they are ineffective and indecisive, then sure enough that's what transpires. Our level of self-efficacy, of belief, equals our power to create our desires. So if we have total belief in our capabilities to do something, we set ourselves up to actually make it happen! This is the power of positive selective thinking. When we're confident in our decisions and abilities, we think, feel and behave in a way that contributes to and reinforces our success.[4]

> *"We find that people's beliefs about their efficacy affect the sorts of choices they make in very significant ways. In particular, it affects their levels of motivation and perseverance in the face of obstacles. Most success requires persistent effort, so low self-efficacy becomes a self-limiting process. In order to succeed, people need a sense of self-efficacy, strung together with resilience to meet the inevitable obstacles and inequities of life."*

Albert Bandura, Canadian psychologist

---

2 Bandura, A. (1977), 'Self-efficacy: Toward a unifying theory of behavioural change', *Psychological Review*, 84, pp. 191-215
3 Bandura, A. and Locke, E.A. (2003), 'Negative self-efficacy and goal effects revisited', Journal of Applied Psychology, 88 (1), pp. 87-99
4 MindTools, 'How Self-Confident Are You?: Improving Self-Confidence By Building Self-Efficacy', http://www.mindtools.com/pages/article/newTCS_84.htm

There's even more substantial evidence to support the theory of belief as a huge factor in determining human potential. For instance, in a large-scale experiment led by the prominent psychologist, Martin Seligman, a group of 15,000 optimists and pessimists were recruited to become insurance sales agents for the purpose of conducting a comparison of their performance.[5] By the end of the second year of the experiment, the optimists had outsold the pessimists by 57 per cent - a significant percentage. While the optimists would persevere to push for as many sales as possible in this difficult and challenging job, the pessimists would usually give up prematurely, causing them to perform much worse overall.

"Commitment unlocks the doors of imagination, allows vision, and gives us the 'right stuff' to turn our dreams into reality."

James Womack, Founder and Senior Advisor of Lean Enterprise Institute

Once you form a decision on which solution to implement, you make a commitment of your personal time and energy. If you've performed all the steps of the Solution Finder correctly, you can have total trust and confidence that you've chosen the correct way forward. Up to this point, you've applied the optimal thinking formula - you've followed a productive process which prompted you to use the appropriate thinking modes at each step so that your thinking has been balanced and objective instead of overly selective, analytical or reactive. Now it's time to put the solution into effect. This is most successfully achieved if you feel passionate about it and have the drive to turn vision into action. Selective thinking is therefore the mode of thinking needed for doing. When you truly believe in your solution, you possess the motivation, conviction and determination you need to strengthen your solution, put together your goals, prepare an effective plan and complete all the action steps necessary for its successful implementation.

"The greatest mistake you can make in life is to be continually fearing you will make one."

Elbert Hubbard, American editor, publisher and writer

---

5 Seligman, M. and Schulman, P. (1986), 'Explanatory style as a predictor of performance as a life insurance agent', *Journal of Personality and Social Psychology*, 50, pp. 832-838

Positive selective belief is instrumental to successful implementation

In brief, the point I've been making up to now is that you create your own success by using positive intention and thinking. When you're confident in your solution and abilities, you can recover quickly from any setbacks or disappointments and persevere in the face of obstacles. People with a low level of belief can be quick to lose confidence in their personal skills and focus on negative outcomes.[6] They close the door to success. Those with high levels of belief aren't afraid to face new things because of the possibility of failure. This notion takes us back to the importance of having an internal rather than external focus (see Chapter 4). An internal focus helps us put in the mental and physical effort to create our external events i.e. to carry out our plan of action, rather than allowing outside circumstances to dictate our progress. We decide what we ought to do and how we ought to do it. In short, we're proactive rather than reactive in our selectivity.

> *"Discipline is the bridge between goals and accomplishments."*
>
> **Jim Rohn, American author and motivational speaker**

Build Up Your Solution

Before getting stuck into any goal setting or planning, you need to strengthen and hone your idea. Your solution may well be a good one but the chances are it will need some crafting and refining before you can use it successfully. There are some instances where the solution arrives at this point in a complete and finished form, but this is usually the exception not the rule.

---

6 Bandura, A. (1994), 'Self-efficacy'. In V.S Ramachaudran (Ed.), *Encyclopedia of Human Behavior*, Vol 4, pp.71-81, New York: Academic Press

In most cases the idea is not yet mature. It's in a budding state and needs the right treatment to help it grow and develop into a robust and workable solution. Your selective thinking is a powerful instrument during this process, compelling you to develop, adapt or change the solution so that it becomes the best it can be, i.e. it becomes 'killer'. Rather than accepting the idea as it is, you ask yourself "How can I make it better?"

This is a crucial exercise for situations where you need to influence people as it provides you with the back-up information you need to gain maximum acceptance for your idea and enthuse others. Later on, you might well find that you have to 'sell' the solution to the people whose approval you require or who will be involved in the actual implementation.

It's best to approach this task in a generative way. Using a divergent tool like Mind Mapping will help you generate lots of ideas for reinforcing and strengthening your solution from multiple angles. Building on the work you did in the analysis (Step 3 of the Solution Finder), ask yourself how you might alter or change the idea to erase any of its 'reds'. And consider how you can build on any of its 'greens'. Also, rethink your idea against your problem and objectives to find more ways of developing it into something truly excellent.

Build up your idea before implementation

It's a good idea at this stage to anticipate any reluctance that other people will have to your proposed solution. You can then garner data to prove its worth and build a case for approval. Consider all the people, places and things that will be impacted by the solution and take them into account while developing it. When your points are structured in a Mind Map, you'll be able to clearly see and understand how everything relates. Use the following pointers to help you:

Boosters – Review the 'greens' (positive attributes) you mapped out in Step 3 of the Solution Finder and examine ways in which each one might be strengthened, emphasised or improved. Is there something you can add to the solution? Can you scale it up? Make it more solid? More cost-effective? Longer-lasting? Are there any other ideas you generated in Step 2 of the Solution Finder that might slot into this idea nicely or extend its impact? Is there anything else the idea might allow you to accomplish? For instance, if your solution to boosting attendance at your seminars and workshops is to 'improve marketing', perhaps there's a possibility of branding your approach to make it more attractive to your target market.

Fixers – Review your 'reds' (negative attributes). Map out all the ways in which each of them might be addressed. How might you overcome your idea's shortcomings and eradicate its flaws? How might you counter other people's concerns about it? Don't be satisfied with simply filling in the holes and patching the cracks. Go further and convert some of the objections into positives. For instance, if your solution involves introducing a new management approach into your organisation, think of how stakeholders might challenge the proposed change initiatives. Then prepare your idea by considering ways to make it better for the company, for employees, for customers etc.

> *"Take care that the honey does not remain in the same state as when you gathered it: bees would have no credit unless they transformed it into something different and better."*
>
> **Francesco Petrarch, Italian poet**

This activity is excellent for arousing your enthusiasm, motivation and faith to follow through on the idea, as well as that of others who'll be involved in its implementation. While refining your idea powers it up with greater strength, flexibility and practicality, try not to overthink and overdevelop it. Keeping it simple makes this an energising, not arduous process.

Next, you'll crystallise your built-up solution into your goals and create a coherent action plan to execute it successfully.

Set Out Your Goal

Good selective thinking is goal-directed. Every achievement of any nature or scale is always preceded by a goal. Before Einstein discovered the theory of relativity he set the goal to look for it; and before a great artist creates a masterpiece, they set the goal in their mind to do so.[7]

So, if you want to make your idea happen you need to first project forward into the future and look at desired results.

Goal setting is a powerful way to envision the success of your solution. The act of establishing your target gives you the initial inspiration to begin your implementation journey. And while on your journey, your goal provides a constant reference to your ideal outcome, keeping you motivated to make it a reality.

> *"Nothing can add more power to your life than concentrating all your energies on a limited set of targets."*
>
> **Nido Qubein, Motivational speaker and President of High Point University**

There are lots of strategies for goal setting and you should use whatever works for you. The following technique is one that we've found to be particularly effective in our organisation for helping us meet new challenges and problems. Using a Mind Map, create a well-formed outcome by specifying:

1) Target - Your target outcome/goal. What exactly do you want the solution to achieve? Where do you want to be at the end of the process or journey? As Edward de Bono points out, your target may be far or near, wide or narrow. It follows, therefore, that if a target is both wide and near then success is more easily assured.[8] When designing your target, make sure that it's actually achievable and not unrealistic.

2) Now - Where are you now in relation to your goal? What are your current circumstances? For instance, if your goal is to improve customer satisfaction to a certain percentage, what's the current level of customer satisfaction?

---

7 Mayne, Brian (2006), *Goal Mapping: The Practical Workbook*, Watkins Publishing
8 de Bono, Edward (1982), *Thinking Course*, BBC

3) When - By when, precisely, do you want to have achieved your target? Personal development guru Anthony Robbins defines a goal as a 'dream with a deadline'. It's important to state the date by which you want to achieve the goal to give your task urgency and galvanise you into action. Without a deadline, it becomes easier to procrastinate and allow your goal to fall by the wayside.

4) How - A summary of how you propose to get there. This is a broad strategy; your detailed action plan comes later. An example? If your goal is to design a new product, your broad strategy may be to focus on reliability and performance rather than style and showy features.

5) Next - What will be your next step? Considering the next logical action for your project is a powerful thought process advocated by David Allen, author of *Getting Things Done*.[9] He says, "For any outcome that we have an internal commitment to complete, we must make the decision about the next physical action required." This activity brings an automatic increase in energy, productivity, clarity and focus.

Laying out these factors in Mind Map form provides a powerful physical record of your goals, one which is visual, concise, structured and memorable.

"*A goal properly set is halfway reached.*"

Zig Ziglar, American author, salesman and motivational speaker

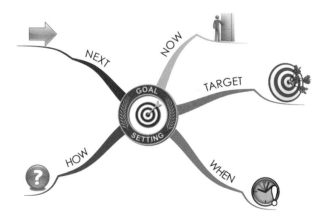

A Goal Setting Mind Map

9 Allen, David (2001), *Getting Things Done: The Art of Stress-Free Productivity*, Penguin.

It's important to come out of goal setting with a clear and concise synopsis of what you want to accomplish and how you propose to do it. This has to be stated in a way that you can actually measure. For example, if one of your personal goals is to achieve excellent physical health, how will you know when you've reached it? Perhaps you might see yourself as being in excellent physical health when you can run two miles in ten minutes, do 100 sit ups or maintain your ideal weight for three months.[10]

A secondary benefit of constructive goal setting is that it not only acts to channel *your* attention on the task, but also that of *others* who will be involved in making it happen. Everyone will be focusing on the same objectives and desired results, and will be better placed to select appropriate tactics to accomplish them.

> *"Define your business goals clearly so that others can see them as you do."*
>
> **George F. Burns, American comedian**

Goal setting alone isn't enough to ensure successful implementation of your solution. Actions must be taken and tactical decisions made to get you there step-by-step. Often we get so fixated on the eventual outcome that we forget to plan all the steps that are needed along the way. This puts us at the mercy of external forces. It also leaves us wide open for the critical aspect of ourselves to take hold - "I'm never going to get this done on time", "This target is impossible" etc.[11]

Once we've set our goals, we need an action plan that helps to focus our attention on the process of implementation i.e. the steps we need to take to get there. As we complete each one and cross it off, we realise that we're making progress towards our ultimate goal. This helps to reinforce our belief in what we're doing. By concentrating on what we can do proactively, we maintain the faith that each step is leading us in the right direction. This is especially important if our goal is really demanding or long-term.

Prepare for Action

Once you've set out your goal or target outcome, it's time to prepare for action! How do you make sure that you cover everything needed to launch

---

10 Wheeler, Jim (1998), *The Power of Innovative Thinking: Let New Ideas Lead You to Success,* Career Press
11 Mind Gym (2005), *The Mind Gym: Wake Your Mind Up,* Sphere

your solution?...You create an action plan.

Action plans are simple schedules of all the tasks you need to complete to meet your goal. They're incredibly useful because they give you a framework for thinking about what's to be done, where, by when and by whom. They enable you to start your implementation journey with adequate instructions, prevent you getting lost or confused and help you persevere in delivering the work needed. Implementing your solution without an action plan is like writing a book without a pre-determined outline for the story. While it can be done, the process will undoubtedly be more of a struggle and could take much longer. Having an outline helps drive the story (launch) and prevents you having to go back and rework different sections.[12]

Draw up an Action Plan to help you execute your solution

Your action plan doesn't have to be intricate and exhaustive, just organised. The idea is that it gives you the opportunity to figure out what you need to do to succeed. Like a map, a plan can never be entirely accurate and is unlikely to foresee all eventualities, but it can help you understand the territory you'll be entering a lot better.

If you involve other people in your planning, you set the groundwork for garnering support for your solution. You allow other people the chance to 'buy in' to the project and claim some ownership over it. In doing this, you gain their commitment in helping you actualise your solution.

"Great things are not done by impulse, but by a series of small things brought together."

Vincent Van Gogh, Dutch post-Impressionist painter

---

12 Adair, John (2009), *The Art of Creative Thinking: How to be Innovative and Develop Great Ideas*, Kogan Page

As with goal setting, you can use a Mind Map to draw up your action plan using the following process:

1) Identify Tasks

Map out all of the tasks you need to complete to achieve your target. It's helpful to start at the beginning and work through your tasks step-by-step. What's the very first action you'll need to take? Once that task is complete, what comes next? Highlight those steps that you feel are most important to the objective and attach numerical rankings so you can clearly see the order in which you need to complete each task.

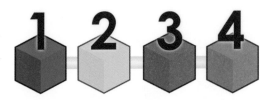

Identify the step-by-step tasks you need to complete

The divergent structure of the Mind Map helps you generate as many action steps as you possibly can – without judging and without censoring. You can then use convergent analytical thinking to make sense of all the possible action steps and decide which ones are needed. Some tasks will be dependent on others and some will be stand-alone actions. Group the action steps that relate to one another together for greater clarity. You'll find that the Mind Map helps you get a sense of both the whole and its parts so you can fully comprehend the bigger project before you.

2) Allocate Resources

Now that you can see all your tasks clearly, examine them in greater detail. What resources will you need in terms of people, money, facilities, time and expertise to do what needs to be done? Use the following pointers to check that you cover everything adequately:

Money – What financial resources will you need to complete all your action steps? Is the money available now? If not, how can you acquire the funds you need? Your response to this might imply additional action steps for your plan.

Time – Add timescales for each of your action steps. This will help you measure progress later on. The Mind Map structure is invaluable here as you can easily pinpoint which tasks might have to be shuffled around to accommodate others that must be accomplished beforehand. If you don't have sufficient time for certain tasks, consider how you might be able to borrow it from other activities.

People – Are there enough people available to make the plan happen? Whose support and contribution can you rely on? Make sure all your tasks are allocated to the right people. A task that's left unassigned can very easily be left undone. People can help you in different ways - some may contribute their time, knowledge, money or influence, others their moral support. Once you've defined who these people are, ask yourself how you might engage them even more. Does this suggest additional action steps for your plan?

Equipment – Do you have the necessary equipment, systems and facilities to work on and achieve the plan? If you have the material resources you need, include them on your Mind Map. If not, map out how you'll go about acquiring them.

Skills – Do you, your co-workers or employees have the necessary knowledge and training to accomplish each action step? How much training will you and others need? If you have to acquire more expertise or knowledge, map out how you'll get it .

This exercise helps you decide wisely and accurately how you'll align resources and assign responsibilities for the tasks you identified. For smaller projects, you may not need to think about all of these factors. For instance, if you're working on a small internal project to create a departmental database, you might only have to consider 'People', 'Skills' and 'Equipment'. For larger, more complex projects, you could find it helpful to use formal project management techniques and tools such as Gantt Charts to manage all your data.

Having considered everything you require, you now have a platform for action.

"Mind Maps have made it easier to manage goals, create action plans and enhance our planning abilities."

The Sports Managers College, operated by the Japan Football Association

3) Communicate the Plan

Using your Mind Map, communicate the plan to those who'll be involved in approving it or getting it off the ground. Outline the merits of the plan, what resources it will require and who'll be affected by it, whether customers, employees or stakeholders of some other kind.

New plans aren't always accepted automatically; most of the time they're resisted. This resistance has lots of sources such as fear of the unknown, lack of information, threats to status, fear of failure and lack of perceived benefits.[13] As psychologist, Kurt Lewin, suggests in his theory of change management, people must be introduced to change before change is introduced.[14] Good communication is vital for getting people to accept the need for the new solution and to bring about successful change. To increase the likelihood of full support for your proposal, it's necessary to communicate the following:

The Problem – Use the output of Step 1 of the Solution Finder to create an awareness of the problem or challenge and make people recognise that there's a need for a solution.

The Solution – Stress the benefits of the idea to the individuals involved using the WIFM factor i.e. 'What's in it for me?' People will only be motivated to accept and adopt the plan of action when they perceive that it's in their best interests to do so.

4) Implement The Plan!

Finally, after all the thinking and preparation comes action. This is the point where you launch the idea for real. Referring back to our earlier personal example, let's say some of the activities you came up with to achieve excellent health included going on a diet, beginning an exercise programme and setting up a support system. This is now the stage where you begin these activities in the order dictated by your action plan. If you're implementing a large-scale solution or change, I would suggest looking into change management skills and techniques to ensure it all goes smoothly.

A key aspect of this implementation stage is the gathering of data (quantitative or qualitative) to help you gauge the effectiveness of your solution. Checking this data as you go along allows you to monitor,

---

13 Lawrence, P.R. and Greiner, L.R. (1970), 'How to deal with resistance to change', in Lawrence, P.R and Greiner, L.R. (eds), *Organisational Change and Development,* Homewood: Irwin

14 Lewin, K. (1958), 'Group Decisions and Social Change', in G.E. Swanson, T. M.Newcomb and E.L. Hartley (eds), *Readings in Social Psychology*, Holt, Rhinehart and Winston: New York

manage and modify your activities to keep you moving in the right direction.

> *"In theory there's no difference between theory and practice. In practice there is."*
>
> **Yogi Berra, Former American Major League baseball player**

Make Sure You Follow Up

Successful innovation thrives on feedback – we set our targets, put our plans into action, track our results and then take advantage of the lessons learned. The 'follow-up' is a critical element of problem solving – ignoring it defeats the entire purpose of going through the creative problem solving process in the first place! At the end of it all, you have to be able to determine whether your idea has been successful in achieving what you wanted.

As part of your follow-up, you need to evaluate both the effectiveness of the implementation plan and the effectiveness of the solution.

1) The Plan

Was the plan carried out according to schedule? If the plan wasn't followed as expected then consider: Was the plan realistic? Were there sufficient resources to accomplish the plan? Were there any aspects that were overlooked? Did any major errors occur? Were people resistant to it? Where did you waste time?

If you think you'll be trying to achieve a similar goal again, determine which steps were successful and maintain these elements as part of your revised implementation. Then modify all the things that you could have done better, for instance, allow more time for certain tasks or obtain extra funds for particular elements of the plan.

2) The Solution

How you track the effectiveness of your solution depends upon the type of solution you're implementing. Some solutions are based on numerical factors and involve comparing changes in quantities, for instance, the frequency of faulty products, complaints/errors before and after the solution is implemented. In such cases, you can take a quantitative approach to your evaluation by collecting statistics and other mathematical information to evaluate your results. Other solutions involve changes in people's attitudes, opinions, satisfaction or morale and these require a more qualitative approach. For example, we can solicit feedback from the people affected by the solution through various methods such as surveys or focus groups. Their responses will give us a sense of how successful they believe the solution is.

Track Progress and Assess Results

Once all the data is in and you have an overall picture of your results, you can then make a decision as to whether the solution should be continued, modified or abandoned altogether. If the solution was generally effective but didn't entirely meet your expectations, are there ways that you can fine-tune it to increase its feasibility in future? Adjustments could include changing dimensions (making something longer, shorter, thicker etc); changing aspects of time or distance; or adding, subtracting, or combining different items.[15]

If the solution was a disaster, you can safely reject it knowing that you went through the appropriate processes to get to this point. Try not to be too disappointed. For innovation to thrive you need to acknowledge that you won't always win them all and get rid of any fears of failure. The important thing is that you take a chance on the ideas you believe in. It's well known that many top business people believe that risk taking should be celebrated, not punished. For instance, former Time Warner chairman, Steve Ross, actually said that people who didn't make enough mistakes shouldn't be rewarded for not screwing up, they should be fired for not taking enough risks![16] If your idea didn't pan out the way you wanted I recommend that you work through the Solution Finder again from the beginning, this time taking into account the lessons learned from this failed attempt. You'll find that these lessons provide valuable pointers to future success.

15 Caroselli, Marlene (1997), *That's No Problem! A Problem-Free Approach to Problem-Solving,* Coastal Training Technologies Corp
16 Stewart, D. and Simmons, M. (2010), *The Business Playground: Where Creativity and Commerce Collide,* Financial Times / Prentice Hall

What if your solution was a huge triumph? In this instance, the next step is to extend that success. You can now move forward to institute the solution wholeheartedly. For example, if the solution was found to work well in a given setting, you can roll it out to other settings, departments, divisions or organisations.

It's a good idea to prepare a short presentation or write a brief report that highlights the success of the problem solving effort and what you learned as a result. You can then share this with your bosses, colleagues and subordinates. It's also important to recognise and reward the key champions and supporters of the innovation. Rewards build motivation and commitment to the solution and encourage others to follow the example.

Innovation can be a complex and time-consuming process. If it's going to be executed successfully, it needs to be organised and managed well. This final step of the Solution Finder is absolutely essential to the innovative process because it involves transforming your creative thinking into creative action. You've been proactive in your thought processes, now it's time to be proactive in your behaviour. Here's a reminder of how to launch your winning solution:

1) Passionately believe in your idea (selective thinking).

2) Strengthen your solution to make it as robust as possible.

3) Set a target outcome or goal.

4) Put together an effective action plan for implementation.

5) Communicate your intentions in a way that builds acceptance and motivation.

6) Execute your solution according to the plan.

7) Follow up on your implementation, making adjustments where necessary.

The fundamental element of this final stage is proactive *planning*. It's by having goals and an action plan behind us that we can move forward confidently, exert the effort necessary to meet task demands and keep persisting, even if we encounter obstacles or adversity. Thus the value of planning is that it makes us better at doing. When you first start working with this approach, it will probably take you longer than more traditional reactive thinking and will involve a good deal more effort (mental and physical). The results, however, will be well worth the extra investment in time and energy. It doesn't completely remove or replace reactive thinking, but it guarantees that all your responses and day-to-day actions will now be in line with your ultimate goal. As you know exactly where you're going, you can click into that wonderful brain activation state known as 'flow' and completely immerse yourself in getting there. Sure enough, success will soon rise into view.

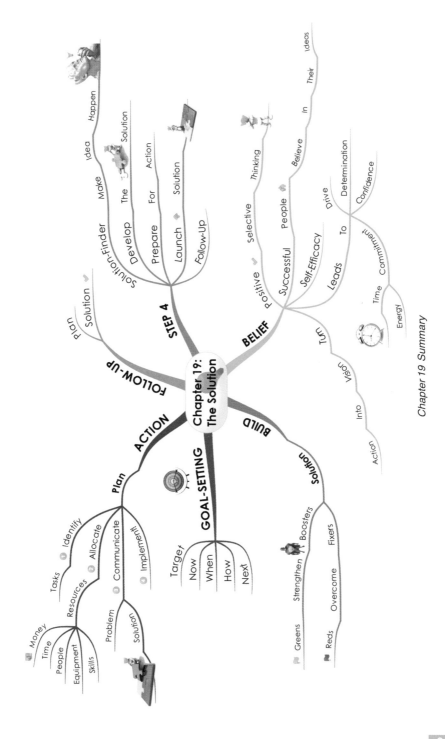

Chapter 19 Summary

IMPLEMENTING THE GTS SYSTEM

Congratulations on reaching the end of this book. I hope you found it to be useful, worthwhile and enjoyable. In particular, I hope that you picked up a few key themes and applications to help you let go of the old and 'grasp' a bright and innovative future.

The next step, however, is the real challenge. It's putting the theory into practice. No book, concept or system can do this for you. It's up to you to determine whether the information you've discovered in these pages can be truly beneficial to your career or business. Whatever you do, don't procrastinate. As you well know, the world is changing. And it's changing at an alarming pace. The development of technology and proliferation of information have been potent factors in bringing forward a more complex, competitive and global culture. But they're no longer factors on which you can depend for success, or even survival!

> *"Creativeness and a creative attitude to life as a whole is not man's right, it is his duty."*
>
> **Nikolai Berdyaev, Russian religious philosopher**

To survive and thrive in today's fluctuating climate you must be able to adapt and evolve. To do this you need the kind of thinking that leads to new opportunities and breakthrough results. The kind of thinking that will help you break away from old habits, expand your vision, perform regular tasks better, question established concepts and meet new challenges.[1] In short, you need **CREATIVITY** and **INNOVATION**.

---

1 Treffinger, Donald J., Isaksen, Scott G. and Dorval, Brian K. (2000), *Creative Problem Solving: An Introduction,* Prufrock Press

The Dawn of a New Age

In chapter 1, we witnessed how the workforce is evolving to encompass a new creative class. We're moving from a knowledge economy in which information was 'king' to a new age - an age which Daniel Pink, author of *A Whole New Mind: Why Right-brainers Will Rule the Future*, has labelled 'The Conceptual Age'.[2] Success no longer depends on what you know, but what you can create. Today's computers can replicate all sorts of logical and information processing tasks, but they can't reproduce the imaginative thought processes of the human brain. Information and logic is cheap, creativity is priceless!

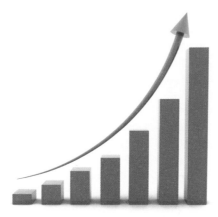

Innovation has a huge impact on long-term success

The leaders of the future know that innovation and creative thinking are mandatory in the new economy. They've gone from being 'desirable' competencies to 'essential' ones. Without a constant flow of killer ideas and solutions our career or business is condemned to the backwaters. Others will progress, while we remain at a standstill. A landmark study by Harvard Business School Professors, John Kotter and James Heskett, validates this point.[3]

Over an 11-year period, they found that the net income for firms with an adaptive, innovation focused culture increased by 756% compared to 1% for those who had not developed a philosophy of thinking creatively. This demonstrates that an innovation focus has a tremendously huge impact on a firm's long-term sustainability and strategic success.

---

2 Pink, Daniel, H. (2008), *A Whole New Mind: Why Right-Brainers Will Rule The Future*, Marshall Cavendish
3 Kotter, J.P. and Heskett, J.L. (1992), *Corporate Culture and Performance*, New York: Free Press

"Paradoxically, the ability to forget the old answers, to unlearn the old ways becomes a decisive factor for success in a business environment which is changing at the speed of light."

Jonas Ridderstrale, Co-author of 'Funky Business'

The approach in this book is about generating the new and different, not rehashing the old. This is something that most people struggle with. Normal reactive thinking has us repeating the past: doing what we've done before in ways that we've used before. Very few of us actually stop to think about what's driving our lives and our thinking. We take it for granted and go through life on autopilot. Most of the time this is fine as it helps us quickly get through our daily tasks. But today we're being thrown new problems and tasks for which there are no routine answers and acting on our default responses can be foolishly dangerous. Innovation requires conscious direction and momentum – our thoughts need to lead events, not follow them! It demands that we be **proactive.**

The principle force of the **Grasp the Solution (GTS) System** is proactive – it forces you to question your habitual ways of thinking and doing, and to look more deeply at how you can bring about positive change. Quite simply, it gives you the principles and tools you need to create the future. The first part of the system involves understanding how you think so you can free yourself from the wasteful and unproductive thinking patterns that limit you **(GRASP)**. The second is about applying the right strategy to unleash your potential to think more effectively and creatively for what you need to achieve **(Solution Finder)**.

We Can All Be Creative

Each of us came into the world with outstanding raw material – a relentlessly active brain. And we can all harness it in the right ways to become more creatively productive in how we solve problems and make decisions. While it might seem that creativity is a special talent or 'gift' bestowed on the few, it's actually a skill. And like any skill, such as chess or athletic ability, it can be developed. We can all be creative; it's just that the majority of us haven't learned how. Throughout our lives we've been taught or encouraged to use logic, reason, analysis and calculation in solving problems and making decisions, but very few of us have been shown how to apply the limitless, creative power of the 'whole' of our brain.

> *"Thinking is a skill, it can be developed and improved if one knows how."*
>
> **Edward de Bono, Author, consultant and inventor of 'lateral thinking'**

In reading this book, you've taken a proactive step towards tapping into the creative functionality of your mind. You've discovered that creativity isn't a faddy or elusive concept, as some would think. And you've become aware that there's a strong need for a purposeful approach to encourage and enhance creativity actively. Without such an approach, creativity will either depend on the best you happen to come up with at the time, or it will be left to those individuals who display a 'rare' talent for it.

Anyone can be creative using the right systems and techniques

When you provide structures, processes and systematic techniques, you dramatically increase people's potential to think creatively so that it becomes a regular, everyday prospect. And the more you apply these processes and techniques, the better you get. Remember what we said about 'purposeful practice'. No skill can be developed to a peak level without consistent strengthening and replication. After reaching a certain level of performance, an athlete, or chess player, even an artist, has to practice just to maintain their existing standards, let alone get better.

What this means is that creativity and innovation require a great deal more than a token gesture, they require deliberate reinforcement. Anytime you need to define a problem, identify new possibilities, evaluate potential alternatives, or find that brilliant new idea, make sure you apply the principles and processes of the GTS System. They will encourage the release of your creative energies and place you in a more productive state for whatever you're hoping to do or achieve.

It's Common Sense

The content of this book is probably not news to you. My intent in writing it was not to hammer you with a radical new theory on how to be more successful. Rather, it was to validate much of what is already known about thinking and problem solving and to define a useful methodology to help people make best use of it. It's nothing more than 'common sense'.

I believe the real value of this book is that it will make it much easier for you to apply this knowledge systematically in a world that's becoming ever more complex and fast-paced. It may be modestly sized but this book gives you the essential components – the key values, concepts and systems – to operate more innovatively and productively.

> *"The three great essentials to achieve anything worthwhile are, first, hard work; second, stick-to-itiveness; third, common sense."*
>
> **Thomas Alva Edison, American inventor**

To be innovative we need to solve problems and make decisions, and in order to do this well we need to be able to think clearly and use information objectively. It's virtually impossible to make the 'perfect' decision but there are ways and means to increase your chances of finding the best possible solution or course of action. The GTS System is one of many approaches you can use, but it's a good one. Its whole purpose is to help you think better – to think more powerfully, productively and creatively while solving problems and making decisions. It's not a magic formula – it won't miraculously give you all the answers, but it will certainly be useful in pointing you in the right direction.

Here are just a few reasons why the GTS System makes sense:

It's Powerful
The GTS System can be applied in lots of domains and integrated into any number of activities. For instance, it can be used to solve complex business matters, propose new products, develop technical solutions, create organisational strategies, resolve conflicts, improve relationships, decide on marketing activities, reduce operational deficiencies and sort out personal difficulties. It works across all organisational departments and industry fields, and is helpful for private issues. In a nutshell, it provides a thinking structure that can stimulate important and lasting changes in any area of your life or business.

It's Supported
The GTS system links the modes of thinking with well-established problem solving processes and creativity techniques. The main themes and components of the system are all backed by scientific and psychological research, and all creativity tools have previously been verified (scientifically and/or anecdotally) in their effectiveness and impact.

It's Easy to Use
It's an easy-to-learn system that can be readily applied by individuals and groups. It's not absolute – it doesn't embrace every aspect of reality, only those that are relevant or useful for creative thinking. It can, however, be used flexibly and adapted to your own needs and circumstances.

It's Focused
The GTS System helps you focus your thinking constructively to release your creative talent. It reduces the complexity of a situation by providing an attention-directing process that will keep you aligned with your task and, at the same time, damp down any distractions.

Please note that the GTS system isn't meant to be a prescription, but more of a framework to help guide you. You don't have to work through the steps of the Solution Finder in painstaking detail every time you need new ideas to address challenges or opportunities. Not all challenges require radically new ideas. There are many circumstances in which conventional, reactive thinking is fine to give you a quick fix or ready-made solution. In other situations, you might want to skip most steps of the Solution Finder and just take advantage of a couple of generative thinking tools to find a satisfactory solution.

The Solution Finder process in its entirety is most helpful when you're looking to identify and solve challenges that are important to you and can be best fulfilled by original and imaginative solutions. For example, it's great to use when you want to attract more customers or empower staff to take on more responsibility. It's up to you to determine whether your particular challenge will benefit by going through the Solution Finder or part of it, or whether an existing solution will do a good enough job.

A Quick Recap –
GRASP and The Solution Finder

Before I leave you to get on with things, here's a brief reminder of the two core components of the **Grasp The Solution (GTS) System:**

1) **GRASP** – an acronym for the different modes of thinking. It stands for:

- **Generative** – Generating thoughts and ideas
- **Reactive** – Reacting to existing influences and ideas
- **Analytical** – Analysing ideas to reach a solution
- **Selective** – Validating and implementing a potential solution
- **Proactive** – The strategy of thinking (encompassing all of the above)

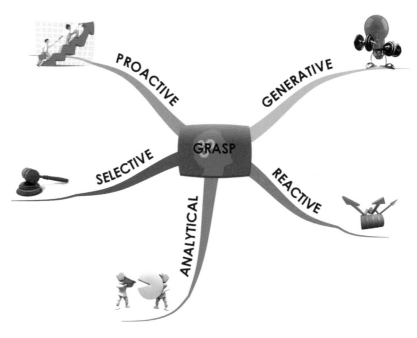

GRASP Thinking Modes

2) **The Solution Finder** – a four-step process for solving problems and making decisions creatively:

1) **Define** the problem.
2) **Generate** lots of ideas to potentially solve the problem.
3) **Evaluate** your ideas and select a solution.
4) **Solution** – build your solution, create your plan and put it into action!

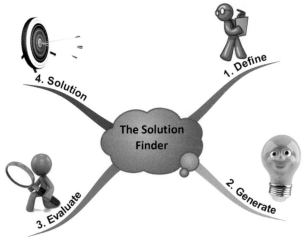

The Solution Finder

GRASP is what puts a context around your thinking. It helps you understand your modes of thought so you can draw on the correct ones for the tasks you want to perform. The Solution Finder is an application of GRASP – it allows you to create a strategy around your thinking. You can take a holistic view of your situation and make use of the appropriate processes and tools to achieve your desired outcomes.

If you take the analogy of your mind as a computer, GRASP is the hardware and the Solution Finder is the software. It's by understanding the hardware that you can design and utilise the appropriate software to operate your computer optimally. The key values that I hope you take away from this book relate to the following two modes of thinking:

1) Proactive Thinking

This is the highest order of thinking (metacognition) and is concerned with putting a strategy around our thinking. Applying a strategy is key to overcoming our natural, reactive tendencies. The normal reactive mode of thinking is useful and necessary for running an organisation and dealing with routine tasks on a day-to-day basis. But if we rely on it all the time, we make it difficult to initiate any real change or innovation. We end up doing the same things and get trapped in old habits and patterns. When we think proactively we give ourselves the time, and set ourselves up with the systems to be more creatively productive in how we make decisions. And to be proactively innovative, we must always define our problem first. Exploring the problem and building a solid understanding of it seriously raises our chances of coming up with the right solutions. While we can skimp on other aspects of the Solution Finder, this stage is the most valuable in setting the scene for creative problem solving and is always worth spending time on.

2) Generative Thinking

In applying a strategy to our thinking, we must aim to be heavily generative in the approach we take and tools we use. Why? Most of us aren't predisposed to be generative when we're solving problems; most of the time we'll be analytical or selective. But generative thinking is a potent force for unleashing our creative energies. It's where those first-rate ideas come from. And it's what helps us imaginatively convert those great ideas into sound solutions which we can actually implement. For this reason the GTS System embraces tactics to help us use our generative thought processes to full advantage.

This is a book to help anyone be more creatively productive, regardless of IQ, training or background. Its aim is to increase your chances of finding, developing and implementing novel solutions via a systematic approach to problem solving – the GTS System. Like I said earlier, this system isn't a magic formula – it won't always help you find the 'perfect' answer, but it will help you find the best answer you possibly can.

Off You Go!

The hardest part of thinking is getting started. The beauty of the GTS system is that it not only helps you get started, it gives you the focus and direction to finish. And the tools to do it time and time again. After working through the system, you'll be a million times more empowered to be innovative – you'll have defined your challenge, generated ideas using a range of techniques and applied whole brain analysis to find your winning idea. Now you can be 100 per cent confident that you're heading in the right direction.

"What you can do, or dream you can do, begin it; Boldness has genius, power and magic in it."

Johann Wolfgang von Goethe, German playwright, poet and novelist

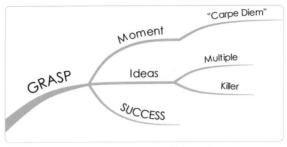

Grasp a successful future!

There are no excuses. It's up to you and you alone to realise more of your creative potential and make your world what you want it to be. People don't get to be successful with boring, run-of-the-mill ideas and solutions. But they do with killer ones. Only by being proactive and thinking about your thinking do you set up the right conditions to achieve real success through innovation.

So make a start now, and enjoy the process.

Chris Griffiths

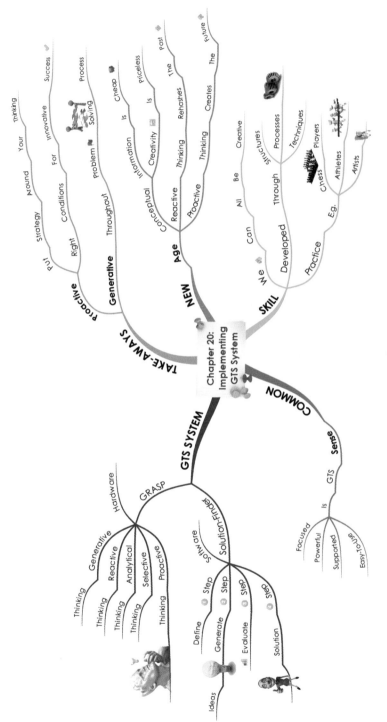

Chapter 20 Summary

BIBLIOGRAPHY

Ackoff, Russell L. (1978), *The Art of Problem Solving,* John Wiley & Sons

Adair, John (2007), *Decision Making and Problem Solving Strategies*, The Sunday Times, Kogan Page

Adair, John (2009), *The Art of Creative Thinking: How to be Innovative and Develop Great Ideas*, Kogan Page

Allen, David (2001), *Getting Things Done: The Art of Stress-Free Productivity,* Penguin

Borg, James (2010), *Mind Power*, Prentice Hall Life

Butler, Gillian and Hope, Tony (2007), *Manage your Mind: The Mental Fitness Guide*, 2nd Edition, Oxford University Press

Buzan, Tony (2000), *Head First! You're Smarter than you Think*, Thorsons

Buzan, Tony (2004), *Mind Maps At Work*, Thorsons

Buzan, Tony and Buzan, Barry (1994), *The Mind Map Book: How to Use Radiant Thinking to Maximize Your Brain's Untapped Potential,* New York: Dutton.

Buzan, Tony and Griffiths, Chris (2010), *Mind Maps for Business*, BBC Active

Carr, Clay (1994), *The Competitive Power of Constant Creativity,* AMACOM, New York

de Bono, Edward (1990), *Lateral Thinking: A Textbook of Creativity,* Penguin de Bono, Edward (2009), *Think! Before It's Too Late*, Ebury Publishing

de Bono, Edward (1982), *Thinking Course*, BBC

Foerster, Anja and Kreuz, Peter (2007), *Different Thinking: Creative Strategies For Developing the Innovative Business*, Kogan Page

Forman, Ernest and Selly, Mary Ann (2001), *Decision by Objectives (How to convince others that you are right)*, World Scientific Publishing

Fries, Amy (2009), *Daydreams at Work: Wake Up Your Creative Powers,* Capital Books

Gelb, Michael J. (2000), *How to Think Like Leonardo da Vinci: Seven Steps to Genius Every Day,* New York: Dell

Guilford, J.P. (1967), *The Nature of Human Intelligence*, New York: McGraw-Hill

Hirshberg, Jerry (1998), *The Creative Priority: Driving Innovative Business in the New World*, HarperCollins

Hurson, Tim (2008), *Think Better: An Innovator's Guide to Productive Thinking*, McGraw-Hill Professional

Johnson, Steven (2010), *Where Good Ideas Come From: The Natural History of Innovation*, Riverhead Books

Kelley, Tom and Littman, Jonathan (2001), *The Art of Innovation: Lessons in Creativity from IDEO*, America's Leading Design Firm, HarperCollinsBusiness

Koestler, Arthur (1964), *The Act of Creation*, Hutchinson, London

Mind Gym (2005), *The Mind Gym: Wake Your Mind Up*, Sphere

Osborn, Alex F. (1953), *Applied Imagination: Principles and Procedures of Creative Problem Solving,* New York: Charles Scribner's Sons

Paul, Richard W. and Elder, Linda (2002), *Critical Thinking: Tools for Taking Charge of Your Professional and Personal Life,* Financial Times Prentice Hall

Pink, Daniel H. (2005), *A Whole New Mind: Moving from the Information Age to the Conceptual Age,* Riverhead Books

Pink, Daniel H. (2008), *A Whole New Mind: Why Right-Brainers Will Rule The Future,* Marshall Cavendish

Proctor, Tony (1999), *Creative Problem Solving For Managers*, Routledge

Robinson, Sir Ken (2001), *Out of Our Minds: Learning To Be Creative,* Capstone Publishing

Shapiro, Stephen M. (2001), *24/7 Innovation: A Blueprint for Surviving and Thriving in an Age of Change*, McGraw-Hill

Souter, Nick (2007), *Breakthrough Thinking: Using Creativity to Solve Problems*, ILEX Press

Stewart, D. and Simmons, M. (2010), *The Business Playground: Where Creativity and Commerce Collide*, Financial Times / Prentice Hall

Syed, Matthew (2010), *Bounce: How Champions are Made*, Fourth Estate

Taleb, Nassim Nicholas (2007), *The Black Swan: The Impact of the Highly Improbable,* Allen Lane

Thompson, Charles (1992), *What a Great Idea! The Key Steps Creative People Take,* New York: HarperPerennial

Treffinger, Donald J., Isaksen, Scott G. and Dorval, Brian K. (2000), *Creative Problem Solving: An Introduction*, Prufrock Press

van den Brandhof, Jan-Willem (2008), *The Business Brain Book,* BrainWare

Wallas, Graham (1926), *The Art of Thought,* Jonathan Cape

Wheeler, Jim (1998), *The Power of Innovative Thinking: Let New Ideas Lead You to Success,* Career Press

INDEX

A

N

NASA, 20
Neurons, 124
Neuroscience, 24, 30, 81,
Newton, Sir Isaac, 191, 194
Nobel Prize winners, 30
Nokia, 208

O

Objective, thinking, 15, 55, 83, 88-89,
240, 250, 271
Objectives, 78, 244, 252, 256
Ollila, Jorma (Nokia), 208
Orbital cannon, Newton's theory, 195
Osborn, Alex, 46, 48, 159-160, 165

P

Paper clip, 48
Peale, Norman Vincent, 94
People, 17-18, 94, 114, 153-154, 248-249
    successful people, 94, 248-249
    most important factor, 17-18,
Perspectives, 108, 159-160, 217-218,
221-223
Perception, story, 62-63
Picasso, Pablo, 209
Pink, Daniel, 268
Planning, 64, 70, 142, 155, 247-248, 257,
264
Plan, of action, 97-98, 116, 247-248, 256-
261
Positive judgement, 75, 235, 239, 240
Post-it note, 50
Point of Reference, change, 217-223
Principles, 46-51, 118-119, 127, 161,
165-166
    for brainstorming/generative thinking,
    46-51, 161, 165-166
Pringles, 180-181
Proactive, 25-26, 39, 40-42, 61, 63-66,
68, 101-108, 117, 264, 269, 273-275
    leader, 66
    planning, 64, 264
    thinking, 25-26, 39, 40-42, 61, 66, 68,
    101-108, 117, 273-5
    strategy, 41, 63, 103-105, 117
Problem solving, 23, 25-27, 38, 40, 113-
121, 271-273
Process, processes, 18, 23, 26, 41, 54-
55, 92-93, 97, 105-108, 115-118, 270
Proctor, Tony, 125

Production blocking, 163
Productivity, 60, 68-69, 151, 172
Psychology, 30, 40, 130
Purposeful, 12, 22, 42, 53-55, 101, 165,
192-193, 199 270
    creativity, 53-55
    daydreaming 192-193, 199
    practice, 42, 101

Q

Quantity, strive for, 47-48
Questions, 149, 173-174, 211-212, 222
    for challenging assumptions, 211-212
    for changing points of reference, 222
    for defining the problem, 149
    for reframing a problem, 173-174

R

Reactive, react 25-26, 39, 59-71, 101,
166, 264, 269, 273
    during brainstorming, 166
    events, reacting to, 26, 59, 63
    follower position, 64
    thinking, 25, 39, 59-71, 273
Reds (cons), 77, 116, 241, 252, 253
Reframe The Problem, 171-177
Relationships, Mind Maps, 52, 139, 239
Resources, 106, 113, 258-259
    equipment, 259
    money, 258
    people, 259
    skills, 259
    time, 258
Restaurant, example of assumptions,
210-213
Reverse The Challenge, 225-231
Right brain, 79, 129-132, 236
    See also brain
Risks, 49-50, 52-53, 262
Robinson, Sir Ken, 21
Rules, breaking, 49-50

S

Salk, Dr. Jonas, 220
Sanders, Colonel (KFC), 94
Screen ideas, 240-241
Select, idea/solution, 244-245
Selective, 25, 39, 54, 87-99, 107, 127,
247, 249-251, 273
    dangerous, harmful, 89-90, 94-96,
    127

T

U

V

W

Also by Chris Griffiths

Books
Mind Maps For Business - Tony Buzan and Chris Griffiths

Software
iMindMap - the user-friendly Mind Mapping tool that ignites your thinking and creativity at home and in the office

ThinkBuzan Training & Accreditation

➡ ThinkBuzan Licensed Instructor Training (Four days)

➡ Mind Mapping Masterclass (One day workshop)

➡ Read and Recall 10 times Faster (One day workshop)

➡ Learn the Secrets of the Memory Master (One day workshop)

➡ Change Your Thinking: GRASP The Solution (One day workshop)

➡ Online iMindMap Training

➡ Bespoke Tailored Solutions – We offer courses on Mind Maps, creativity, iMindMap software, memory, innovation, speed reading and idea generation and will eagerly design a tailor-made programme around your precise requirements. Our training experts are passionate about delivering effective and objective driven courses at your chosen location.

Speaking
Chris Griffiths is available to speak at events, conferences and exhibitions. He is the ideal speaker for organisations and groups who are committed to business and professional development, unveiling remarkably practical and innovative methods that dramatically multiply the chances of success.

Visit: www.ThinkBuzan.com

Look out for other titles by Proactive Press
A selection of superb new books to help you make the best of yourself

www.ProactivePress.com